To Crown the Year

DECORATING THE CHURCH THROUGH THE SEASONS

To Crown the Year

DECORATING THE CHURCH THROUGH THE SEASONS

Peter Mazar

Art by Evelyn Grala

LITURGY TRAINING PUBLICATIONS

Acknowledgments

This book was edited by David Philippart; Deborah Bogaert was the production editor. It was designed by Kerry Perlmutter and typeset in Sabon and Fritz Quadrata by Jim Mellody-Pizzato. Printed by Interstate Graphics.

The translation of Psalm 65 on page *v* is from the *Liturgical Psalter,* copyright © 1994 by the International Committee on English in the Liturgy, Inc. (ICEL). Used with permission. All rights reserved.

Library of Congress Cataloging-in-Publication Data

Mazar, Peter.
To crown the year: decorating the church through the seasons /
Peter Mazar; art by Evelyn Grala.
p. cm.
1. Church decoration and ornament—United States. 2. Interior decoration—United States. 3. Catholic Church—Liturgy. I. Title.
NK2192.U6M38 1994
246—dc20   95-6923
CIP

ISBN 1-56854-041-8
CROWN

PSALM 65

Praise is yours, God in Zion.
Now is the moment
to keep our vow,
for you, God, are listening.

Happy are those you invite
and then welcome to your courts.
Fill us with the plenty of your house,
the holiness of your temple.

You give victory
in answer to our prayer.
You inspire awe, God, our savior,
hope of distant lands and waters.

Clothed in power,
you steady the mountains;
you still the roaring seas,
restless waves, raging nations.
People everywhere
 stand amazed, at what you do,
east and west shout for joy.

You tend and water the land.
How wonderful the harvest!
You fill your springs,
ready the seeds, prepare the grain.

You soak the furrows
and level the ridges.
With softening rain
you bless the land with growth.

You crown the year with riches.
All you touch comes alive:
untilled lands yield crops,
hills are dressed in joy,

flocks clothe the pastures,
valleys wrap themselves in grain.
They all shout for joy
and break into song.

2-3, 5-14

Contents

PREFACE   viii

HOW TO USE THIS BOOK   x

GETTING STARTED

Four Principles   2

Obstacles to Getting the Work Done   9

A Sense of the Year   15

A View of the Whole   18

LENT

A Sense of the Season   42

Overview   45

Welcome the Lenten Spring!   60

The Lenten Veil   64

The Cross   67

Palm Sunday   69

THE PASCHAL TRIDUUM

A Sense of the Season   74

Overview   78

Holy Thursday Evening   88

Good Friday   98

Easter Vigil   104

Easter Sunday   118

EASTERTIME

A Sense of the Season   122

Overview   124

The Ascension of the Lord   143

Pentecost   145

Easter Flowers   149

SUMMER ORDINARY TIME

A Sense of the Season 154

Overview 158

Summer Festivals 169

AUTUMN ORDINARY TIME

A Sense of the Season 176

Overview 180

November 192

ADVENT

A Sense of the Season 200

Overview 204

The Advent Wreath 222

CHRISTMASTIME

A Sense of the Season 230

Overview 234

Evergreens and Lights 246

The Nativity Scene 250

The Tent 256

The Christmas Tree 259

The Mystical Marriage 262

WINTER ORDINARY TIME

A Sense of the Season 266

Overview 268

Candlemas 275

Ashes 278

OCCASIONAL CELEBRATIONS OF SACRAMENTS 282

Preface

I've always enjoyed gardening, and I take it seriously. To be a better gardener I got a master's degree in horticulture. I still don't know what infects the tomatoes every summer.

Somehow for the past ten years I've been writing about or editing other people's writing about liturgy. And not once has anyone said, "Why, you're nothing but a gardener." After managing to pass calculus, biochemistry and cytogenetics, I tend to think, "Why, I'm only a liturgical writer."

And, to use a botanical term, I'm a hybrid. Although both my parents are Hungarian, Dad is Roman Catholic and Mom is Greek Catholic, with a good share of her relatives Orthodox. All of this made for loud discussions around the family table. For instance, regarding the grave subject of human sinfulness, the family was in agreement that one of the most heinous sins a Hungarian could commit was buying cheap *kolbász* at Easter.

In this book you may recognize a Byzantine influence and a horticultural one, too, but mainly the book is liturgical. This adjective is borne by many churches, and there's plenty here that will be useful in any communion that keeps a liturgical calendar.

I've been a member of parishes in several states, and these communities have been urban, suburban or near-rural. I've learned a lot of critical (if arcane) details. For example, in South Florida white *bauhinia* blooms in early spring and is a more fragrant and longer-lasting Easter flower than the lily. Or (this I learned in Minnesota), if you try to cut down a Christmas tree when the temperature is 25 below zero, it will shatter like glass.

Thanks to the details, I have also learned that it's dangerous to make generalizations (of which this book is full).

In preparing *To Crown the Year,* again and again I wanted to digress into personal anecdotes, for instance, about the time the pastor asked me to remove the mice from the nativity scene (he was convinced I had put them there to add a Disney touch), or about the server who merrily marched a processional banner right into a chandelier, where it stuck and hung for the rest of Mass. (Later, some folks wanted to know what it symbolized.)

The stories would have been fun, and they would have assured you that the notions here have been put to the test.

Today—the day I complete this book—is August 6, the Transfiguration of the Lord. On this day I make a point to listen to Alan Hovhaness's Symphony No. 2, "Mysterious Mountain," wonderful music made even more wonderful by its allusions to Armenian chant. It got me thinking about how hard it is to communicate in words what I most want to tell you about the "atmosphere" surrounding our seasons and feasts.

Today the garden's first swamp mallows have come into bloom, red and pink, the size of dinner plates. Through the screen door waft the aromas of basil and dill and last night's squabble between a raccoon and a skunk. After the morning run to a farmer's market, there are pole beans, sweet corn and Michigan blueberries, in the kitchen.

I believe, despite all the good work here, that this book cannot possibly do the mystery of this holy day as much justice as your gazing for a while at the loveliness of swamp mallows or fixing yourself a bowl of blueberries. That's just what I'm going to do for myself right now.

How to Use This Book

To Crown the Year begins with an introduction, *Getting Started*. It's enough to read at one sitting but also enough to keep coming back to and mulling over. *Please don't skip it.* It provides the basics.

The rest of the book can be read part by part, season by season. Each season of the year or portion of Ordinary Time has its own section.

Lent, Triduum and Eastertime are at the beginning of the book because they are the most important seasons of the year and will occupy most of our time. They are the church's springtime. These seasons ought to be understood as a whole before they are considered separately. So if you are responsible, say, for Lent, please look over all three of these sections.

Summer and autumn are discussed in separate sections (even though they both fall within Ordinary Time). Then come Advent, Christmastime and the winter weeks of Ordinary Time, the weeks before Lent.

Advent and Christmastime are also prepared best as a unit. They are discussed toward the end of the book because Christmas and Epiphany are loaded with images of the fulfillment of time and the renewal of creation.

A final section covers sacramental celebrations other than Sunday Mass. Sacraments are best observed within the context of the season in which they are celebrated. If, for example, you're preparing a Christmastime wedding, besides this section on the sacraments you might also look over the material on the Christmas season.

Each season's section is divided into chapters. "A Sense of the Season" and "Overview" are standard chapters in each section. "A Sense of the Season" offers for reflection images from scripture, poetry and folklore. The information is meant to get imaginations in gear and adrenaline flowing (like a pep talk).

If you want to get down to basics, read "Overview." This may or may not be a list of the top ten things to consider when preparing the worship environment for a season, but it's close. "Overview" contains a walk-through of liturgical areas and the accoutrements of the sacred rituals:

> The assembly's place
> Altar, ambo and chair
> Vessels and vesture
> Font
> Shrines
> Seasonal corners
> Vestibules, doorways and outdoors

And then, as needed in each section, additional chapters cover special occasions as well as other topics that deserve attention, such as the Advent wreath or the veiling of statues during Lent.

This book does not cover all the day-to-day material things of liturgy—such as the lectionary, the altar or the communion vessels. In 1978 the United States Bishops' Committee on the Liturgy issued *Environment and Art in Catholic Worship (EACW).* This document is necessary reading. It's filled with a wealth of foundational principles, often wonderfully stated. In LTP's *The Sacristy Manual,* G. Thomas Ryan does a remarkable job of introducing and providing practical suggestions regarding the many year-round essentials of worship.

To Crown the Year *is about seasonal decorations, but it is not a recipe book.* There are no blueprints for arranging flowers, hanging banners or sewing vestments. There are, however, some principles and a host of practical ideas. Evelyn Grala's illustrations flesh out and amplify these principles. Of course, the ideas in this book need to be balanced against your own parish's architecture and its own blend of human resources.

This book was written for pastoral ministers. A key ingredient in your work is compromise and coordination, the matching of talents to tasks. This is what some call the pastoral role of "enabling." If anyone musters up the courage to offer help, then it seems that it should be a pastoral minister's duty (in other words *your* duty) to figure out how this person can contribute to parish prayer in a way that matches both the person's level of skill and the parish's need for good liturgy. A willingness to help is too valuable not to direct toward a fitting role.

Don't take yourself too seriously. We'll all be healthier if we accept, at least for the moment, many of our limitations and skimpy budgets and especially the idiosyncrasies of our parish—maybe the person most willing to sew happens not to be very good at it, maybe our nativity scene is old and chipped, maybe the orange carpet the parish council installed is now the dominant visual element in the church. We can push toward improvements, but in any given year we also need to adapt to much that needs improvement.

Don't take this book too seriously. We've all seen damage done when good ideas are applied heavy-handedly or inappropriately. So right up front, here's a "buyer beware":

> **Warning:** The author based this book on sound principles, but all of the ideas in this book are not intended for every parish.

This book often uses the words "perhaps" and "maybe" instead of "must." Ideas are presented to be wrestled with and puzzled over. The book can spark dialogue, imagination and a truly local tradition. Please write and tell LTP how you think the book is helpful and where it's wanting: *To Crown the Year*, LTP, 1800 North Hermitage Avenue, Chicago IL 60622.

Balthasar Fischer's wonderful little book *Signs, Words & Gestures* begins with a quotation from the German poet Goethe: "In every new situation we must start all over again like children, cultivate a passionate interest in things and events, and begin by taking delight in externals until we have the good fortune to grasp the substance."

"To delight in externals until we grasp the substance" is at heart the purpose of *To Crown the Year*.

Getting Started

Four Principles

We usually use the word "decoration" to mean balloons and streamers and other colorful materials that create a mood of festivity at parties. Liturgical decorations also are used to foster a mood, sometimes of festivity and at other times of penitence or anticipation, but always of dignity and hospitality.

The word "decoration" can suggest materials that are cheap. Worse, the word suggests stuff that is nonessential, merely added for the fun of it. In this book, "decoration" is used often, despite the troublesome associations. It's too good a word to abandon. "Decoration" (and the related words "decorum" and "decorous") can mean "appropriate honor." That's what the Latin *decorus* means: "seemly," "decent," "fit for its purpose." *Decoration is used to make a place fit for the liturgy.*

The liturgy is where we begin when thinking about seasonal decorations.

ONE: WORSHIP REQUIRES A FIT PLACE

> In the earthly liturgy we take part in a foretaste of that heavenly liturgy celebrated in the holy city of Jerusalem toward which we journey as pilgrims, where Christ is sitting at the right hand of God. . . . We sing . . . to the Lord's glory with the whole company of heaven.
> —*Constitution on the Sacred Liturgy,* 8

We can almost see the words "laity" (meaning "people") and "energy" (meaning, at its root, "work") in the word "liturgy." Liturgy comes from a Greek word meaning "the work of the people."

Liturgy is the public ritual prayer of the church. *Ritual* means "repeated action." We perform rituals again and again, and so we learn them by heart. Introducing something new into the liturgy, even a new decoration, may put an obstacle in the way of ritual, in the way of the repetition necessary for people to take part in their liturgy. That's good to keep in mind.

Shrines and homes are places of private prayer. But *public* prayer requires useful public spaces that are not just big enough to hold a lot of people but are arranged so that we can hear and see and move around in order to participate in our many rituals.

These different rituals (including sacraments and blessings) may need different kinds of spaces: not just a large hall (what we usually call "the church") but at times also a baptistry, at times a large gathering area in addition to the church, at times a spacious area close to the front doors, and at times even a street (for processions).

Not having the right spaces is an obstacle to liturgy—a big one. Our liturgical rites were renewed almost a generation ago. Thus our buildings need authentic renewal too, not just to fix a leaky roof but to help us carry out our liturgy.

Much more is required by the renewed liturgy than simply turning the altar around. In recent years a lot of adjustments to church interiors have been inadequate. For the sake of better worship, most churches still need better acoustics, wider aisles and more accessible entryways. Most churches are still arranged like theaters, giving the impression that worshipers are an audience rather than participants. So that shrines can function as places of private prayer, they need to be large enough and located in places that do not compete for our attention to the liturgy. Liturgical norms call for the tabernacle to go in its own noble chapel instead of being stuck in some odd corner.

Anything we might do with seasonal decorations will be bolstered or diminished by the permanent physical arrangement, especially the church's floor plan. In recent years we've been learning from experience how interior layouts, loveliness and the beauty of construction materials can facilitate participation in the liturgy. Some seating arrangements and acoustics help people sing better and may even help build a sense of community. Equally important is how these elements offer a sense of mystery, a sense of how the people, gathered with their pastor and involved in their holy rituals, can be an image of God's reign—of Christ praising the Father in the unity of the Holy Spirit.

We're learning why we need large baptistries to do baptism well. We're recognizing the usefulness of big "gathering spaces" and even the possibilities opened up by having a place big enough for everyone to gather on certain occasions (such as the Easter Vigil) in preparation for a procession to the church. Many of us are getting a better appreciation for the *private* spaces within our churches, too—the shrines and chapels that are accessible to but separate from the body of the church.

Parish decorators may need to be the movers and shakers for renovation. Our responsibility might be seasonal arts, but at nearly every turn we might wish we had a more appropriate place of worship to decorate.

We struggle with the limitations of our buildings but enjoy their potential. We feel most strongly the frustration of accomplishing the church's rituals in inadequate spaces or learn most quickly what wisely designed spaces make possible.

Two: Worship Requires a Climate of Hospitality

Seasonal decorations help set the mood for liturgy. Preparing these decorations is good and necessary work.

Environment and Art in Catholic Worship speaks often about the importance of what it calls the "climate," "atmosphere" and "mood" of liturgical celebration. Regarding a particularly important mood, paragraph 11 of this document says:

> Liturgy flourishes in a climate of hospitality: a situation in which people are comfortable with one another, either knowing or being introduced to one another; a space in which people are seated together, with mobility, in view of one another as well as the focal points of the rite, involved as participants and *not* as spectators.

Seasonal decorations must contribute to a climate of hospitality that leads to participation in the liturgy. A "climate of hospitality" is more or less what we're trying to form when we set a dinner table with candles, flowers and other signs of affection for those who will gather around it. This atmosphere of good will (adapted to the scale of the space, to liturgical tradition and to the requirements of the rituals) can be brought to our preparation for worship.

To create a climate of hospitality means that we don't set up barriers to movement (especially the ability to walk around the altar) or block sightlines (which means we need to have a working knowledge of liturgical movement and gestures).

We don't treat the church as a theater where liturgy is a show (which means we should think twice before focusing decorations up front around the altar and ambo, because too much here tends to make the area look like a stage). And we don't use decorations in ways that suggest that some members of the assembly are more welcome than others (which means, for instance, that every worshiper at a wedding is just as important as the bride and groom).

Three: Worship Is Filled with Images of the Reign of God

There's a Greek word, *ephemerata*, for things (such as seasonal decorations) that are "here today, gone tomorrow." "Ephemerata" makes a good word for the serious spirit of the Book of Ecclesiastes or of Job, perhaps, or of psalms that remind us that life is fleeting:

> You turn us back to dust,
> and say, "Turn back, you mortals."

> For a thousand years in your sight
> > are like yesterday when it is past,
> > or like a watch in the night.
> You sweep them away; they are like a dream,
> > like grass that is renewed in the morning;
> in the morning it flourishes and is renewed;
> > in the evening it fades and withers.
> —*Psalm 90:3–6*

Some ephemeral things we use at worship—ashes, for instance—literally hit us right between the eyes with the truth of life and death. This sacramental sign summons us to set priorities straight.

We might say that seasonal materials are meant to summon us to face reality. They certainly aren't to be used as rose-colored glasses to make the world more pretty. Decorations need to be able to "bear the weight of mystery" (this splendid phrase is borrowed from *Environment and Art in Catholic Worship*). Such a mystery resists a single definition.

For instance, flowers that bring us joy and that we sometimes use to offer comfort or soften harsh surroundings can also be signs of the frailty of God's creatures, of mortals who are "few of days and full of trouble, who come up like a flower and whither, who flee like a shadow and do not last" (Job 14:1–2). But even that is not the final word, not of the book of Job, nor of the gospels, nor of flowers, which communicate even as they are dying a presentiment of paradise.

At heart, Christians have a split perspective on the passing of time. We recognize how it carries us to our graves, but we anticipate that it will bring us to the fullness of time.

This attitude stands in contrast to much classical mythology, whose poets spoke of a golden age long ago, an era when people were decent to one another, governments just, life wonderful. It was the age of Saturn, also called Chronos, meaning "time." This backward-looking philosophy remains strong in our day. At Christmas especially, at the year's end, advertisers offer a heavy dose of a hankering for some imagined good old days. Ads are steeped in nostalgia, a word meaning "homecoming". (Every New Year's Eve old Chronos makes a reappearance.)

The hymn-writer Isaac Watts, in his much-loved paraphrase of Psalm 90, knew that Christian nostalgia looks not to the past but toward the reign of God:

> O God, our help in ages past,
> > Our hope for years to come,
> Our shelter from the stormy blast
> > And our eternal home.

Our days are not dwindling into oblivion but are leading us forward to justice, to wholesomeness, to an endless Easter. For us, the "ghost of Christmas yet to come" is not a specter of death but a brightly clothed angel who asks, "Why do you search for the living among the dead?"

Seasonal liturgical materials at worship must point toward the kingdom. Decorations for the liturgical seasons need to be in some way images of heaven, signs of the reign of God and of the fullness of time. Through their use in the liturgy, they need to be windows into mystery.

"Icon" is Greek for "image" or "mirror." Gospel parables overflow with icons of God's reign. So does the liturgical year. So too must the materials we use in celebration of the year. These must point us toward the holy city. And they must offer us a foretaste of our destination.

Some seasonal images are abstract, such as water, a bonfire or the color red. Some are figural, such as a cross, wreath or star. Some figural images are nearly literal depictions of a person or event, such as statues, and these images are usually used devotionally as objects of veneration rather than to contribute to the mood of worship.

A seasonal element can function simply as a mood-setter. An array of fabric strips can be used simply to convey a mood of merriment. That's all this decoration is intended for, and that's fine. The liturgy needs its mood-setters, as *Environment and Art in Catholic Worship,* 100, reminds us:

> Their purpose is to appeal to the senses and thereby create an atmosphere and a mood rather than to impress a slogan upon the minds of observers or deliver a verbal message.

A seasonal element also can fulfill several functions at once: mood-setter, iconographic image and tool within the liturgy. For instance, a paschal candle contributes to the mood of the liturgy through its beauty, its light, its noble presence, even its aroma. At the same time, the candle is an icon of the risen Christ and of the fire of the Spirit. Further, it is like a pillar of fire to lead us into the promised land.

The way the paschal candle is used within the liturgy complements this iconography and atmosphere. At the Easter Vigil, the candle is carried before us into the church. It is placed by the ambo to illuminate the pages of scripture. It is carried to lead the soon-to-be baptized to the font. It is plunged into the font's water as a sign that the baptized are reborn through the passionate power of the Holy Spirit, as a sign that this font is a womb, as a sign that on this night the church is in labor.

To consider the candle's contribution to the liturgy, we might ask: Is the candle beautiful? Is it large and glorious? Does it have a beeswax fragrance? But to consider the candle as a ritual tool, we might ask if it burns brightly (and safely) and if it can be carried with grace and even hoisted high. If the answer to any question is no, we have a problem.

FOUR: THE MATERIAL THINGS OF WORSHIP MUST BE TRADITIONAL

The church's use of imagery is governed by the discipline of tradition. A big part of your job as an art minister is to learn this tradition. Liturgical imagery is not a matter of whatever our imaginations come up with at the moment; the church's imagery has been handed down from one generation to another, like language. What would happen if every generation invented a new language?

If a generation fails to adopt and adapt a tradition (a word that literally means "hand-me-down") that tradition is lost. Of course, hand-me-downs quickly turn into useless junk without the right alterations and repairs. Each generation must learn as much of the tradition as possible, grapple with it and make an attempt to apply it to current situations. That's the often messy way that tradition (or language or any of the arts) is handed down.

If tradition is like an evolving language that's handed down from one generation to the next, the Roman (or Latin) rite is our own dialect. The rite is described in the *Constitution on the Sacred Liturgy* and other official texts. (LTP has gathered these in its 1991 anthology *The Liturgy Documents.* Think of these as the liturgy's grammar books.)

We might characterize the Roman rite with the words "noble simplicity." The *General Instruction of the Roman Missal* uses this phrase to describe how churches should be decorated and calls noble simplicity "the perfect companion of genuine art." *Environment and Art in Catholic Worship,* 17, gets to the point:

> It does require a persevering effort to respect the Church's mind in terms of its . . . simplicity, for example, by not drowning the action in a flood of words or by not making the action more complex than necessary in order to signify the gospel essentials.

Over its history, the Latin rite has borrowed from other rites (like the way languages borrow words from each other). For instance, centuries ago Palm Sunday's procession and Good Friday's veneration of the cross were "borrowed" from the Christian East. So were certain festivals, such as Assumption and Holy Cross. This history can help us get a better handle on the appropriate "atmosphere" of a ritual or a feast day.

We still borrow elements from other rites; for instance, the use of icons. Some people think this tendency to borrow is one of the strong suits of the

Roman rite because it helps the rite adapt to new cultures and times. But some wonder about this tendency because on occasion it fails to show respect for the traditions from which the Roman rite borrows. Also, especially at first, such borrowings can feel foreign to a Roman-rite parish and may even be artificial to it. Keep that in mind.

Obstacles to Getting the Work Done

In accomplishing their work, parish decorators have a number of road-blocks. These obstacles undermine efforts, and there may not be a lot that can be done to remove them.

The church doesn't have many specific guidelines for the use of seasonal elements, and the few we do have often are presented as options, not as essentials. For instance, there are no rules that require banners or Advent wreaths or nativity scenes. The *General Instruction of the Roman Missal* doesn't even mention flowers. Only four of the 107 paragraphs in *Environment and Art in Catholic Worship* deal directly with seasonal decoration. Nowhere is the role of a custodian of seasonal arts defined.

Especially in recent years, musicians and servers and readers have had their tasks described in pastoral guidelines, but decorators haven't. Some ministries have their own national organizations. Decorators do not.

We're not even sure what to call ourselves. "Environment minister," besides sounding like jargon, might sound more like someone concerned with hazardous waste than with flower arrangements. "Decorator" sounds lightweight, like someone who puts the icing on a cake. But this ministry has much more to do with the cake than it does with the icing.

IS THIS NECESSARY

Art ministers in particular suffer from "minimalism," which has been a plague on liturgy. Minimalism is the attitude of, "What's the least we can do to get this over with?" That's not the "noble simplicity of the Roman rite." It's laziness.

For example, using abundant water and chrism at a christening, including communal singing and having everyone walk from door to font to altar (as the ritual describes)—these are definitely not as easy as simply skipping participation and processional movement or using miserly amounts of sacred substances.

Another manifestation of "minimalism" is to think that environment and art ministers are nice but not necessary to the celebration of the sacraments. Paragraphs 26 to 32 of the *Constitution on the Sacred Liturgy* lay this notion to rest by stressing the necessity of the interplay of roles.

Often enough some people act as if beauty, quality and appropriateness are, like the ministry of art, nice but not really necessary. How else are we to explain the homeliness of so many church interiors or the ugliness of so much vesture? Why would parishes be content year after year to worship in a gym, auditorium or other space not designed for the liturgy?

Environment and art personnel can be a "thorn" in the parish's side, spurring it toward fulfilling its responsibility to celebrate all forms of liturgy with fullness, gracefulness, authenticity and, most importantly, with active participation.

EXCESS

Is there such a thing as overdoing it in liturgy? Yes. *Environment and Art in Catholic Worship,* 103, tells us to stand back and review the seasonal decorations as a whole:

> Both beauty and simplicity demand careful attention to each piece of furniture, each object, each decorative element, as well as to the whole ensemble, so that there is no clutter, no crowding. These various objects and elements must be able to breathe and function without being smothered by excess.

Another form of excess stymies participation by turning worship into a spectacle. We all might be able to recall rituals that became superhuman in scale—perhaps a wedding or funeral or installation of a bishop where it was hard not to be aware of the money spent on lavish display, where the imagery of power and politics got mixed up with liturgy. That's never right.

There is a line between "triumph" and "triumphalism." How do we tell the difference? The first is the community's joy at being the promised inheritors of the victory of Christ. The second is self-assurance in this victory or anything that suggests that we have it and others don't.

The *Constitution on the Sacred Liturgy,* 32, offers this counsel:

> The liturgy makes distinctions between persons according to their liturgical function and sacred orders. . . . Apart from these instances, no special honors are to be paid in the liturgy to any private persons or classes of persons, whether in the ceremonies or by external display.

BROKEN TRADITION

Many of the traditions of the material things used at worship—especially seasonal ones—have gotten confused or lost. That's a formidable obstacle in our work as parish decorators. This loss has a complicated history, but its key player has been an old and stubborn attitude that keeps resurfacing—the belief that God's creation is not good, no matter what Genesis has to say, and so isn't a good image of the Creator.

The few traditions that have survived the years are leftovers from a rich and full liturgical way of life. But the bits and pieces no longer fit into a satisfying whole. For example, the Catholic year used to be filled with blessings, often linked to feast days or memorials of saints. In most parishes today, the only saint's day blessing is of throats, on February 3, the memorial of the martyr Blase. Observing the year with a host of blessings on a host of saint's days reflected an attitude of thankful wonder offered in the company of "a great cloud of witnesses." But what are we to make of the blessing of throats without all those other blessings on all those other days? What had been an expression of a wholesome stance toward life is now mostly a relic of the past.

Many parishes are only part way toward a consistent approach to liturgical tradition. Consider the ways we baptize: In many parishes adult baptism is celebrated with plenty of water, full robes and fat candles, with communal singing and well-choreographed processions. At least there's evidence that traditions are being wrestled with and are regarded as important.

But what about infant baptism on a Sunday afternoon? In most parishes there's no singing, a few drops of water are drawn from a mere bowlful, a handkerchief-size cloth is offered as a "baptismal garment" to a child already robed in yards of beautiful fabric, and a thumbprint of scentless chrism from a greasy wad of cotton is all that suffices as a sign of the Spirit.

In recent years seasonal decorations in many parishes may have been rather awful. Most church basements have a boxful or two of unfixably bad materials: purple burlap with the word "repent" glued on it, a plexiglas terrarium used for Easter water, a hollow metal paschal candle with a gizmo on top that burns butane, a red, white and blue chasuble for Independence Day, plastic holly garland and polyester ferns.

At the time, many of these might have seemed the right thing to make or buy. And although they don't show a good sense of tradition, they probably make evident that there was enthusiasm and communal spirit.

While we may have outgrown what now seems poor, we can't forget how we got to where we are today. There was an evolution, and it can remind us that improvement is built upon improvement. This is important to remember as we enable the parish to "own" its traditions of worship.

That being said, in all of this experimentation we may have created a kind of "tradition" of gimmickry, a habit of change for its own sake. As a consequence, even when we try to break this habit and adopt ways that reflect authentic traditions, they can appear to some folks as this year's "angle." The only way around this dilemma is to keep coming back to the practices that have worked. Year by year they will seem less novel and more our common property.

We are still in a time of transition. In much of liturgy since the reforms, we have been feeling our way. We're still not exactly sure how to use, much less construct and even decorate a baptistry, a tabernacle chapel or a room for the catechumens. But we're learning. We're struggling toward renewal. We have good ideas and they're getting better.

GOOD TASTE

Other obstacles in the way of our ministry are the often insurmountable issues surrounding "style" and "taste." These are gray issues we must learn to live with.

Perhaps one trick to developing taste and judgment (and expressing them) is to become familiar with a wide array of styles of liturgical design. A way to do that is to tour churches and to make it a point to visit those that are known for their design.

Another way is to spend as much time as possible "armchair traveling": From the late 1920s to the early 1970s, Maurice Lavanoux edited *Liturgical Arts Quarterly.* You might squirrel yourself away (say, in a seminary library) and browse through this journal, if only to look at the pictures! LTP's *Environment and Art Letter* (published monthly) continues the conversation begun decades ago by Lavanoux. Reviewing these periodicals old and new makes a fine exercise in developing appreciation for quality and appropriateness and certainly for the wide range of visual styles used by the church.

Concerning style and judgment: The *Constitution on the Sacred Liturgy,* 123, reminds us that "the church has not adopted any particular style of art as her very own; it has admitted styles from every period according to the natural talents and circumstances of peoples and the needs of the various rites."

Each style is governed by its own "aesthetic," a set of principles and traditions (or sometimes a set of definite rules) that establishes what is appropriate and beautiful and what is not—for instance, the principles of Japanese flower arranging or of Byzantine iconography. In making use of a particular style within the liturgy, we need to balance and join the style's own aesthetic principles with the principles of liturgy. Every decision that goes into preparing worship requires the exercise of such balanced judgment, and each judgment has the potential for being faulty.

In making judgments, we would do well to choose our battles wisely. And we would be wise to present our judgments carefully.

As an example, say that the parish has gotten accustomed to putting the nativity scene under the altar (where it doesn't belong; for a discussion about that, see page 251). And so based on sound principles, you have made the decision to move the scene to a shrine. How do you part from parish custom in the way that's least likely to cause a ruckus?

For one, we shouldn't present decisions (or make them) as if they were simply a matter of personal taste. After all, this really isn't a choice based on taste. It really isn't even a "choice" but is rather an observance of the church's norms (see the *Book of Blessings,* 1544). It's also a return to tradition, even if it parts from recent practice.

Decisions regarding liturgy, if at all possible, should put the emphasis where it belongs—on liturgical tradition and church norms, which are "community property," and not on any individual's personal opinion. In the matter of where a nativity scene is located, the church has a wonderful tradition that makes the scene a private place to visit before and after worship. That way we make a journey in spirit to Bethlehem.

In carrying out a decision, we also need to follow the proper "aesthetic" (the principles governing appropriateness and beauty) of the particular form of art. What is the customary aesthetic of a nativity scene? For an understanding of that, we can study the forms this folk art has taken.

We can be glad to know that by putting these principles into practice (which results in greater beauty and authenticity), a parish is far more likely to accept changes in its ways of doing things. In the case of a nativity scene, most traditions suggest creating a delightfully complicated scene with plenty of flowers, animals, stars and other elements. If done well, this results in something most people fall in love with. And it will only stand to reason that such a delightful array can't fit under an altar and would look best in its own shrine.

In choosing from among the many styles available to us, the parish decorators at least should try to complement the style of the parish buildings. If the architecture is Gothic, go with that. Explore its possibilities. Even if it's not your taste, you are obliged by the discipline of your ministry to work with your church building's own architectural style.

You might think that this goes without saying, but the failure to match the style and scale of seasonal decorations (and other liturgical furnishings) with the style and scale of the building is an all too common mistake. For instance, a paschal candle covered in baroque ornamentation might fit in a baroque church but not in a church with a modern interior.

When all is said and done, we don't have all the answers, and that's just fine. Our best efforts will be a kind of grand compromise juggling the limitations of the spaces we have, our budgets, our judgments and the people with whom we work—and that's just fine.

A peculiar advantage of dealing with the materials of worship is that limitations keep crashing through to make us humble. Christmas trees fall over. Pumpkins rot. A cable snaps and the Pentecost mobile comes down in a twisted heap.

The mayhem is what's missing from the pages of this book; it really belongs here somewhere, along with a first-aid manual. Mayhem makes a wonderful image of the incarnation!

THE MYSTERY OF LIMITATIONS

As a lesson in humility, apprentice icon-painters learn their art by first reproducing the icon of the Transfiguration. This event teaches them about the necessity of limitations. Recall what happened at the Transfiguration of Jesus: When he began to shine like the sun, and Moses and Elijah joined him, Peter said, "If you wish, I will make you three booths." Suddenly a cloud surrounded them and God's voice was heard and the disciples fell down in fear. But "when they looked up, they saw no one except Jesus alone" (Matthew 17:8). The vision was over.

An icon-painter is creating a kind of "booth," a fragile tent for the cloud of God's presence. This is almost unimaginable, certainly audacious, like Peter's proposal; and the painter prepares for this labor through prayer, fasting and almsgiving, the practices that dispose us to "fall down in fear" in the face of mystery.

We, too—when we decorate with flowers and banners, bring into worship ears of golden corn or set up an evergreen tree—are building "booths" to contain the uncontainable. But ponder the Transfiguration. Before our booths can be built, the cloud may disappear and God's voice grow silent, and looking up, we will see Jesus alone. And that is enough.

A Sense of the Year

The church doesn't put spring, summer, autumn and winter into a box marked "secular" and then put Advent, Christmas, Lent, Triduum and Eastertime into a box marked "sacred." In every corner of the year the church celebrates the mystery of Christ, the paschal mystery.

THERE ARE MANY PASSOVERS

Every moment is sacred, though naturally the year's moments of transition, of "passover," receive special attention. These are times within the seasons of nature that we have named as the liturgical feasts and seasons.

We give most attention to the weeks around the spring equinox, when days grow longer than nights. With zeal we count the days of springtime— first the 40 we call Lent, then the three we call the Paschal Triduum, then the 50 we call Eastertime. We reserve the spring for the annual telling of the death, burial and resurrection of Jesus. Spring is also put to the purpose of initiation, which is our entrance into this passing over of Christ.

Another turning point, the time before and after the winter solstice, is Advent and Christmastime. Here too is a time of passing over, now reflected in the stories of the nativity and baptism of Jesus and celebrated with light in darkness, with evergreens and flowers in the dead of winter, with dancing and singing in a time of heightened anxiety and fear.

Summer and autumn are less structured by the church, but again the paschal mystery gets clothed in the garments of the year. That's easiest to sense in the festival days; for instance, the Birth of John the Baptist (June 24), the Assumption of Mary (August 15) and All Saints (November 1). The turning of the year has many such "passovers," as does the turning of the day (for example, morning and evening) and the turning of the week (for example, Sunday).

Sunday brings its own imagery that we layer upon the imagery of the year. Sunday is the first day of creation and the "eighth day" as well, the day that leaps altogether out of time. It is the day of resurrection, the day of the outpouring of the Spirit, the Lord's Day that will usher in the end of days and the fullness of time.

Every Sunday can come dressed in seasonal garb. In much of North America, Sundays in January come clad in bare branches and icicles, in June can wear roses shining in the sun, and in September are adorned with ripe apples and goldenrod.

The seasonal images we use at worship should be true to what we observe around us—whether in Vermont, Virginia or the Virgin Islands, whether in rural, suburban or city neighborhoods. Even so, a rural parish cannot be divorced from the concerns of the city, an urban parish separated from the imagery of the countryside, or a suburban parish content to surround itself with middle-class comfortableness.

In our use of seasonal images, we're under obligation to unite and not separate peoples. The images are used in celebration of the dominion of God and not only of a community's heritage or surroundings.

Environment and Art in Catholic Worship, 32, addresses this balance between what we are and what we aim to be:

> The action of the assembly is . . . not merely a "celebration of life," reflecting all the distinctions stemming from color, sex, class, etc. Quite the contrary, liturgy requires the faith community to set aside all those distinctions and divisions and classifications. By doing this the liturgy celebrates the reign of God. . . . When the assembly gathers with its own varied background, there is a commonness demanded which stems from our human condition. The commonality here seeks the best which people can bring together rather than what is compromised or less noble. For the assembly seeks its own expression in an atmosphere which is beautiful, amidst actions which probe the entire human experience.

Scriptural images are touchstones that all the earth's people can claim in common. Yes, these images are mostly agrarian and not necessarily close to many North Americans today. But we cannot lose this language. Even in our own day it unites poor and rich, the powerless and powerful, those who produce the daily bread and those who eat it.

This being said, it is important to note that the liturgical year of the Roman rite is an invention of people in the middle latitudes of the Northern Hemisphere. Much liturgical imagery (which is at heart biblical imagery) fits best with the environs of the Mediterranean Sea (which, while geographically limited, spans three continents).

What are the "passovers" within the turning of the year in other latitudes? It's hard to imagine a more dramatic "passing over" than the beginning of the monsoon in India after weeks of oppressive heat, or the coming of the rains in east Africa, when so much life erupts out of the wet earth.

In this book we stick closely to the seasonal imagery inherited from the Bible, which happens to work well in much of North America. Readers, say, in New Zealand should dismiss what's said in this book about Advent being a time of deepening darkness as well as what's said about almost every other seasonal association. However, we who make our home in the

Northern Hemisphere ought to be convinced that *our* dismissing this legacy of images is not the way to maintain communion between North and South.

Maybe the world's peoples need to claim their right to use local imagery as emblems of the paschal mystery, even if that means reinventing their liturgical calendars. We know there's more to communion than which days we call holy. Or maybe the calendar could keep its form, and an Australian, South African or Argentinean could come up with all sorts of splendid associations for their harvesttime Easter, their spring festival of All Saints or their summer Epiphany.

None of us, no matter what our climate, should be content with fake snow at Christmas. Liturgy abhors the artificial. Look around you. There's plenty that is real that can be used as seasonal expressions. Open up your imagination. Maybe Floridians (and others in the subtropics) can make a Christmastime image of fulfillment from orange trees, which is not too hard to imagine considering that in winter the trees bear the blossoms that will grow into next year's crop on branches still hung with last year's fruit.

At issue here is this: Liturgy requires our ability to see in the seasons signs that point toward the reign of God. Of course, the imagery takes us only so far and then falls apart. Heaven will not be contained.

Our icons aren't supposed to make convincing idols, which is why our favorite iconographic images—the substances of the sacraments—are wind, water and other things that fall through our fingers, drift into the air, ferment or rot. But chief among our holy signs is that least decay-proof substance, the human body, and that most impermanent commodity, time itself.

At the very least, this work of ours with materials that are "here today, gone tomorrow" will keep us humble—a word rooted in "humus," the brown, crumbly component of soil. "Humus" also gives us "human." That's good to keep in mind when plans go awry or things fall apart. At those times—*mirabile dictu*—we can be very close to the paschal mystery.

A View of the Whole

Think seasonally. Each liturgical season can have its own decor that does not change from week to week within the season. Any special days within a season might have some special elements, but even these days would, in the main, be celebrated as part of and not separate from their season.

Preparing the worship environment for each season (rather than for each Sunday) does more than avoid unnecessary work. It helps the parish better "own" the season. We get to know that Advent or Lent has a particular look and that this look is something we've seen before and will see again. It's part of the "ritual" (the repetition) necessary for public prayer.

Any changes from year to year would happen as a gradual evolution toward improvement, never just for the sake of change itself.

MARK CALENDARS

You can count on being busy at the turning of the seasons, just before:

> The First Sunday of Advent, when Advent begins
> Christmas Day, when the Christmas season begins
> The day after the Baptism of the Lord, when Ordinary Time begins
> Ash Wednesday, when Lent begins
> Holy Thursday evening, when the Paschal Triduum begins
> Easter Sunday, when the Easter season begins
> The day after Pentecost, when Ordinary Time resumes

In the two stretches of Ordinary Time (all those green-vestment days), changes might come gradually to reflect the shift from summer into autumn. These subtle shifts (a lot more subtle than the changes between the liturgical seasons) might happen around some prime festival days within Ordinary Time (which happen to occur in pairs):

> The Conversion of Paul (January 25)
>   and the Presentation of the Lord (February 2)
> The Birth of John the Baptist (June 24)
>   and SS. Peter and Paul (June 29)
> The Transfiguration of the Lord (August 6)
>   and the Assumption of the Virgin Mary into Heaven (August 15)
> Holy Cross (September 14)
>   and SS. Michael, Gabriel and Raphael (September 29)
> All Saints (November 1)
>   and All Souls (November 2)

PREPARE DECORATIONS AS A UNIFIED WHOLE

In this book we deal separately with the various areas in a church—the entryways, the baptistry, the assembly's place, and so on. However, in preparing the environment for worship, you are creating an ensemble. No one element is as important as the effect of the whole.

As in outfitting our bodies, this regard for the whole means more than matching elements. An interplay of contrasts and complementarity is necessary. Respect for scale is especially important. Too often we don't think big enough: Flower arrangements are too small, banners are too small, Advent wreaths are too small.

A sense for the whole involves thinking in two different directions: Thinking big (so elements look good at a distance) and thinking small (so elements look good up close). It helps to have an understanding of the graphic arts useful, say, in decorating shopping malls and airports. And it can help to understand the arts peculiar to setting a beautiful table. But it's essential to understand liturgy and to appreciate that we do not invent this mystery but enter into it.

DON'T DECORATE A MESS

Usually the first stage of preparing a home for a holiday is putting junk away and giving the place a good scrubdown. Only then do any decorations go up. The same can happen in church. Put clutter away and clean what remains. Then worry about decorations.

"Clutter" in church means more than just stuff that's out of place. Clutter means anything that isn't being used for a particular liturgy. Part of the "noble simplicity" of the way we worship is to pack away any furniture, candles or anything else that won't be used. That way the things that remain get heightened attention.

When dreaming up how the church will be decorated for a season, don't neglect to imagine the church filled with people in the act of worship. They're not only the intended beneficiaries of these decorations, but their physical presence is one of the main components of the worship environment. (That's one of the reasons why we put such fancy clothing on our ministers.)

DON'T CREATE A STAGE SETTING

Limiting decorations to the area around the altar and the ambo can create the feeling of a stage setting—but an assembly of worshipers is not an audience. Also, a lot is already happening in this area, and enough is enough. Maybe the area is perfect just with a beautiful cloth on the altar. Any additional visual elements (such as flowers) have to be positioned with the presence of the ministers in mind. Don't hinder movement.

Figure out how you will decorate the assembly's place. That's the biggest area to deal with, so it requires large materials (and maybe the greatest outlay of time and money). Then turn your attention to where you might use smaller-scale elements. These might go in shrines, vestibules and doorways. (Baptistries are a special situation; see the advice beginning on page 31.)

Be careful where you put figural images. They're hard (and sometimes impossible) to use well. For example, in Year B on the Twelfth Sunday in Ordinary Time (which falls in late June) we hear about Jesus calming the sea. It would not be a good idea to set up a rowboat in front of the ambo just because the gospel mentions a boat, or even to use lots of images of boats in special decorations for this one Sunday.

The problem with doing this isn't the image of the boat (a rich image, to be sure) but its location and literalness, which can exaggerate it. Something as assertive as a rowboat in church strikes many folks as ridiculous, lacking any subtlety. A boat next to the ambo is something of a brat. It demands attention instead of inviting it.

In the right spot, and without being too literal, boats and the sea make wonderful summertime images. Throughout June and July they almost wondrously keep recurring in the liturgy. Perhaps each year throughout these weeks there's a place for hangings in the vestibule or high over the assembly that suggest sails or that evoke various kinds of boats, nets or fishes. Or, even better, a parish near water might choose a summer Sunday (or the solemnity of SS. Peter and Paul) to bless God for the gift of fishing or boating, and any decorations could then be carried in a procession to the water.

MAKE RITUAL ITEMS A PRIORITY

We know we're on the right track when we are able to integrate decorations with liturgical ritual. That way the decorations are more than something static to look at. They become vehicles for public prayer.

Instead of coming up with decorations that sit there for their own sake, come up with ones that adorn the items we use at worship. For instance, instead of putting flowers in a bouquet, attach them to the staff of the processional cross. Instead of hanging a banner on a wall, carry it down the aisle. Instead of potfuls of flowering branches to celebrate a festival, put the branches in people's hands as they arrive for worship.

No matter how interesting a decoration, there's rarely a good reason to interrupt worship to explain it. Most explanations do not contribute to good liturgy (or to good art), mainly because they turn the assembly into a captive audience. Education is a good and necessary part of parish life, but it is a part separate from the liturgy.

In the parish bulletin you might offer a few words about the seasonal decorations, and some homilists are gifted at associating the decorations with scriptural images when breaking open the word. But these efforts should happen in a way that doesn't restrict imagery to one or two interpretations. After all, imagery is best left to imaginations.

THE ASSEMBLY'S PLACE

This is the area where the people stand, sit and kneel. In general, put this area on the top of the list of places to receive seasonal decoration.

There are two areas here to consider. One is the space over everyone's heads (at least in churches with high ceilings). This area grabs our attention when we first enter, but after we are seated we can mostly ignore it. It doesn't compete for attention with the liturgy, which makes this space excellent for all sorts of decoration.

The other area is lower down, such as the walls that surround a congregation. Decorations in this area make less of an impact when we first enter the building and are harder to ignore during the course of the liturgy. This area is good for decorations that create a mood, such as strips of color or botanical patterns, but not so good for strong figural images that tend to demand attention with their fascinating designs.

Pews or chairs can be decked with flowers. We're accustomed to doing this at weddings, so why not decorate the seating areas at Easter and at other high festivals? But even at weddings these decorations really should not be used to emphasize the aisle or to set apart special seating but to offer gracious hospitality to the entire assembly. The materials should be big and bold enough for the space.

Poles bolted to pews or attached directly to the floor can be ornamented with candles or wreaths of flowers. (Of course, they need to be positioned so that they don't block the people's view of liturgical action or get in the way of movement.) Bear in mind that anything on a pole involves the physics of torque: A small force (such as a bump) near one end can result in a great force on the other end. So the pole and anything attached to it had better be attached securely.

Locating candles among the people is beautiful but risky, not so much because of fire but because of melted wax. Candles can be enclosed in glass vessels such as hurricane lamps. For votive candles, there are glass cups with stems that can be inserted into ordinary candle holders.

With votive candles, eventually a faulty wick will tip over and touch the glass, bursting it and usually snuffing the flame in the process but often releasing a messy stream of wax. That's almost guaranteed to happen if you don't remove the burned-out candle's leftover metal base from the cup before inserting a new candle. As a precaution, put glass-enclosed candles within larger glass vessels or sit them in glass bowls.

Walls and pillars can be ornamented with banners and baskets of flowers or branches. This is done to surround the assembly with an atmosphere appropriate to the feast or season. Use colors that complement the principal colors of the vesture. More should be going on here than simply hanging a lot of the correct liturgical color. The textures, patterns and other aspects of the materials are just as important as color.

Decoration along walls can contribute to a busy effect, however, if materials are too small and numerous for the space.

Banners usually don't look good if they are overly stretched to hang flat against a wall as if they were billboards, probably because most fabrics ripple and allow some light to pass through. Why fight that? After all, it's cloth, not lumber. Rippling fabric looks better when hung unobstructed, several inches away from a wall or hanging freely so that the fabric can be appreciated from both sides.

The area high over people's heads may be excellent for all sorts of imagery, but it's difficult or nearly impossible to reach in churches with high ceilings. All that open space with its rich potential requires large (usually expensive) materials and hardware. Many parishes simply don't have the scaffolding or ladders (or skilled personnel) required to gain access to high places.

Heights are inherently dangerous; it's not just a matter of finding someone brave enough and skilled enough to climb ladders and scaffolds. Accidents occur even among the most skilled. The best safeguard against accidents is figuring out how to avoid putting people at risk.

Suspending materials over the assembly is also dangerous. Heaven forbid that a bolt cracks or a cable breaks. Even light materials would disrupt worship and possibly injure someone if the materials fall.

Consider the one-time trouble and expense of having professionals install line-and-pulley systems so that you'll have year-round access to some high places in the building. Such a system has to be the work of professionals using professional equipment and supplies. The materials are not particularly expensive but they must be suited to their purpose, which requires lines that do not kink or snag and that descend and ascend smoothly with pulleys positioned and anchored correctly for the load they will bear.

Professionals know ways to make such systems barely noticeable, but you will need to communicate exactly how the systems will be used. For instance, say you want to be able to hang a large Advent wreath from the center of the church ceiling. Should it be able to revolve or not? How heavy will it get with candles and fresh evergreens? Maybe you have plans to add a large cut-glass star to the center of the wreath at Christmas, or you intend to use the line for other purposes, such as a set of banners for Pentecost. And how will the wreath, star or banners be illuminated? Hash these matters out before installing the system.

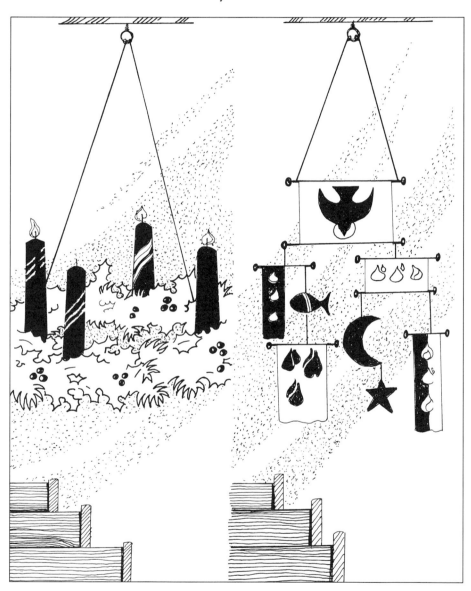

Even a single line from the center-point of the church enables a great range of decorations to be used.

ALTAR, AMBO AND CHAIR

The most common mistake decorators make is concentrating decorations in this area. This space (what Roman Catholics call the "sanctuary") often is sufficiently "decorated" with a beautiful altar cloth and well-vested ministers.

In years past altar cloths were put down in multiple layers of starched and even waxed linen, and some altars had seasonally colored frontals. All of that may have been beautiful (if it was maintained, which it often wasn't) but tended to make the altar appear to be something other than a table. The image of a table is too important to lose. The altar cloth should enhance, not obscure this image. The cloth could be the seasonal color or a complementary color, or a shade of white. Colored strips or appliqué figures on top of the altar cloth complicate something that should be simple and elegant, and may even turn the altar into a billboard. Don't do that.

Some parishes use a large, full cloth for festive seasons and something simpler for other times. A simple cloth allows the parish to see the altar's materials and structure. A full covering can appear regal and even nuptial. A full and flowing covering can hide an ugly altar or hide a beautiful one, so if your altar is beautiful, you might sometimes cover it fully and sometimes cover it very simply so that its structure is revealed.

The area around the altar usually includes the cross and candles. (For a discussion of the parish's cross, see page 67.) In the old days candles were put on the altar (along with a whole battery of other objects). Today, out of respect for the altar, we usually try to keep it free of anything (including candles) except the bread and cup—and these go on the altar only during the liturgy of the eucharist.

Floor-standing candles can be beautiful, and hanging lamps can make marvelous decorations for festival seasons. Real candles (or oil lamps) are the only lanterns appropriate to liturgy. Two or three might be used for ordinary days, and larger groupings (seven, eight and twelve are holy numbers) might be set up for feast days. (The missal's *General Instruction*, 79, says seven candles are used when a bishop presides.)

As long as they don't prevent a minister from walking around the altar or otherwise create a hindrance to the liturgy's necessary actions, floor-standing candles might be arranged

- on either side of the altar
- at an appropriate distance from the four corners of the altar
- in a single grouping to one side of the altar

- in one or more groupings that look appropriate in relationship to the altar, ambo and chair

- gathered around or under the cross (ordinarily a processional cross is flanked by candles)

A good place to locate seasonal flowers is in connection with the cross or candles. For instance, instead of putting a flower arrangement near the altar, put it near the cross. Or instead of a flower arrangement, use a garland or wreath of flowers to ornament the cross and perhaps the candles, too. Or gather flowers at the base or on the pole of each floor-standing candle. Not only do these groupings look less busy than locating these items separately, the flowers appear to adorn a ritual item rather than simply be sitting there for their own sake.

Some parishes also have candles around the ambo. However, there's a stronger tradition of acolytes holding candles during the proclamation of the gospel. (For that matter, they could also hold them around the altar during the eucharistic prayer.) In fact, our practice of holding lamps during the liturgy (for ourselves and to illuminate others) is a more ancient custom than using them for mere ornament. What do candles signify but the light kindled in us at baptism to keep burning until the bridegroom arrives?

In other words, when it comes down to it, maybe candles as "static" ornaments are a leftover from the days of inactive participation in worship. Maybe hand-held lights in any form are more true to the "active" spirit of the liturgy.

One hard and fast rule is to avoid putting anything around the altar that prevents ministers from walking around it. We have a tradition of circumambulating the altar to incense it. Even flowers around an altar can make it appear that it's the flowers that are being incensed and not the altar.

In the old days flowers also went on top of the altar, sometimes banked in grand displays. Today, flowers on the altar would put a barrier between priest and people, so there's less temptation to do this, but it still happens. Flowers do not belong on the altar.

The notion that flowers don't belong on or in front of the altar may take getting used to. For some folks, "altar decoration" is a synonym for any decoration in church. An "Altar and Rosary Society" is made up of people who decorate the church. If you asked most anyone where a big cut-flower bouquet belongs in church, you'd probably get the answer, "in front of the altar." Funeral home personnel and florists, especially, can be told of alternative locations for flowers.

Even with these cautions about using decorations on or near the altar, there are wonderful feast-day traditions for decorating the altar and the area around it with cut flowers and herbs. In some churches at Easter, clusters of sweet blossoming olive or orange would be woven into garlands and festooned around the altar. On the anniversary of the church's dedication the altar's corners or incised crosses would be honored with bunches of herbs and blossoms. In some places the floor around the altar was covered with straw at Christmas and fresh cut alfalfa at Pentecost, with rosemary and lavender on Assumption Day and basil on Holy Cross Day.

What seems to be happening here is an amplification of the fragrances of incense and chrism. The flowers and herbs lend visible support to the invisible aromas that are used to consecrate the altar and give glory to God. Notice that in these traditions the altar is treated as a table, not as a flower stand or backdrop. Think about that. There might be a way to use flowers and greens that gives honor and loveliness (and added fragrance) to the altar and that respects its purpose.

Keep in mind that these traditions were what people also were doing at home with their kitchen tables. Any revival of such customs in church could be accompanied by a renewal of an affectionate attitude toward our supper tables and all who gather around them.

Some parishes cover the ambo with a cloth as the "table of the word." A cloth-covered ambo and a cloth-covered altar can appear confused with one another. While it's possible to use cloth to ornament an ambo handsomely, the point shouldn't be to make it match the altar. An ambo is a very different piece of furniture. There's no need to coordinate the altar and ambo (or anything else) with matching fabrics like some people do with the fabrics in a bathroom.

The better your ambo looks and the more space there is around it, the more you can do with seasonal decorations at this site. Most churches don't have adequate space here. Sometimes the ambo is the right spot for a wreath, a spray of harvest produce or a basket filled with asters. The ambo, like the altar, is not the best place for a great quantity of decorations. In this position, decorations tend to shout, "Hey, look at me."

In some churches the cantor's lectern looks nearly as important as the ambo, and in some churches with imposing pulpits there's actually a second, smaller ambo set up. What's going on here? If you're stuck with multiple lecterns, don't draw the eye to any but the principal ambo. Leave the others free from flowers or hangings. (Better yet, get rid of them).

The area around the altar and ambo is the most visible part of the church. So it is naturally where we think we should put anything we want others to see. In some churches this area is the *only* place where there's room to put holiday flowers.

That's why creative compromise is essential. We need to do our best to balance liturgical principles with the legitimate expectation that lots of flowers really do contribute to the atmosphere of certain holidays. Are you *sure* you can't find other visible and appropriate spots for some of those wonderful flowers other than around the altar?

One thing that's never right is to set up a "shrine" near the altar or ambo. We do that when we put an Advent wreath there, a nativity scene, the All Souls' Day remembrances or a pile of class symbols for a baccalaureate Mass. Find a more appropriate location where these things can be better appreciated and where they would be more in scale, such as in an entry-way or alcove.

Another thing that happens a lot but really shouldn't is the creation of "communion rails" made out of decorations. For instance, a bank of flowers gets put between the people and the altar. This can reinforce the notion that the altar is unapproachable or is the exclusive domain of the ordained. Maybe because for so many years people were forbidden to approach the altar, many parishes make it a general rule never to put *anything* between the altar and the people. This is a good rule.

Strong seasonal visuals in the area around the altar (such as a grouping of lilies or poinsettias) tend to reinforce the notion that liturgy is something to watch and not something to take part in. That might be our best reason for finding other spots for these signs of festivity.

On occasion something is used in the liturgy that deserves a location in the vicinity of the altar and ambo: for instance, ashes, chrism, the oil of the sick. (The list isn't much longer.) Instead of putting these things on the altar of sacrifice, maybe the best place is on a pedestal near the presidential chair, or, if the pedestal isn't easily knocked over, in an aisle. Four big floor candles set in a square around a pedestal can be very handsome.

Different sizes of pedestals are useful objects to keep on hand. They don't look like little altars, they don't take up a lot of space, and they have a natural grace and beauty.

VESSELS AND VESTURE

We're accustomed to using precious metal vessels. But liturgical vessels might be of any material, including glass, clay, wicker, wood and stone. A parish might use certain materials for its vessels during certain seasons of the year, perhaps using earthenware during Advent and gold during Christmastime. A museum gift shop no doubt offers inspiration on the array of possibilities. Parish artisans and other local craftspeople might be the best sources for splendid vessels.

Religious goods stores are getting better at putting parishes in touch with artisans. Still, the goods available are often overpriced, not attractive and not even serviceable. Why is that? And why would anyone purchase, for example, a water bucket from a religious goods store when a local department store likely has buckets with more style and more usefulness, bearing more the stamp of the artist, and all at a more affordable price?

Perhaps some people think that a holy water bucket needs to have a cross or *chi-rho* carved into its side, that a bucket has to be advertised "for holy water" to be used for this purpose. Perhaps some people fail to recognize the usefulness and beauty to be found at craft shows, import houses and gift shops. "Church goods" don't have to come from an ecclesiastical supplier.

Vestments are strong contributors to the atmosphere of worship. Any baptized person may wear an alb (meaning "white," the baptismal garment). Albs might be the proper vesture for readers, servers, eucharistic ministers, cantors and choir members. Deacons, priests and bishops have specific vesture proper to their order.

A vestment's design and texture and the way it hangs are just as important characteristics to consider as color. Add to that the effect of any trim or other ornamentation. Evaluate vestments (and other fabrics used in church) by looking at them in actual use from the vantage point of the assembly. A church's light and shadows affect how fabrics are perceived.

The more these vestments fulfill their function by their color, design and enveloping form, the less they will need the signs, slogans and symbols which an unkind history has fastened on them.
—*Environment and Art in Catholic Worship*, 94

It's strange that we began putting symbols on vestments. What other clothing has insignia? Bowling and baseball jackets, T-shirts and sweatshirts, and military uniforms. But vestments themselves are symbols. What's the sense of putting symbols on symbols?

In any case, most of our stuck-on symbols—such as the cross, a flame, a dove—have been overused. And things that are hackneyed from overuse lose their impact.

If the parish owns vestments with symbols and too much damage would be done by removing the symbols, bear in mind that a red chasuble with appliqué flames makes no sense on any other day than Pentecost. Purple vesture with a crown of thorns makes no sense during Advent. (And it barely makes sense during Lent, which isn't a six-week-long Passiontide.)

Many parishes make it a point on Sundays and feasts to wear a specific set of vesture at specific seasons of year. For instance, at Christmas they don't just wear any white set but a particular set that either was designed for the season or that happens to look good at that time of year. This practice means that presiders and deacons (the regular staff as well as visitors) are cued in and cooperative. Following this practice, a parish *could* have

- a white set for the Christmas season

- a white set for the Easter season (and perhaps funerals, too)

- a white set for white-vestment days in Ordinary Time,
  such as Holy Trinity (and weddings, too)

- a violet set for Advent

- a violet set for Lent (and penance services)

- a rose set for the two days this color may be worn

- a deep red set for Palm Sunday, Good Friday, Holy Cross Day,
  and the memorial days of martyrs

- a bright red set for Pentecost, SS. Peter and Paul
  and the other feast days of apostles

- three different green sets for winter, summer and fall

Maybe the "Ordinary Time white" also is worn on Holy Thursday evening to contrast with the first use of the Easter set on Holy Saturday night. To make connections among days, maybe the "Easter white" also is worn on Transfiguration, Assumption, All Saints and All Souls. Maybe the "Christmas white" also is worn on Presentation, St. Joseph, Annunciation, and the Birth of John.

Black vesture may be worn at funerals and on All Souls' Day. (White or violet may be worn, too.) Most parishes have gotten away from using black, but something has been lost here. Black has an intense and beautiful significance as the color of night, of rest, of what St. Francis called "Sister Death." Interestingly, in some places black was Advent's color. It's hard to think of a better one.

Perhaps the choice of vestments makes only a subtle connection between days not likely to be noticed. Maybe it smacks of fussiness. Yet subtleties have power. To begin using certain sets at certain seasons, start by reviewing the vesture the parish already owns.

One caution: Some parishes have matching sets of vesture, book covers, seat cushion covers, altar cloth, tabernacle veil and other fabric arts. Some of this matching or complementing works well, but sometimes the overall look is artificial. Clothing too much in the same color can have a deadening effect on the whole ensemble.

The Roman rite continues to use white, red, green, purple (and sometimes rose, black, silver and gold) for its vesture. This color scheme isn't very old—just a few centuries. Take a look at a museum's collection of medieval vestments. The range of color and design is enormous.

Older than the association of specific colors with particular seasons is a simpler pattern: somber colors for times of fasting, bright colors for times of feasting.

Judging from antique vesture, it appears that the colors of Lent, Advent or funerals could be deep browns, purples, blues, rusts or black, or a mixture of these. It wasn't as if a fabric maker could run to a store and pick up a particular shade of dye. Available dyestuffs varied from region to region.

The use of clothing to enter into a mood has never been special to liturgical ministers. If someone died, neighbors would wear mourning clothes. If a couple was being married, neighbors would wear festive clothes. In wearing somber or jolly vesture, liturgical ministers were matching the spirit of the assembly gathered around them. Today some parishes ask people to come to worship dressed in certain colors. Why not? Why shouldn't everyone come attired in fiery reds, oranges and pinks in celebration of Pentecost?

A parish can't be content that just because its vesture is the official color, it has therefore achieved a fitting atmosphere for seasonal worship. Certain shades of violet are extremely festive, even gaudy. Certain fabrics, regardless of color, are associated with parties. The color, the shade of color and the texture of the fabric ought to work together to contribute to the liturgical atmosphere.

It is only right to honor the church's scheme for vestment colors. A small book called an *ordo* gives the options for each day. Adherence to this scheme shows respect for the Catholics of the Roman rite who have gathered to worship.

But don't allow the scheme to signify more than it does. It's accurate to say that the color of Ordinary Time is green. It is not accurate to say that we wear green vesture to signify "life" or "growth" or "hope" or anything at all. But then why do we wear green vesture in Ordinary Time? Because that's the church's scheme, at least for the present.

Of course, colors have natural significance. Green is the color of chlorophyll. The sky is blue. Blood is red. There's nothing too strict here: We've seen the sky turn red and skin turn blue. Be wary of saying, "Red means such and such." Instead, on a red-vestment day we can enjoy and puzzle over the associations of a color that conjures up images of a sunset, a flame, a rose, the flash of a cardinal's wing, a blood-soaked sheet.

FONT

It's hard to make recommendations about seasonal decorations for baptistries. From church to church they're constructed in enormously different ways and may even be absent entirely. They can be large and roomy, chapel-like, or merely located in an area with almost no space around it.

In some churches the font is put in a room completely separate from the main body of the church, so that when baptism is celebrated the water bath takes place rather privately. (This is an ancient tradition from a time when people took off all their clothes before entering the water.) Or, the font is positioned near the main entrance, so that people need to turn and face the entrance to witness a baptism. Or it is put to one side of the altar.

The rituals of baptism are supposed to involve processions—from the doors to the ambo, from the ambo to the font and then from the font to the area around the altar (where the newly baptized are sealed with the gift of the Spirit). This walking is itself a sign of "passing over" into Christ. A font located too near the altar or too near the entryway makes it hard to have a proper procession.

The paschal candle (as a "pillar of fire") is used to lead these exodus-like journeys. This candle is kept near the font except during Eastertime, when it goes near the ambo.

A font located in its own proper area means we have another space to consider for seasonal decoration. The imagery of baptism is tremendous. In this book, some of this imagery is introduced each season. The images might be changed as the seasons come and go; and some images can be returned at appropriate times during the year, such as the figure of John the Baptist; or an image can evolve from season to season, such as the story of the Exodus, which can unfold gradually from Ash Wednesday to Pentecost. Obviously if the area around the font is roomy, the materials we use need to be appropriately large.

A baptistry may look a lot like a chapel or shrine, but it's not. Even a tiny baptistry is a site of liturgical action, not only private prayer. Just as in the area around the altar and ambo, any seasonal decoration in the baptistry must complement the liturgical action and not compete for attention, hinder movement or be set up merely for show.

We might take a second look at our use of flowers and plants around baptismal fonts. Do they convey what we are after here? Are they a bit too domesticated? Read Aidan Kavanagh's story of baptism in ancient times (reprinted beginning on page 171 in LTP's *The Three Days*). It's hard to imagine how beribboned pots of hothouse flowers would have any place in such a raw and robust celebration, although perhaps field flowers or branches cut from an orchard would seem right.

Our decorations really shouldn't create an atmosphere of coziness. We're not after charm but mystery, an atmosphere not of a recreation room but of the meeting place of life and death.

All too often ambries are put near the baptismal font. But why? Oil and water don't mix, either physically or liturgically. Catechumens are not anointed near the font. Neither are the sick. And the baptized are confirmed front and center in the midst of the assembly. Also, reserving oils and chrism together doesn't make much sense. The oil of the sick, the oil of catechumens and the sacred chrism are put to very different purposes.

We also might call into question the newfangled practice of reserving the oils in glass cases that behave like "monstrances." We wouldn't do that with the consecrated bread, so why are we doing this with consecrated chrism? It seems that chrism, being the sacramental sign of the Spirit, deserves an extraordinary vessel distinct from the two oils as well as its own place of reservation.

Especially silly is putting the oils in beautiful vessels in a beautiful ambry but then never actually using these oils and instead relying on stocks kept in a safe in the sacristy. Oil vessels need to be more than beautiful; they need to be practical for pouring and accessible to those who use them.

No matter where the ambry is located, it should be kept sparkling. And it can be decorated for the seasons. Certain images are especially fitting: the anointing of David, the gifts of the magi, the baptism of the Lord, the descent of the Spirit. (Notice that some feast days seem to call for ornamentation of the oils.) Fragrant flowers and a leafy wreath can complement the significance of chrism. An ambry can be graced with oil lamps. A few drops of oil-based flower essences rubbed into wood furniture can be used to "decorate" the entire worship space, especially at celebrations of initiation and throughout the festive seasons.

In times past, the light that burned in front of the tabernacle was an oil lamp fueled with the previous year's supply of holy oils—that tells the great quantity parishes used to keep on hand. Acquiring an adequate supply of oils from the cathedral may take some careful arranging, especially during those final, busy hours of Lent.

SHRINES

In recent years we have been learning the differences between public prayer (the liturgy) and private prayer. (The two had gotten mixed up: Some people's initial reaction to participation in the liturgy was that it interfered with their prayer!) We're learning from experience how good public spaces assist public prayer. But are we realizing the value of places of private prayer?

A shrine is a place of private prayer. It is a great loss that many churches don't have real shrines. They may have statues, say, of Mary and Joseph set into wall niches, but these aren't real shrines. They are not successful as places for private prayer because they lack the necessary intimate surroundings.

A real shrine is a chapel-like room or deep alcove set apart from the main worship hall so that it doesn't draw attention away from public liturgy and yet provides a quiet spot for people to pray.

Real shrines are wonderful. They can be places for people to bring flowers, to light candles, to pour out their hearts to the ancestors. Shrines satisfy the human penchant to make a fuss, to juggle imagery, to build a walled-off world that is orderly and yet cluttered.

We puritanical North Americans may have forgotten the art of shrine-building, but it is an art worth rediscovering. Whether from Guatemala, Ghana or Germany, shrines are places to display homemade arts, which, like images of the saints, also can be objects of contemplation and windows into heaven: batik Easter eggs, garden flowers and bowls of seasonal fruits, a quilt with the names of the dead, detailed crochet work and embroidery, wood carving, basketry and paper-cutting. In these and other arts the parish needs the same honesty and beauty that are required of the materials used in the main hall of the church, only here they can be on a more intimate scale.

In one parish a widows/widowers' group keeps up the Marian shrine. The building has a fine private spot for it, and the group has free reign to do their best, even if sometimes the results are peculiar. They take their duty seriously, and their principal responsibility has been to invite parishioners to contribute to and to interact with the shrine as a place of prayer and almsgiving.

For Advent, Mary's statue is dressed to look pregnant, and parishioners are invited to add photos of their mothers, their children or themselves when they were pregnant! Gifts are gathered there for a women's shelter. For Lent, the statue is veiled in purple, a large sword hangs over it (an allusion to Simeon's prophecy), and the parish alms basket is kept nearby. At the Assumption, the statue is robed in gold and surrounded with herbs, fruits and other garden produce, which eventually gets distributed at a food pantry. During November parishioners fill the shrine with mementos of the dead. Again, all of this is usually fine and fitting because it happens in a shrine—not in a place near the altar.

The church has strong traditions surrounding the use of sacred images, whether statues (three-dimensional images) or icons (two-dimensional ones). Let's look at some of these:

An image of a saint represents the presence of this holy ancestor. Images may be located in shrines for private veneration, or they may be placed surrounding the assembly at public worship. There they function as our liturgical companions. They are signs that we are in their spiritual company as fellow worshipers.

If icons and statues are placed in the sight of people gathered for the liturgy, they become part of the environment for public prayer. If statues or paintings face the altar (in other words, if during worship the images and the people face the same direction), this arrangement can better represent the union of the living and the dead in the communion of saints. The images more clearly can be understood as signs of the presence of our heavenly companions, a word that means "those with whom we break bread."

And if that's what they signify, the more images the merrier! In ancient times, Coptic hermits would paint their cells with a horde of angels and saints. They may have been hermits, but as baptized Christians they still stood alongside the whole company of heaven.

Two or three statues can't begin to represent this multitude. If that's all the church possesses, it would be better to use them in shrines apart from the main hall. An exception is the parish patron. An image of the patron might belong best where it seems to stand in the midst of the people or in some other companionable spot.

We give pride of place to images of our parish patron and also to the Virgin Mary, who is called the mother of the church. St. Joseph has been named patron of the universal church. In any parish, St. John the Baptist also is especially deserving of a sign of his presence among us.

Many Roman Catholic churches have a statue of the Sacred Heart. Strangely, some ancient and still well-loved gospel images of Jesus are almost never seen in Roman Catholic churches, such as Jesus the teacher (always a predominant image in Byzantine churches) and Jesus the good shepherd (often found in Protestant churches).

Even without statuary a church already is filled with images of Christ—the people gathered around their bishop, the altar, the cross, the paschal candle, the proclamation of the gospel and the eucharistic sacrifice. Why add figural images of Jesus to compete with these holy signs? It seems that figural images of Our Lord (such as a statue of the Sacred Heart) would be most appropriate in a private shrine and not in full view of the gathered assembly.

When many images are in view at once, it doesn't seem right that images of the saints should be of the same scale as an image of Jesus. Jesus Christ is Lord, but St. Joseph is not. You can tell this at a glance in much medieval art, where depictions of Jesus are larger than those of others, but our use of images has lost this discipline.

It happens, but it just isn't good to use iconographic images as mere decoration. A sacred image deserves better treatment. It is, after all, a sign of the presence of the holy person or event it depicts. What sense is there in using a sacred image on program covers or anywhere the image can't be given due honor?

Because of custom or law, many Jews and Muslims avoid creating figural images. Byzantine Christians avoid creating three-dimensional iconography. All of this is the respectful distance they keep to avoid constructing anything that might be turned into an idol. Jewish and Muslim traditions also forbid printing the scriptures on surfaces that will be discarded or defaced. Perhaps we also might avoid placing holy images or the words of sacred scripture on materials that will be thrown away.

There are circumstances when the use of images in shrines can intersect with their use in the liturgy. An example is a procession with a statue, perhaps on the saint's feast day. Another example is the blessing of a nativity scene. (Ordinarily these scenes belong in a shrine where they don't compete for attention with the liturgy. People can visit the shrine before or after worship.)

In the case of blessing, the "public" ritual enters the "private" shrine for a moment. In the case of a procession, the image is carried out of its private shrine into the public sphere of liturgical procession.

Moving a statue or icon for any reason—even a cleaning—is an occasion for a procession. When the procession ends, the image can be enthroned among the people and positioned to face the altar. Then the image becomes a sign that we are united with the saint in giving God praise. It wouldn't seem right to take an image out of its shrine and then move it into a position facing the people, which would only create a new "shrine" for the image that competes with our attention to the ambo and altar.

For instance, say the parish is having a May crowning and Mary's image ordinarily is located in a private shrine. The liturgy of May crowning could include carrying Mary's image out of the shrine and into the midst of the assembly. The image could face the altar rather than the people, and everyone could turn toward the image during the crowning (the way we turn to face a bridal party walking down the aisle).

Don't set up shrines where they don't belong. Some examples: Locating the nativity scene under the altar; fastening to the ambo a poster with the photos of the first communion class; setting up a flowery arch for the bride and groom to sit under. These gimmicks turn a nativity scene, a poster or even a couple into "shrines" that turn our attention away from the altar, ambo and presidential chair.

Let's face it: The reason we set things around the altar usually has more to do with catechetics than liturgy. We might be trying to teach or demonstrate something instead of helping each other participate in our common prayer. Or we're setting things up for people to stare at and contemplate, creating a kind of show-and-tell. There's a place for this teaching, such as a vestibule or parish library or even a shrine that we can visit before or after worship. But the right spot for catechetics is not in competition with worship.

SEASONAL CORNERS

Almost every parish has bulletin boards and book racks. A parish may have a library, a place to donate money and goods, and a place for folks to write down requests for prayer and remembrance. The parish might display the photos and names of newborns and their parents and godparents, newlyweds, those celebrating baptism, confirmation and first communion, those who are sick and those who have died.

Also worthwhile is a place to learn about and acquire materials for prayer in the home, as well as a place to display books and arts of the season.

(There's a tremendous task here: opening up the ways our tradition bids us to live a liturgical way of life.)

All of these areas need to be kept up. They're part of the environment for worship and contribute loosely or directly to the ways we pray as a community.

Sometimes these places function as information centers and sometimes as small shops, but sometimes they function as shrines (as sites of private prayer) when they call the parish's attention to its life of prayer and intercession. For instance, an alms box (a receptacle for donations to charity) could have a fitting place in a shrine, perhaps alongside an image of the Good Samaritan. Here might be the right spot for information about the institutions that receive parish gifts. This information, besides enlightening the parish, acts as a call to prayer.

As an art minister you may take on the responsibility for these areas in the church. Someone should, so that they are kept orderly and handsome. They would be changed or decorated for the changing seasons and would be part of the overall liturgical decor, the things that make the place decorous, "fitting," for worship.

VESTIBULES, DOORWAYS AND OUTDOORS

These are undervalued sites for decoration. The atmosphere for public worship often begins and concludes in the church parking lot. At Easter, what good is it to fill a church with lilies if outdoor planters are filled with a winter's worth of cigarette butts? Shouldn't the church exterior reflect the mood of our holy days and seasons?

An attractive landscape rich in trees and gardens creates the loveliest and most fitting exterior seasonal environment. Thanks to the way windows are positioned in some churches, people inside can see the outdoor gardens; then the gardens themselves become a strong element in the interior environment. Maintaining these gardens might involve something close to a full-time job! See page 168 for more on this subject.

You know how it would stir your heart to drive by a church that's hung with red bunting for Good Friday. It would stir your heart to pass by a synagogue decorated for Rosh Hashanah or a city hall decorated for Independence Day. Outdoor decorations can be signs of hospitality and neighborliness.

We Christians can make it a point to avoid decorations that seem emblematic of power. Of course, there's an important distinction between "triumph" and "triumphalism." An enormous illuminated cross can conjure up frightening images for some parish neighbors that an image of the Good Shepherd would not.

Classic decorations for outdoors are wreaths, garlands and bunting. It's hard to imagine more appropriate designs than these time-tested ones. The outdoors are more "forgiving" in the use of materials, because outdoor decorations don't compete for attention with the liturgy. Within limits, certain materials such as polyester or nylon, that probably would not look elegant indoors, can look just fine outside. Certain graphic figures—for instance, fishes or stars—that might be too dominant indoors can be perfect for banners hung, say, in a parking lot.

Of course, outdoor materials need to be in scale with their surroundings, which usually means thinking big. And outdoor materials need to accommodate the weather. Big materials combined with bad weather can be especially dangerous: In a windstorm even a piece of fabric becomes a projectile.

Doorways especially are valuable sites for liturgical action (and decoration). Most liturgies include rites that are supposed to be held at the doors. Our entering is emblematic of homecoming, of communion, of gathering in the new Jerusalem, of passing over from time into timelessness. Our exiting is emblematic of our being commissioned as apostles, of new birth in the Spirit, like the disciples on Pentecost spilling into the streets.

Marking the seasons with seasonal ornaments hung on doors is increasingly popular in homes and in churches. Of course, at church the materials would be larger or fuller than the ones we use on our front doors at home. Even more, the materials for church doors should be less fussy. For example, at home it's fine to ornament a clump of Indian corn with ribbons and bows, but at church, instead of hiding the wire with ribbon, maybe a plain raffia or hemp cord would be a simple but attractive alternative. That way the corn is emphasized, not any secondary adornment.

Learn the importance of a "gathering space," if only as a place for folks to mingle before and after worship. Maybe your church has one; maybe all you have are small vestibules; maybe the only "gathering space" is the parking lot. Still, there's something happening here that deserves attention. At least be sure that the area is well lighted and free from safety hazards.

Many of the decorations that we're accustomed to putting close to the altar may be better located in the vestibule or gathering area. Here the scale usually is more adaptable.

An interesting tradition makes the church vestibule the customary site for catechumens to meet, with the baptistry separating this area from the main body of the church. That tradition has given the vestibule a liturgical function as a large enough place where everyone, including the catechumens, can be seated for the liturgy of the word. Imagine that. (In this scheme, for the liturgy of the eucharist the catechumens remain in the "vestibule" and the baptized go into the eucharistic hall.)

In planning for the future, consider the possibilities opened up by a large space that can accommodate everyone who has gathered for worship. Think about how the entrance into liturgy could better involve real processions with everyone participating.

The vestibule is customarily decorated with sparse but specific imagery of founders and patrons. It's an especially good place to display mementos of the parish's history.

A traditional icon sometimes offered for contemplation in vestibules has Jesus the teacher surrounded by John the Baptist and Mary. John points toward Jesus, and Mary stands with arms wide open. It teaches the essentials of the Christian stance toward mystery. Like John, we are to give witness to the Word, ready to direct others to the Lamb of God, even at the risk of our own necks. Like Mary, we are to be receptive to the Word, with senses kept fully open, ready even for the visit of an angel.

Lent

A Sense of the Season

The world in late winter seems awash in mud, like Jeremiah in the cistern, like Esther marked with ashes, like the blind man at the pool of Siloam.

Cabin fever may be getting the better of us. But being stuck indoors so long can make it easier to imagine what it is like to huddle aboard a stinking ark. Throughout the winter we may have spent too many nights in a lions' den, in a fish's belly, in Lazarus's tomb.

But the hibernation is over. It's time to roll off our duffs and roll up our sleeves! There's work to be done "by the sweat of our brow." The children of Adam and Eve must make the most of being outside of Eden, among the thorns and thistles.

This is plowing and planting season, when the sower goes out to sow, when the grain is buried in the earth, when the farmer spreads manure in the hopes of a fruitful yield. Now is the time buds grow fat. Farm animals are born. Birds lay eggs. Creation is at its most vulnerable.

The span of days from late winter to early spring is a birthing season. How stupid, we may think, that in nature's design the young come into the world at the most violent time of year.

There is in Lent's customary abstinence from meat a sympathy with this fledgling generation. We will not add to its struggles by butchering it. Together all creation will bide the time aboard this ark called "earth," even as we grow hungry for a fresh harvest.

Lent's fast is like a long table grace at the beginning of the agricultural year, a thanksgiving not for what we have in hand but for what is promised in the future. For now, we have ashes, the dirty leftovers of life. Dust we are and to dust we will return. That's how Lent begins. It will end, thank God, with Easter baptising near a pool of clean water.

It's not quite accurate to say that prayer, fasting and almsgiving are Lenten disciplines. They are, rather, the year-round regimen of Christian living, the disciplines that, many would say, form us as disciples. During Lent we try the best we can to get back to these basic disciplines.

Fasting usually means eating less food and skipping meals. Sometimes it means abstaining from certain foods, such as eggs or meat, and replacing these with vegetables, grains and legumes. Late winter and early spring fit fasting the way the harvest fits feasting.

But fasting means more than dietary restrictions. Customarily it is accompanied by silence and reflection, by less relaxation and less entertainment. John Chrysostom called fasting a "medicine." It's meant to be healthy.

For this medicine to be effective, fasting must be accompanied by prayer and almsgiving. "Alms" comes from a Greek word meaning "compassion." The Book of Tobit reminds us that "prayer with fasting is good, but better than both is almsgiving with justice."

For many in the church, Lent is lived as a time of final preparations for baptism at Easter. Lent also is a time for those who have broken their baptismal vows to seek reconciliation. Through communal prayer, fasting and almsgiving, the already baptized link arms with the soon-to-be-baptized, and together they march toward Easter.

The march is rarely merry. We are a long way off from where we want to be. The prodigal son would have been happy to eat pig food. And the exiles have hung up their harps, for how could they sing the Lord's song in a foreign land? Sometimes silence is the only fitting response to the world. Sometimes hunger helps bring prodigals to their senses.

In most of the Lenten scriptures, people are on the move. "Leave your country and kinsfolk," God told Abram and Sarai. And so they set out in search of the promised land. Their children and their children's children continue the adventure.

Often the number 40 gets connected to the stories. In the days of Moses it took 40 years for the generation of former slaves to die out so that only the freeborn would enter Canaan. Forty has come to represent an unsettled life spent hungering and thirsting for justice. Maybe Lent is a rehearsal for living this kind of life.

Lent is like a retreat. Throughout the year the church is to be directed out to the world, but during these 40 days we pull back into ourselves for reflection and self-examination. "Physician, heal thyself," we say, and Lent is the season when the church must face its own unhealthy ways. The word "quarantine" is an old word for Lent—40 days of imposed recuperation.

Jonah shouted to the inhabitants of Nineveh: You have 40 days to repent! And they did. Even their cattle fasted. Like the story of Noah's flood, creation conspired to save itself. (And in case we miss it, a pun makes clear the connection between the stories: "Jonah" is the Hebrew word for "dove.")

The Hebrew word for repentance is *teshuvah,* which also means "return." The dove returned with great graciousness to Noah to announce the reconciliation of heaven and earth. Jonah, however, was far less gracious at announcing forgiveness. God had to force him to go to Nineveh—with the help of the big fish.

At the end of his story we read that the vine that shaded Jonah withered, so he whined like a brat. Elijah did the same thing while sitting under a broom tree. Self-denial can teach us what we'd rather not know. Happily,

an angel brought Elijah a little refreshment, and soon the prophet was off and running 40 days to Horeb, God's holy mountain. Lent, too, has its oases, its moments of refreshment.

Amazingly, when Lent is completed we will find ourselves right in the middle of what we have been hearing all along. During the Paschal Triduum we will gather around the cross—a tree of life, an ark, a burning bush where we learn God's name. In joy we will fill the font—a flood, a sea, a great fish that saves us from ourselves.

There the Judiths of the parish will lop off the heads of the demons of death. And the Jonahs will get spit up on the seashore, safe and sound.

Overview

The Paschal Triduum is the heart of the church's year. Lent is the preparation for it, and Eastertime is the 50-day celebration that flows from it. Together, Lent, the Triduum and Eastertime make up the "paschal season," the springtime of the church.

Think about the days from Ash Wednesday through Pentecost as a whole before preparing its parts. It is probably best if one group coordinates the entire span of days. We begin our work by preparing the Triduum. Once these preparations are underway, we can turn our attention to Eastertime and to Lent.

Many of the seasons' liturgical traditions follow a principle that is a good way to think about visuals throughout these days: During Lent we emphasize some things by their absence, which can create in us a holy hunger for things to be set right; in the rituals of the Triduum we welcome back that which was absent; at Eastertime we give what was absent pride of place.

Some Lenten traditions are "musts," such as not singing *alleluia*. Some are optional, such as veiling or removing the cross and other sacred images. Some are what might be called experimental, such as draining and sealing the baptismal font, done in many parishes because it seems to reflect an anticipation for baptism. It will help you to prioritize your plans if you keep in mind whether what you would like to do is obligatory, optional or experimental.

Throughout the paschal season, give some attention to the same particular locations: the font and the cross, certainly, and doorways perhaps, including all the areas we come and go in, even the parking lot. These are natural sites for extra effort throughout this time of "passing over."

Here's where you might begin to focus your efforts for Lent:

1. Put clutter away and give the place a cleaning. That includes entryways, bulletin boards, and especially the furniture or candlesticks that get used on occasion but not every day. Put these away and bring them out only for the times they will be used.

2. Put away all flowers and tropical plants. (You'll need to find the plants a sunny "vacation home" until after Easter.)

3. Decorate (and clean) outdoors to welcome the neighborhood into the holy season. (See page 54.)

4. Indoors, introduce a few elements that are unique to Lent—for instance, a large thorny branch of honey locust on a back wall,

a series of black, purple and gray fabric hangings suspended from the ceiling, or a woodcarving of Noah's ark in the middle of a vestibule. But keep the area around the altar and ambo free from distraction.

5. This is optional but traditional: Veil or put away images of the saints. (This custom is explained beginning on page 64.)

6. This is becoming a tradition in parishes that try to hold off on baptisms during Lent: Empty the font and the ambry. (See page 50.)

Hospitality demands that a church be clean and free from clutter, including the disarray that sometimes surrounds bulletin boards, music racks, lost-and-found cabinets, the parish library, etc. Worship requires orderliness. Anything not used at a particular service should be stored, even if that means a bit of rearrangement between services. If clutter is a problem, then Lent is a good time to set things right.

Throughout the season the physical plant can be given a spring cleaning that will be finished by the Triduum. Windows can be washed, woodwork polished, stonework scrubbed. Sometimes this is the work of professionals who know the proper techniques, have the right tools and chemicals, and have the right insurance.

Of course, there are other jobs in preparation for Easter. During Lent there might be a sign-up board in church with a list of tasks and an estimate of the time required for each. Don't neglect the landscaping. In many regions, planting season is here or is just around the corner.

Lent requires something more than good order: austerity. Lent demands an apparent plainness that says, "This is a time to get back to basics." Our efforts are meant to make more evident what is important about these 40 days: the assembly of the faithful, the penitents seeking reconciliation, the candidates preparing to enter into communion, and perhaps most of all, the catechumens elected for Easter baptism.

Lent's traditions include a ban on any instrumental music not used to accompany singing. Its visual counterpart is the Lenten ban on flowers. The ban has nothing to do with gloominess; the silence makes it easier to think straight, and the lack of clutter makes it easier to give the place a good cleaning.

It's not only music ministers who should be concerned about silence. Environment ministers also have a role: Is Lent the time to fix banging doors and kneelers so that they function quietly? Is now the time to repair the hum in the sound system?

During Lent the vessels, vesture and other materials we use in worship can share this simplicity. Communion vessels can be stone or clay or wicker instead of ornamented metals. Candles can be unbleached wax.

Lent and the upcoming Triduum is the ideal time to renew liturgical reverence. We can use home-baked bread instead of wafers or replace fake candles with real ones. Reform and renewal may be easier at this time because people expect to be distinctive, because change itself is in the air. St. Leo advised, "What Christians should be doing at all times should be done during Lent with greater care."

Focus your efforts on the material requirements of the church's rituals. For example, if you have a limited amount of time, energy and money for Palm Sunday, it's better to concentrate on the processional cross and its festive ornamentation rather than to worry about banners.

Lent requires a fitting atmosphere for the trembling and tears that may accompany repentance, forgiveness and healing. In general, it's easier to achieve a fitting Lenten atmosphere with non-figural elements than with literal ones. For instance, a pile of sand with cactuses and a steer's skull is a literal image, maybe too literal (and it will make some people laugh); earth-tone-colored fabrics can be used to evoke a similar atmosphere without thumping folks on the head with the image of a desert.

However, a great volume of dark-colored fabrics or gnarled thorns can create an exaggerated atmosphere. The season isn't melodramatic.

Lenten decoration can be "transfigured" somehow for Eastertime: For instance, the same spot where a large container of bare branches was put during Lent would be where a pot of flowering branches is maintained through Eastertime.

Early on in your preparations, for each area of the building—the assembly's place, the font, a shrine—roughly sketch how you plan the area to look during Lent, on Good Friday, at the Vigil, during Eastertime. How will the decorations reflect the unity of these days? How will the decorations (or their absence) reflect what is unique about Lent, about the Triduum, about Eastertime? What elements will be special to certain days, such as Palm Sunday and Pentecost?

Lent should look pretty much the same as the previous Lent and the Lent before that. Keep what worked; change what didn't.

That said, this year the Lenten spring may unfold in a parish going through an upheaval or within a community torn by tragedy. One year there may be many preparing for baptism; another year there may be no one. Some years Lent begins as early as the first week in February, and in other years

as late as the second week in March. What does Lent look like outside your own window?

What's often needed in our plans and experimentation is the difficult but necessary balancing between the tradition of the season and our adaptation of it. The more we have lived the tradition—Lent's rituals, scriptures, songs and all that the season encompasses—the more they can help form our decisions.

What decorations are in need of repair? What needs to be new or to evolve? Was there anything in the past that caused concern or complaints? What would benefit from a few words of explanation in the parish bulletin? Make sure homilists are cued in to plans.

THE ASSEMBLY'S PLACE

The area high over the heads of the congregation or along the walls is usually a good area for strong decoration that signals the season. For example, a cluster of large branches of weeping willow or an array of purple and gray fabric hangings grabs people's attention when they first enter the worship space, but it does not necessarily demand attention during the liturgy.

The purpose of ornamenting this area is not to teach something or to provide a focus for prayer, and so this often isn't a good area for decorations with a lot of detail or figural imagery. The strongest effect of decoration in this area is to create what *Environment and Art in Catholic Worship*, 100, calls "an atmosphere and a mood."

What will you do to decorate the assembly's place? How will it conform to the building's style? What mood will it set? How will it relate to what is planned for Eastertime? See the discussion beginning on page 60 about

some of the imagery of winter-turning-into-spring that may be useful in this area during Lent.

Baptism is at the heart of Lent. Initiation governs the entire time from Ash Wednesday to Pentecost. Yet initiation is in many ways the church's year-round way of life. The Lenten Sunday gospels from John—the Samaritan woman, the man born blind, the raising of Lazarus—express powerful, archetypal images of water, light and life. But keep in mind that these (and other) baptismal images are woven throughout John's gospel and are hardly unique to any one story.

In some parishes, each week of Lent, symbols of light or water are used as decorations because the gospel that week includes light or water as a central image. This is not a good idea. We will surround ourselves with these sacramental signs in abundance at Easter—not as secondary decoration but as primary ritual necessities, the blessed material of the sacraments.

The Lenten way of emphasizing baptismal materials is through their absence, an absence that does more than make the heart grow fonder. It can make us hunger and thirst for Easter.

ALTAR, AMBO AND CHAIR

This is a good area to keep as free as possible from added adornment. The visual focus here is almost always on the proclamation of the word and the celebration of the eucharist, as well as on the ministers and materials of these rites.

Will there be a particular altar cloth used during Lent? At the eucharist, is it possible to place the cloth on the altar during the preparation of the gifts and then remove it after communion? What candles are to be used during the gospel and during the eucharist? Can they be brought out only when they are used?

How will the cross be treated during Lent, the Triduum and Eastertime? See the discussion beginning on page 67.

VESSELS AND VESTURE

Take an inventory of the material things used for worship. Are these the best they can be? What improvements can you make?

Now more than ever the lectionary and other books should be in good repair. Would it be good to use seasonal book covers? If the lectionary has a festive cover year-round, for the sake of Lenten plainness you might want to cover the book with a simple fabric.

The book of the elect: Those who are already baptized keep Lent in company with the "elect," those catechumens chosen for baptism this coming Easter. The choosing, called "the rite of election," ordinarily takes place at the cathedral on the afternoon or evening of the First Sunday of Lent.

In many parishes, at Sunday morning eucharist the elect enroll their names in a special book. This "book of the elect" is brought to the cathedral for the rite of election and is then brought back and kept somewhere in the church throughout Lent. There the book becomes a wordless call to prayer for the sake of the soon-to-be-baptized.

Where might this be? The area around the altar or ambo is not good. Too much else is going on there. The baptistry may be the right place, or, in some churches, the vestibule. Keep in mind that whatever spot is chosen becomes the place for the book year after year.

The book of the elect would go where parishioners can flip its pages and learn the names inscribed there. Perhaps photos of the elect are included. Perhaps candles are kept burning nearby and a small token of spring flowers is there, too, as a foretaste of Easter. This is a fine place to keep images from John's gospel that are part of the scrutiny rites: the Samaritan woman at the well, the cure of the man born blind, the raising of Lazarus.

If the parish has a set of vessels that it uses only during Lent (or perhaps during Lent and Advent and at no other times), what care do they need? Will there be a particular bread recipe, variety of wine or incense used?

On most days purple vesture is worn. That's true even when celebrating the memorial of a saint during Lent. Red is worn on Palm Sunday. White is worn only on feasts and solemnities (and at most there are only three of these during Lent). Dusky rose may be worn on the Fourth Sunday of Lent.

Is the Lenten vesture in good repair? Is the color and fabric attractive? If purple is used elsewhere in the church, do the shades of color match or at least complement one another? If you want all the ministers to wear the same purple set throughout the season, take the other purple sets out of the sacristy and put them away.

Is the red vesture also in good shape, free from inappropriate ornamentation (such as Pentecost symbols)?

FONT

Many parishes have adopted a general policy that, as much as possible, baptism, confirmation and first communion are not celebrated during Lent.

Also part of general policy is that every year, if possible, baptism, confirmation and first eucharist are celebrated at the Easter Vigil, and confirmation (for teenagers baptized as infants) and first communion (for children baptized as infants) are celebrated during Eastertime.

There is no law that forbids the sacraments of initiation during Lent. Church documents, however, presume and prefer that we celebrate baptism, confirmation and first eucharist at the Easter Vigil. So it simply makes sense that during Lent baptism is not celebrated. This is a good parish policy.

Perhaps, then, the baptismal font is drained, cleaned and sealed in a noble manner before Ash Wednesday. The ambry is emptied of its chrism; the paschal candle is put into a closet and brought out only for funerals.

There is no historical precedent for sealing a font or emptying an ambry. But such a custom makes sense, speaking clearly of the experience of exile and the longing for the Easter bath that are at the heart of Lent. It is not a good idea, however, to fill the font with sand, stones or anything else.

In some places strips of cloth are placed over the empty font, or the font's lid is bound in cords and a wax seal is set in place. The best way to seal the font is bold and simple enough to make it appear that its emptiness is intentional. (Simply to leave it empty of water may make people think that its emptiness is accidental.)

If the font is emptied, then holy water stoops are also emptied. Like the font, the stoops may need something more. Filling them with sand or ashes can make them look like lobby ashtrays. Perhaps like the font, they can be covered. In some places, they can be removed.

Certainly font and stoops need cleaning, and vinegar or a stronger acid will help remove encrusted lime. A grease remover such as trisodium phosphate may also be necessary.

Explain to the parish why there is no holy water during Lent. It is an image of the desert, of the Lenten fast, of our thirsting for baptism at Easter.

The first few times this is done, it may feel like a gimmick, which is unfortunate because gimmicks have no place at worship. If the practice is kept up, in a few years this feeling may pass. However, if the font is drained one year and not the next, the practice in fact will be a gimmick and might as well not be done at all.

CATECHUMENEON

Throughout the year, when catechumens are dismissed from the liturgy, where do they go? How will this place reflect the seasons? There once were strong traditions about this room, called the *catechumeneon*. Customarily, it is a place that is under the same roof as the eucharistic hall but separated from it by a wall; in this way, when catechumens are dismissed from the assembly of the baptized, they are not sent out of the "church."

When they were first accepted as catechumens, these people were signed with the cross and became members of the church. They cannot be shut out, and this truth can be represented in the building's layout. In Byzantine churches there are simple forms of decoration for this space, such as images of Jesus the teacher and of Mary, mother of the church.

SHRINES

Will the parish cover statues and other iconography? If so, how will this be done, and how will the images be unveiled during the Easter Vigil? If not, how else can the shrines reflect Lenten sobriety? (See the discussion of the Lenten veil, beginning on page 64.)

SEASONAL CORNERS

You might create an area (or areas) for highlighting the ways in which the parish is renewing its life of prayer, fasting and almsgiving. Such "seasonal corners" can serve a number of purposes: as a place to advertise intentions for prayer, as a place to accent the ways the parish is preparing for Easter, and perhaps as a place to display seasonal imagery.

Whose job is this? Creating seasonal corners is a joint venture. Pastoral ministers, catechists, school teachers and janitors could join forces with artists and others. Environment and art ministers would try to make sure that the place isn't messy looking, that any materials or decorations are noble and appropriate, and that everything is handsome and fits the scale of the space.

Choose a spot that is easy to visit before and after worship; keep it well lit and call attention to it with decoration. Invite people to use it. You want a practical space that invites churchgoers to linger awhile, but you also want a space that doesn't compete with the liturgy for attention.

Keep seasonal take-home materials in this area. Advertise prayer services. Swap recipes for meatless meals. Sell worthwhile books and items to foster domestic prayer. Especially in this place, advertise the services of the coming Triduum.

Include literature that describes whatever might have been agreed upon as a focus of parishwide almsgiving. In a spot that can be secured, you might keep tended a large hamper for canned goods, clothing and other donations to charity—a parish alms box. Here too can be distributed alms boxes for the home table, such as the cardboard "rice bowls" or plastic "love loaves."

You might even sell piggy banks. These originated as alms boxes, a visual reminder that Lent's fast prepares for a feast. The pig gets cracked open on Holy Thursday, and the money is brought to church to purchase an Easter feast for others. The word "pyg" is an old word for clay—that's what the banks were made of. It's a good Lenten image.

The "seasonal corner" can serve as a kind of community bulletin board, as a place where prayer intentions are made known and where help is asked; for example, here you would find requests for volunteers as well as information about forms that community action can take. An image of the Good Samaritan would be fitting in this place.

Here could go photos and names of the elect and of their families and godparents, as well as photos of parents preparing for the birth of a child, couples preparing for marriage, the newly married, young people preparing for confirmation and first communion, people who are sick, and people who have died or are in mourning.

Preparing a seasonal corner requires an eye for attractiveness of both design and function. It also takes dedicated upkeep. The trick is to keep the place useful (which usually means a lot is going on there) and at the same time tidy.

A seasonal corner might be graced with some of the smaller-scale imagery associated with Lent —a clay bowl of ashes, driftwood, a mobile of fishes,

a pot of crocuses, folk art images of a journey, a desert or winter turning into spring. They would be here to offer delight, to stimulate imaginations, to educate and inform the parish about its paschal treasury.

In the eucharistic hall, these images can appear frivolous because they would be out of scale or out of place. But in a single site somewhere out of the arena of the liturgy, imaginations may be well served by a collection of seasonal art. On occasion (outside of the liturgy) there could be a kind of show-and-tell with folk arts of the season.

One such tradition, a nice one for parish schools, is a "burning bush," a cousin of the "Jesse tree." Branches are set into a pot of sand or gravel (red-twigged dogwood is beautiful). Day by day, onto the twigs are hung representations of characters from the Lenten scriptures. These are our companions on the journey, and their stories are heard at daily Mass.

Jewish tradition includes calendars for counting the days between the festivals of Passover and Shavuot. Christians might take a cue from this custom. A paschal calendar running from Ash Wednesday to Pentecost can grace a vestibule or classroom. The calendar can be a construction of cut paper, cloth or wood, perhaps made into a series of cards to announce the count each day or perhaps made more elaborately with small doors, as in an Advent calendar. It would designate both the day of the week—say, Monday of the second week in Lent—as well as the day of the count—in this case, the ninth of the Forty Days of Lent.

LTP publishes a Noah's ark with windows to open for every day from Ash Wednesday until Easter. The books of LTP's *Sourcebook* series are anthologies of seasonal prose and poetry arranged day by day through the seasons. Perhaps a place can be found to leave *A Lent Sourcebook* (and then *Triduum* and *Easter*) open to the day's entries as an invitation to prayer and meditation.

VESTIBULES, DOORWAYS, OUTDOORS

The paschal season can be compared to a journey, a trip that will leave some of us exhausted. The Lenten leg of our march takes us from Egypt to the sea, from the wilderness to the garden on Calvary's hill. During Eastertime we travel to Sinai, where at Pentecost we meet God face to face.

Spring is a time for outdoor processions. They are at the heart of our seasonal rituals. In fair weather, processions can be acts of thanksgiving; in foul, they can be acts of hope.

There is another form of "procession" that deserves our attention: the weekly gathering of the church. The walk through the parking lot might benefit from outdoor decorations. Even if the plan is to keep the interior of the church as austere as possible throughout Lent, outdoor decorations can serve as an announcement that business-as-usual has been suspended, that the paschal season has become our preoccupation, and that all are welcome to the adventure.

Ways of doing this might be with a monochromatic array of purple hangings near the main doors; a large vine and pussy willow wreath could be hung near the sign that bears the church's name; or even a collection of fish-shaped nylon windsocks fluttering from bamboo poles could be set up. One parish suspended purple, rose and green nylon kites from the lights in their parking lot. Most of this kind of decoration would be inappropriate inside a church, but outside it can communicate the hospitality and enthusiasm of the parish.

A "triumphal arch" is a traditional seasonal decoration worth returning year after year. The arch—a handsome and sturdy wooden trellis constructed to complement the architectural style of the church building—is set outside the main doors from Ash Wednesday to Pentecost. It receives changing ornamentation: purple fabrics and bare vines during Lent; red fabrics, palms and other spring branches added for Palm Sunday and the Triduum; a switch to pastel fabrics and flowers for Eastertime; and green branches and bundles of fresh grasses at Pentecost.

Something of an arch can be created more simply from a large swag of fabric used as bunting over the main doors. This is a customary emblem of triumph or mourning.

OTHER LOCATIONS

What attention will the grounds require? In what ways can the school, parish hall, library, rectory and other places, indoors and out, reflect the season (and not jump the gun on Easter)?

Classroom windows are a favorite place for seasonal decorations. Folks who drive by can catch the spirit reflected in the windows. Lenten images are not too hard to imagine: How about construction-paper fishes in an array of purples? What about snakes? Or phoenixes? And let's not forget those wonderful Lenten readings about Noah and Jonah and Esther and Daniel. Lent is overflowing with stories to hear, tell and act out.

SPECIAL OCCASIONS

Ash Wednesday may have an atmosphere all its own, one that is not sustained throughout Lent. Perhaps Ash Wednesday, in the context of the paschal season, is a kind of slap in the face with our mortality, a shaking up that sends us running to Easter. The day after Mardi Gras is not tragedy's mask replacing comedy's; it is a time without cosmetics, without masks of any kind.

The liturgy offers several traditions for this day of lamentation: empty bellies, long silences broken by the penitential psalms, kneeling and even prostration, a stripped-down space, the procession for the imposition of ashes.

The parish really should have a special set of vessels to contain and distribute ashes. Rough clay or stone or even bone seems a fitting material for these vessels. The ashes might be set in the midst of the assembly on a pedestal (not a table, the altar is our table), perhaps canopied in grays, browns or purples, perhaps with candles set around it (such as an old funeral set with unbleached beeswax candles) and burning incense nearby.

It is inappropriate to put vessels of ashes on the altar. Another place needs to be set up, so why not choose the place that the coffin rests during a funeral? An urn is the usual container for ashes. On Ash Wednesday all that has died is bound up in that dust.

In some places the beginning of the 40 days is marked by a penitential procession. Some of this spirit might be reflected by carrying a decorated processional cross, banners or a flowering branch during the entrance procession of Mass on the First Sunday of Lent.

The third, fourth and fifth Sundays of Lent have the rites of scrutiny and exorcism of the elected catechumens. The laying on of hands is the strong physical gesture here. In some parishes the elect and their godparents stand down the aisles or around the room in the midst of the assembly for these rites. Portable banners, simple strips of color, might be carried by servers who flank the elect during these rites.

The Fourth Sunday of Lent, Laetare Sunday, is a crest in the hill from which we catch our first sight of Jerusalem, the motherland where we shall keep the Passover. This Sunday gets its name from the Latin entrance antiphon: *"Laetare Jerusalem: et conventum facite omnes qui diligitis eam"* ("Rejoice, Jerusalem, and come together all you who love her.").

Lent is a preparation for our homecoming in the Holy City. Will this homecoming take place at Easter or at the end of time? There is a splendid ambiguity here. Thanks to the liturgy, in England this fourth Sunday became "Mothering Sunday," a day for honoring Mother Jerusalem and Mother Church and one's own mother. The day is meant to make us eager for Easter.

Halfway through the Forty Days, on this Sunday of rejoicing, flowers are permitted in celebration of spring, and in some parishes flowers are handed out to everyone. Rose-colored vesture is customary (although not required). The color is not pink but a dusky rose, a softening of Lent's purple.

Like those of Carnival, the traditions of Laetare Sunday were formed by people for whom Lent was important. If Lent is kept with vigor and care, perhaps we truly need this mid-Lent Sunday to muster our resolve to finish the journey.

After the Fourth Sunday, the gospels at daily Mass are all from John, as they are during the Easter season. In some parishes, in the parish library a Bible is kept open to the year's evangelist. From now through Pentecost the book would be open to John.

The final Sunday of Lent, called either Palm Sunday or Passion Sunday, is the subject of its own section, beginning on page 69.

Three days can fall during Lent on which white vesture is worn and flowers are used as signs of festivity: the Chair of St. Peter (February 22), St. Joseph (March 19), and the Annunciation of the Lord (March 25). Check the calendar; in some years the March solemnities are transferred to another day.

The feast of the Chair of Peter is a celebration of the apostle as bishop of Rome. Joseph is remembered on the final day of winter. His name evokes the patriarch who was also "a dreamer of dreams"; so it seems fitting that he is honored when the earth itself awakens. On Annunciation Day, when daytime has grown longer than night, when winter has passed over into spring, we remember how Mary's "yes" undid Eve's "no."

The Lenten array would not be altered much on these days, if only to underscore these days' place in the church's paschal season. However, if a

parish has a special set of vesture for Christmastime, why not put it to use on March 19 and 25?

The angel's annunciation to the sleeping Joseph or to Mary is a favorite subject for artists. So is the commissioning of Peter with the "keys of the kingdom." Are these images found in the church building in a picture or stained-glass window? Can they be highlighted for the day with flowers, candles and other illumination? (Carnations, meaning "flesh colored," are the "flowers of the incarnation" and are customary in some places on March 19 and 25.)

If images of Peter, Joseph or the Annunciation have been veiled for Lent, they might be unveiled for their respective days, or an appropriate painting or statuary might be put on display in the vestibule.

Memorials of the saints (and there are only a few on the calendar at this time of year) are all optional during Lent, and if one is observed the vesture stays Lenten. That means, perhaps surprisingly, that the liturgical color for St. Patrick's Day is purple. The memorials of the saints are not meant to be interruptions in the observance of the season.

Much of the imagery associated with the day is also associated with Lent and might be useful in parish schools that day, but not used weeks ahead of time as the card stores do. A liturgically responsible way to reflect St. Patrick's Day at worship is to bless and distribute shamrocks.

The shamrock was a teaching device for catechumens preparing for Easter baptism. The legend about chasing the snakes out of Ireland is an image of repentance and purification. Even the "wearing of the green," besides being a greeting of spring for some and a support of one's heritage for others, is the color once worn by penitents being reconciled with the church on Holy Thursday.

In most parishes, communal celebrations of the sacrament of reconciliation are especially well attended during Lent. This sacrament is one of the destinations of the Lenten journey.

Any stations for individual confessions—with attractive and sturdy chairs and kneelers—might include a large burning candle and a small cluster of spring flowers. Make sure reconciliation rooms are in good order, that any liturgical art in them is appropriate and well made, and that vesture used during the sacrament is full-sized and of excellent quality.

During private confessions, try to make sure the church is quiet and clean and safely lit—but not necessarily brightly lit—and that candles are burning (perhaps floorstanding ones could be near the door of the reconciliation chapel or confessional) as a sign that this, too, is a liturgy of the church. It would not be inappropriate to decorate the entrances to the reconciliation chapel or confessional with a palm or olive wreath or a cluster of forsythia branches as a foretaste of Easter.

During the times of the sacrament of reconciliation, the church entrance is a good spot for an image of the prodigal son's return. Perhaps a trough of sand and a basket of small candles can be placed nearby so that people can leave a burning candle in the sand on their way out.

Welcome the Lenten Spring!

> Lenten is come with love to town,
> With blossoms and with bird's song,
> That all this bliss bringeth:
>> Daisies in the dales,
>> Notes sweet of nightingales
>> Each fowl its song singeth.
>
> −from the Thirteenth century

In some places the Lenten spring comes to town with plenty of bird songs, but in other places it arrives with blizzards. Spring has many faces. Sometimes it looks like an orchard, pink with blossoms and butterflies, and sometimes like a flooding river engorged with mud and drowned animals. Throughout the paschal season death and life are never far apart.

Take a Lenten walk in the wild. You'll likely return with clods of dirt stuck to shoes, hair messed by the wind, muscles stiff and sore, eyes blinded by the strengthening sun.

The word "Lent" is English. Thanks to the northerly latitude, day lengths in England vary dramatically, from just a few hours of sun at Christmas to almost endless light at the summer solstice. In ancient times people divided the year so that solstices and equinoxes didn't mark beginnings and endings of seasons, as they do now, but their midpoints. Spring, by this definition, began at Candlemas and ended on May Day. This was the *lencten* season, the quarter of the year that daytime lengthens rapidly.

Lent is a spring not of settled warmth but of change—of transformation, conversion and passing over—when the northern hemisphere of the planet turns toward the sun, the source of life. In the lengthening brightness from Ash Wednesday to Holy Thursday—our Lenten spring—we are called to turn away from sin and death. We are called to turn to God as our source of life.

Many parishes decorate for Lent with bare branches. That makes sense in regions where trees are still leafless at this time of year. Branches can evoke the wilderness, the burning bush, the fig tree given another chance to bear fruit. They also can reflect the time of year when buds are preparing to open.

Locust and hawthorn branches are handsome; so are brightly colored osiers. Pussy willows are customary on Palm Sunday, but not much earlier in the season. (Don't put them in water or the catkins will fall off.) Small branches can look good arranged in a large pot of vermiculite or sand. A large branch may look good hung against a wall, but this has to look natural, without contrivance.

Branches should be set against a contrasting background; otherwise, they disappear. Exotic species—such as corkscrew willow or contorted hazel, two favorites of florists—can look bizarre and out of place in church.

Willows are among the first trees to green up. In Christian poetry their thirst for water is compared to the catechumens' longing for baptism. Weeping willows are mentioned in Psalm 137, the song of exile; the species name shows the link—*Salix babylonica.* They look best suspended from a ceiling with invisible wire, with their stump ends anchored against a wall. If hung high, this can be a good decoration for the assembly's area.

Some parishes include among the Lenten decorations a kind of "work in progress." For example, week by week a bare tree is hung with flowers and fruit; or a banner, say, of a mountain in the desert gradually takes shape with features added each week. This is done to represent transfiguration—in Greek, *metamorphosis.*

This might sound like a good thing to try, but it's usually not effective. Only the alert church-goer who attends every week would notice the changes. Otherwise they need to be explained, and that makes it contrived. This sort of decoration may be appropriate in a parish hall or vestibule but never near the altar; it draws too much attention to itself. If you have limited time and energy, this is not where it should be spent.

Some people set branches or small trees in water to leaf out over a several-week period. But even with a suitable species, such as poplar, what's likely to happen is that within a couple of weeks new leaves emerge only to die soon after—hardly a sign of transfiguration and, in any case, one that won't last the season.

It seems that in every parish the metamorphosis from caterpillar to chrysalis to butterfly has been a favorite, if overused, image. Frogs also undergo transformation; an ancient Christian tomb is decorated with a carving of a frog and the words "in the twinkling of an eye," from Paul's First Letter to the Corinthians, which speaks of the metamorphosis of the dead "at the last trumpet."

In much traditional religious art such things as butterflies or frogs would be added to a composition in secondary positions, say, tucked into a corner. The primary images (of Jesus or the saints) must conform to a strict accepted pattern because they are expressions of the church's communal faith. But the artist takes a lot more leeway in using secondary images, which the artist can use to offer a kind of personal commentary on the primary

images. And these secondary images can delight the viewer who happens to notice them.

The same principle can apply to the worship space. A Lenten caterpillar that is transformed at Easter into a butterfly is best in a place that doesn't demand attention—an out-of-the-way spot where the image can surprise us, perhaps in a shrine or in the vestibule but not hanging over our heads or near the altar.

Scripture stories of the season are tales of transformation. The animals aboard the ark, the Hebrew slaves marching through the Red Sea, Jonah in the fish, Daniel in the lions' den, the three children in the fiery furnace, the prodigal son—these tales can be depicted in some way and the depictions changed from Lent to the Triduum to Eastertime.

As an example, on a bulletin board in the parish school, perhaps during Carnival the animals are shown marching aboard Noah's ark; during Lent they huddle inside the boat; at the Triduum, Noah releases the raven and the dove; and during Eastertime the animals come out of the ark and the rainbow appears.

We ban flowers from church during the Lenten spring. Northerners might regard this as a reflection of the time of year, but not Southerners, for whom Lent overflows with daffodils.

We ban flowers because they are signs of festivity. But when you think about it, flowers are emblems of many different things. They are signs of festivity, of consolation, of life and even of the shortness of life. The flowers of very early spring are harbingers—they point to something even more wonderful to come.

What always would be avoided throughout the season is the use of flowers as emblems of festivity—except on the Fourth Sunday, on the feast of the Chair of Peter, on St. Joseph's Day and on Annunciation Day. The ban on festive flowers should be explained to anyone thinking of scheduling a Lenten wedding. At this season weddings are without verbal or visual alleluias, which is enough of a reason to postpone them until Lent is past.

Of course, flowers also are signs of consolation, which is why they are used at funerals throughout the year and are permitted at funerals even during Lent. But give away leftover flowers after the funeral liturgy.

Red and silver maple, elm, willow, hazel, birch and a few other species bear small, peculiarly shaped flowers during the first warm days. The flowers are not showy—hardly recognizable to most people as flowers—and certainly are not merry. But they do have a strange and welcome beauty that seems to fit the season. They can be signs of the brevity of life, and perhaps even heralds of the life to come.

A few branches might go in a crock of water put in a place where they can be appreciated up close. Perhaps each week of Lent one or two snowdrops or crocuses or daffodils can be put in a place where those few "harbinger flowers" would be in scale, such as near the book of the elect.

The Lenten Veil

By the rivers of Babylon—
there we sat down and wept
   when we remembered Zion.
On the willows there
   we hung up our harps.
For our captors
   asked us for songs,
and our tormentors asked for mirth, saying,
   "Sing us one of the songs of Zion!"
But how could we sing the LORD's song
   in a foreign land?
   —Psalm 137:1-4

A generation ago, the custom of veiling crosses, statues and sacred pictures during the final two weeks of Lent was the year's most ambitious alteration of the worship environment. Here was a custom with visual clout.

In the early Middle Ages the cross was crafted as a richly jeweled emblem of triumph. During Lent the bright cross was hidden from view. That's the origin of the custom of veiling the cross, but the veiling of other sacred images has a different beginning.

In ancient times at the start of Lent, penitents were marked with ashes and then expelled from church. They were expected to keep Lent in strict fasting before being welcomed back during the Triduum. Almost everyone kept the fast out of compassion for the penitents: There but for the grace of God go we. The whole assembly stopped short of being expelled from church, but in many places the altar was hidden from view throughout Lent with a curtain (called in some places a "hunger cloth") or solid panels, which came down in joy on Easter Eve.

The Lenten veil is a strong image of exile. Ever since we were thrown out of paradise, death deprives us of the company of our ancestors, the saints. A veil keeps us from seeing heaven, a sight that religious art is meant to anticipate. In Isaiah's words, on the day that death is destroyed, gone also will be the veil that veils all people, the web woven over the earth.

In the liturgical reforms of the late 1960s, word came down that Lenten veiling was "suppressed." However, in the 1985 edition of the sacramentary the practice was reintroduced as an option. The rubrics are located on the Saturday before the Fifth Sunday of Lent.

Perhaps the celestial significance of the two-week period before Easter is enough of a reason to distinguish it: Because Easter's date is determined by the full moon, the coming of Easter is heralded by the new moon waxing ever brighter each evening during the 14 days before it grows full. This is the astronomical origin of "Passiontide."

But Passiontide is gone from the reformed calendar so that Lent is undivided. If the parish reintroduces the custom of veiling sacred images during Lent, it's probably best to do this at the beginning of the season. Bear in mind that the custom has a ritual purpose. If the cross and statues are veiled for Lent, the cross is unveiled during the Good Friday liturgy. The images of the saints are unveiled during the Easter Vigil. (See page 112 for more about the unveiling.)

Although there is no tradition for this, perhaps the veiling itself can be part of the liturgy. Veils might be put in place at the end of Evening Prayer the night before Ash Wednesday.

If the custom is taken up again, there is a responsibility to continue it year after year. It's too distinctive to try one year and ignore the next. But don't make too much of it; it's simply a part of the other ways we simplify the worship environment during Lent. It's an image of exile and of sorrow for sin.

Perhaps the custom comes down to this: During Lent we don't need our shrines, those places of private prayer. For a season, we turn aside from private concerns to focus on the community.

A Lenten "veil" is not sheer. It is a covering that removes an object from sight. If circumstances permit, it might make more sense to remove the cross and images rather than cover them, except that moving anything involves risk. Is it worth it? Also, removing a statue, even for a few weeks, will generate anxieties that would not be raised if instead the statues were to remain in place and be covered with fabric.

By custom, the coverings would be of the liturgical color of the day, which meant they could be purple, white, red or black. Coverings might be made of a fabric that matches or complements the vesture, but a gray or earth-tone color or the color of the walls may help the veiled object disappear into its background—which is the purpose of the veil. To cover flat surfaces, panels could be made from fabric and stapled to lightweight frames that fit over the flat surface.

A veiled picture or statue has a cocoon-like appearance, which in a sense communicates that a transfiguration is soon to occur. Another odd effect of the veiling is that it can look as if a place is being repaired or renovated—which in a way comes close to the truth.

The Cross

> A cross is a basic symbol in any Christian liturgical celebration. The advantage of a processional cross with a floor standard, in contrast to one that is permanently hung or affixed to a wall, is that it can be placed differently according to the celebration and the other environmental factors.
> —*Environment and Art in Catholic Worship*, 88

It may seem strange to veil the cross during Lent. But absence can put a powerful emphasis on something. A reason for removing the cross from sight is to make us long for its return on Good Friday.

It was in a garden that Adam and Eve ate from the tree of wisdom and brought death upon themselves and their children. Here in Lent's desert we fast from eating. On Good Friday, when Lent is past, Eden's gardener will plant the tree of life in our midst to welcome us home to paradise.

Ideally, the main cross in the worship space is the one venerated on Good Friday and the one used as the processional cross throughout the year. That way our worship space has one cross, and one cross only.

But in many places the main cross is unmovable and inaccessible for processions or for veneration (making it liturgically useless, if that isn't too blunt), and so a special cross, which spends most of the year in a closet, is used on Good Friday.

The first choice would be to set things right so that the cross we honor all year becomes the cross we honor with great affection on Good Friday. This cross would be processional and made out of wood to conform to Good Friday's invitation, "Behold the wood of the cross."

If this cannot be done—a great loss—we at least might put the priority on avoiding having more than one cross in view at the same time. A way to do this: During Lent and Eastertime the (unmovable) main cross is kept covered with a screen or curtain (but not with old-fashioned veiling, which can turn the cross into a huge purple kite). This screening is done in a way that complements the church interior (which, admittedly, may be impossible to do well). On Good Friday a large wooden cross is used for the liturgy. This cross would be kept in a place of honor through Eastertime, perhaps hung in front of the curtain that screens the main cross from sight.

This won't work in many situations, especially if hiding the main cross for a quarter of the year is insensitive to parish regard for it. Although this is a

job for professionals, in some parishes a beloved crucifix is relocated to a shrine so that it doesn't compete with the cross used in liturgy and yet is still accessible for private devotion.

Some parishes use a cross as a decoration during Lent or at Easter or throughout the whole paschal time. Sometimes it is placed near the altar (where it is often redundant to the main cross); sometimes it goes in the vestibule or outdoors; sometimes it gets purple bunting during Lent and more festive ornamentation during Eastertime; and in some places this is the cross venerated on Good Friday.

Here are a number of things to consider before using a cross as a seasonal decoration:

1. Lent is not a six-week long Passiontide. The liturgy does not focus on the passion of Christ until the final days of Lent. The tradition during Lent has been to hide the cross from view, if only to make us eager to see it once again during the Triduum. There is, however, a good, strong tradition for honoring the holy cross throughout Eastertime, because once the cross is carried into our midst on Good Friday, it is not carried out.

2. Throughout the year a cross is used within the liturgy to "christen" the space (or the route of a procession) as well as the assembly of worshipers. But a cross can be used in a shrine as a focus of private prayer; these are seen outdoors all over Latin America and Europe. There's often a place to kneel, to put flowers, to linger awhile and pray.

3. If you plan to use a cross in a seasonal shrine, does its setting allow people to give it reverence? If used outdoors, will the cross be an affront to neighbors of another or of no religious tradition? Considering that the cross has been abused as a sign of hatred, how will your cross convey inclusivity and charity?

4. Creating a seasonal shrine for the holy cross, which requires a bit of privacy for meditation as well as isolation from the liturgical space, can put a cross to a worthy purpose. Using a cross as mere decoration does not.

Palm Sunday

Ride on, ride on in majesty!
In lowly pomp ride on to die.
O Christ, your triumphs now begin
O'er captive death and conquered sin.
—Henry Hart Milman

For those who prepare worship, Palm Sunday can be "schizophrenic Sunday." An austere Mass has a merry beginning.

The liturgy for this day is a hybrid of Eastern and Western traditions, and it has the typical vigor (and peculiarity) that often results from hybridization. The day's Mass had its origins in Rome, which titled this day "Passion Sunday" and centered the liturgy on the passion and death of the Lord. However, the Commemoration of the Lord's Entrance into Jerusalem, whose full form is an outdoor procession, is borrowed from the Christian East, where Palm Sunday marks the festive conclusion to Lent.

After the procession, the liturgy focuses on the passion. A visual way to make this distinction is to limit Palm Sunday decorations to the outdoors, the entryways and the vestibule. The interior of the church would remain the same as during the previous weeks of Lent. However, it might be appropriate to add, very simply, some red to the Lenten purple and perhaps, if this can be done simply, with dignity and without melodrama, a large wreath of thorns or other emblems of the passion.

The entryways where people receive palms would be decorated, and palms could be made available in large, handsome baskets. An icon of the Lord's entrance into Jerusalem could be enshrined there.

Most of the outdoor decoration—perhaps red and purple bunting and ribbons, leafy crowns and clusters of palms and pussy willows, a triumphal arch and decorated poles—probably can stay in place throughout the coming week as an invitation to the neighborhood to enter into the Passover of the Lord.

The liturgical color for Palm Sunday is red, not purple. Red is associated with blood, with the cross, with the passion and death of the Lord, with the Spirit that Jesus breathed forth on Calvary. But red replacing the Lenten purple may send the wrong signal—that Lent is over—although it also may suggest that the Pasch is near.

In the old liturgy, the vesture color was red for the procession and purple for the Mass, a pattern that still can make sense. Purple and red are royal

cousins. The poet Venantius Fortunatus (†609) wrote of the holy cross: *"Arbor decor' et fulgida, ornata regis purpura."* ("Fit and shining tree, hung with purple majesty.")

Is the parish's red vesture in good condition? Is it worthy enough for the great days on which it is worn? The red vestments especially should be free from applied symbols, such as a dove or a crown of thorns, so that they can be used on Palm Sunday, Good Friday, Pentecost, Holy Cross Day, SS. Peter and Paul and on the martyrs' and apostles' memorial days.

The sacramentary suggests that the processional cross be "suitably decorated" for the entrance rites. A handsome way to decorate the cross is to ring it with a wreath of flowers and to attach ribbons to the wreath. In some countries, this day is called "flowering Sunday" or "Passover of the flowers" because of the abundance of flowers used in the procession.

A procession looks more like a procession if as many people as possible are carrying banners and other signs of festivity. Bunches of palms and blossoming branches tied to large sticks are easy to fashion.

From Guatemala to Germany, there are splendid customs for weaving clusters of palms and branches with ribbons and other ornamentation for Palm Sunday. The clusters are often ten feet tall and just as wide, but even under massive ornamentation—sometimes the branches are hung with food—their significance shines through in strong ritual action: The branch clusters are lovingly fashioned at home, the household carries them to the great ingathering in Jerusalem (the parish church), and then the assembled community marches into the streets and eventually on to the cemeteries to announce to the dead that Easter is coming.

That is where most of these fantastical "palms" wind up—stuck into graves. No wonder the branches are festooned with food. It will be, God willing, the Easter breakfast for the newly risen.

A wonderful part of the procession might be a donkey piñata hoisted high on a pole. Using a donkey in the Palm Sunday procession is as old as the day itself. A donkey is a scriptural sign of humility and service. It calls to mind Zechariah's enigmatic words about a humble king who will arrive to end war and "command peace to the nations." There are other great scriptural images for this day: the phoenix, the rooster, the olive tree and Noah's dove, crowns, the lamb, the holy city. (LTP's *Lent Sourcebook* can help us recognize the wondrous imagery of this occasion.)

It is important to remember that the procession is not just a reminder of a past event but a sign of the advent of God's reign. In this liturgical act, as in every liturgy, the past, present and future get rolled up into heaven's timeless "today." If a donkey helps us pretend we're back in Jerusalem two thousand years ago, that's not liturgy. But if a donkey and branches and banners and singing and marching are part of our celebration of Christ among us, who comes to establish peace, that's both good worship and good news.

Ordinarily, all the things used in the procession are left outside the church doors when the procession enters. These things might be used outdoors throughout the coming week as a visual declaration that this holy house is now Jerusalem, that God's people are gathering here to keep the Passover.

However, the decorated processional cross would be used to lead the people into the church. During the opening prayer and the liturgy of the word, perhaps instead of being put in its stand, the cross could be held by someone standing in the main aisle and facing the people.

Receiving palms creates a bond between home and church. Strengthen this bond: Don't skimp on your order. Order the palms whole and rip them up yourself into sizable pieces if the only "pre-shredded" palms available are torn to smithereens. Greeters can invite people to take as many as they want.

Decorate with whole fronds so that you can make an association between the actual leaf and the torn piece in people's hands. Decorate with a few (usually expensive) date palm fronds, *Phoenix dactylifera,* which is the desert species that has such strong religious associations for Jews, Christians and Muslims as an emblem of resurrection. (The plant used in much of North America is cabbage palm, *Sabal palmetto,* a native of the Gulf Coast.)

Also decorate with the budding branches of spring. After Jesus marched into Jerusalem, he spoke of spring branches as heralds of the coming of the day of the Lord.

The date palm, as its Latin name implies, is a reminder of the phoenix, the legendary bird of paradise that landed in the fronds of a palm tree and then burst into flames. Soon, from a single egg left in the ashes a new and more beautiful phoenix arose. Early Christians enjoyed this legend as an allegory of the resurrection.

Peacocks, too, became emblems of Easter because they renew their bright plumage each spring. In some regions wooden phoenixes are carved for Easter—a marvelous folk tradition that can be part of the decoration from now until Pentecost. Peacock feathers can be mixed with the palms and used as decorations (a Mediterranean custom).

In past generations, on this day people carried in the procession branches from whatever trees and bushes happened to be greening up in their own backyards. In many places these other kinds of branches have come to be called "palms." Because they are heralds of Easter, they often have been planted in cemeteries, and the plants there also became a source for Palm Sunday branches.

The biblical significance of olive branches makes them favorite native "palms" in lands around the Mediterranean. Lilacs and forsythia (both relatives of the olive) are favorites in the north. Almost everywhere, pussy willows are strongly associated with this day. In many communities the significance of the ceremony demands that people cut their own branches and carry them to church.

Throughout Lent, you might invite people to bring backyard branches to church on Palm Sunday. Mention that we cut our own branches, whatever we have, to welcome the Messiah into the Holy City. These will be joined with the palms. In places where spring needs hastening, a week or so earlier the branches can be cut and brought inside and placed in water to force them to bloom.

Palms and other green branches are pledges of resurrection. They are signs of faith in the risen Christ, and on this final Sunday in Lent we cling to them as we proclaim Christ's suffering and death.

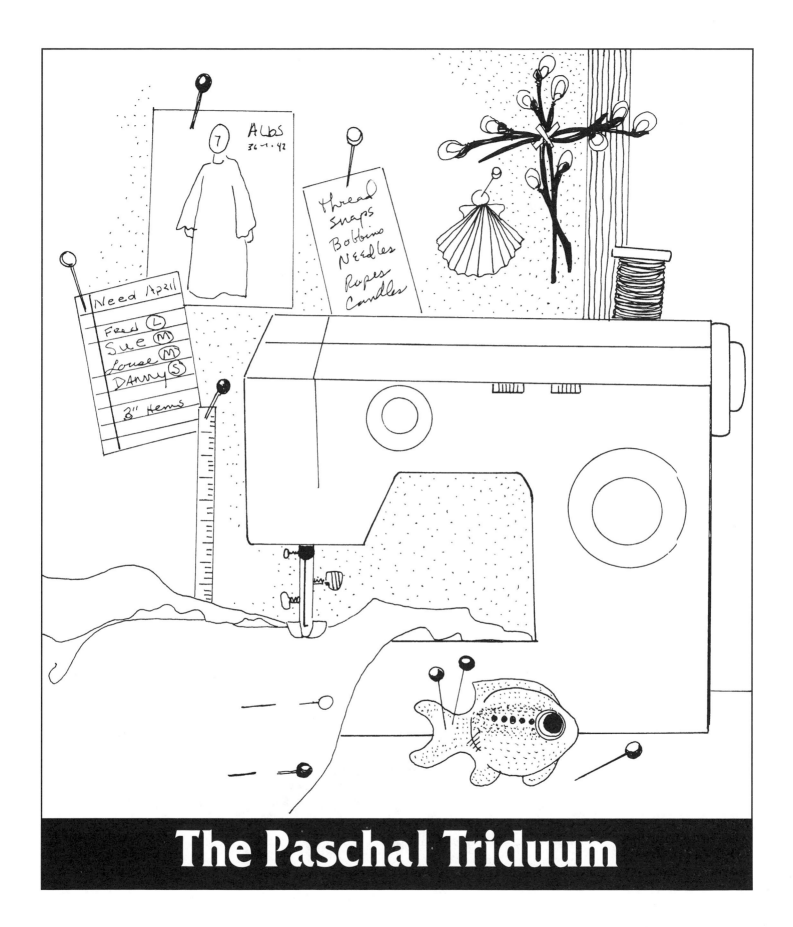

The Paschal Triduum

A Sense of the Season

Christian poets have said that the liturgical year is like a wedding ring we wear to remember our covenant with Christ. The Paschal Triduum is its jewel.

As the word signifies, the Triduum is a three-day observance. Lent is a preparation for it. Eastertime is a continued celebration of it. The three days begin Holy Thursday at sunset and conclude on Easter Sunday at sunset.

Notice that the Triduum is not Holy Thursday, Good Friday and Holy Saturday. It would be more accurate to say that the Triduum is Good Friday, Holy Saturday and Easter Sunday, except that the three days are counted in the Jewish manner, from sunset to sunset, to correspond to three of the biblical days of creation. These three days are the "sixth day" (when God finished creation), the "seventh day" (the sabbath, when God rested), and the "first day" (when God began creation).

On a "sixth day" Jesus died. On a sabbath Jesus lay buried in the tomb. On a "first day" Jesus was raised into glory. That's why we take these three days to observe the Christian Passover. We witness a new creation.

It's no wonder that the date of Easter is set to fall in spring (at least in the northern hemisphere). Spring isn't incidental to the imagery of the Triduum. It's foundational. Spring is an image of creation, perhaps the strongest image we have.

And it's not just spring's nice weather and flowers but also the harsher elements of the season that are bound up with the Triduum—elements that reflect the struggle between order and chaos, liberty and oppression, life and death. Poets have seen these elements as signs of the paschal mystery. If you've ever kindled an Easter fire during a snowstorm, you'll have witnessed something of this imagery.

Christ crucified, buried and risen—Augustine said that this is the mystery of the Triduum. Most specially in those who are baptized, we celebrate the body of Christ that struggles and suffers and dies, that is buried in the oblivion of death and that is risen from chaos into inextinguishable light.

Notice that we use the present tense in speaking of this mystery. Nowhere in the liturgy of the Triduum is there any notion of trying to re-create first-century Jerusalem, of pretending we're there again. That's not the liturgy's goal, and it shouldn't be our goal either. Something even more wonderful than that is happening in the liturgy of the Passover. The boundaries between past, present and future dissolve.

And so we can sing on Easter Eve, "This is the night" that light is created, the rainbow appears, Isaac's life is redeemed, the Red Sea opens, the Jordan parts, and the three children sing God's praises in the midst of a fire. In the words of the Exsultet, this is the "most blessed of all nights, chosen by God to see Christ rising from the dead."

Church tower bells are not rung from the Gloria of Holy Thursday until the Gloria of the Easter Vigil. This is an old custom that remains a part of the way we worship. The bells ring out to welcome the Passover and then again to signal its completion. But in between, they are silent.

The point here is that time stops. In some places all clock faces are veiled and the hours are not sounded, because once the sun sets on Holy Thursday the entire church is swept into its Passover. As wondrously strange as this may seem, we enter eternity.

In medieval villages only a few of the rich could afford timepieces, and so the paschal silencing of the bells had consequences. It meant business-as-usual was brought to a standstill. During these most sacred days, people would show up at church early in the morning and then spend the day there. They didn't need bells to summon them; they were there waiting.

The Christian Passover will not be understood apart from keeping watch, waiting, anticipating. The Paschal Triduum requires of us a liturgical piety that prods us to put everything else aside—even time itself—in the presence of the awesome mystery.

The Triduum is observed by the church with a single, three-day-long liturgy. That's something we have to get into our hearts and minds and even into the mechanics of how we prepare for the Triduum: how we

organize our schedules, when we decorate, when we rehearse. We are making ready for a three-day-long liturgy, not a series of liturgies.

"Mass of the Lord's Supper," "Celebration of the Lord's Passion," "Preparation of the Elect," "Easter Vigil," "Easter Sunday Mass," "Easter Evening Prayer": These phrases are a kind of shorthand we use to describe certain moments in the paschal liturgy. But notice that Holy Thursday's eucharist has no dismissal rite. Good Friday's service has no greeting and no dismissal. The Easter Vigil does not have an entrance rite. The notion is that once the paschal liturgy begins on Holy Thursday, the church remains together in spirit to see it to its conclusion.

The Triduum is not too far removed from other human adventures. Weddings, family reunions and funerals often unfold over a series of days. There are several meals, occasional lulls, catnaps, shifting moods, quiet times and raucous ones, and there is a main event. The main event of the Triduum is the Easter Vigil.

The ideal is to enable the parish to join in conclave for these three days each year. We can aim toward that and at least not thwart it. For example, from year to year the different groups in the parish can schedule their activities so that they do not conflict with the three days. Perhaps communal meals in the spirit of the fast are prepared for Good Friday and Holy Saturday. Child care is provided. A round-the-clock vigil is organized. *The parish does not lock its doors.* Outdoor lights are left on and security staff is provided.

Does this involve environment and art ministers? You bet, and not just in ways we might expect! A lot more is possible than just getting up the Easter decorations. (And those eventually might be last on our list of priorities.)

We can see that the other sites around the parish are decorous—"fitting"—to their purpose: for a fasting supper, a parish Easter breakfast, for child care. One area you may need to prepare is a "paschal chapel"—a focus of prayer for people keeping watch in prayer between the liturgical high points of the Triduum liturgy. This chapel is discussed beginning on page 94.

Rather than disturb those keeping vigil, the paraphernalia of liturgy could be set up as much as possible before the Triduum begins and kept "waiting in the wings." Once the Triduum begins, the church complex can then be maintained in a prayerful atmosphere. The quiet hours between the principal services can be "decorated" with times of music and of silence, with subdued lighting and with bright candles.

There are, of course, a few jobs to be done in the midst of the Triduum, but even filling an empty font or unwrapping flowers can be an act of worship, a way we keep vigil. It's gracious to advertise the times you will be decorating so that others may join in this activity as one of the ways we keep our Passover united as a parish.

The Triduum is a fast and then a feast. Fasting is one of the ways we keep watch. This paschal fast is part of the "liturgy" (a word that means the "work of the people") that begins on Holy Thursday night and continues through Good Friday and Holy Saturday.

Fasting is something the Triduum has in common with weddings and funerals. It's what we do when our stomach is in knots, when we are overwhelmed with emotions. The paschal fast unites this time at home and in church. Then on Saturday night into Sunday morning we pass over from fasting into feasting.

Fast and feast are helpful ways to think about the atmosphere within the church. The simplicity and cleanliness of the interior on Good Friday and Holy Saturday are like a visual fast. Easter decorations are like a feast.

Overview

LTP's book *The Three Days,* by Gabe Huck, addresses most everything about the Triduum liturgy. You need that book to cover what won't be covered here. Here, we focus on the worship environment.

Putting things away is a meaningful gesture. A couple generations ago, altars overflowed with candlesticks, cloths and altar cards throughout the year. On Holy Thursday after Mass, while Night Prayer was sung, the cloths, candles and cards were taken away, leaving the church with a dramatic barrenness. But many, many generations before that, in ancient times, this stripping was a daily routine all year long, not a special ceremony for this one night: Throughout the year, unless something was being used, it was put away.

This practice waned except at the Triduum, days that conserved many ancient practices. And the lack of clutter on these days came to be understood as the proper atmosphere for reading the book of Job, for chanting the Lamentations of Jeremiah and for proclaiming the passion of our Lord according to John.

The emptiness also came to be seen as an image of *kenosis,* of Jesus "emptying" himself in his passion, like a vessel poured out so that it could be filled with something else. That something else is the Holy Spirit, the Lord of life. The whole church participates in this expectation of fulfillment.

Nowadays, well-kept places of worship are free from clutter year-round. In many places, in keeping with sound liturgical practice, candles, cloths and liturgical books are removed when not needed.

So what's left to strip on Holy Thursday? Perhaps a more important question would be, what is the atmosphere in church during the hours of the paschal fast? We decorators might phrase the question, just what should the church look like?

During the Triduum the church interior "looks like" the great gathering of the parish with all its ministers. It looks like a church that keeps watch in fasting and in prayer, that washes feet, that venerates the cross of Jesus Christ, that kindles a bonfire, that listens to the word, that christens its newborns and that gives thanks around the altar.

There's plenty in all of this to keep parish decorators busy with the physical requirements of the rites. The Triduum liturgy is complicated, sometimes overwhelming.

What should grab our attention first? Consider a few suggestions: Churches that retain a great number of fixtures, hangings and shrines

might maintain the old custom of stripping or veiling as much of this as possible. The logical time to do this hard work is well before the evening Mass on Holy Thursday, not in the wee hours of Good Friday. Some parishes will want to do much of this "stripping" even before Lent begins.

One purpose of this stripping is to make the eucharistic hall reflect the paschal fast. And a purpose of the fast is to free us to focus on our participation in the rites. There is nothing puritanical here. The physical beauty of the rites will need extraordinary care.

Do what you can to take away clutter. This is a yearlong job, but it's especially critical to these days. Emptiness and cleanliness is special to the worship environment of the Triduum. But be sensible. Moving or veiling items must be done carefully to avoid damage.

Bulletin boards, book racks and other parish message centers could be stripped (check with the various responsible parishioners first), the notion being that day-to-day concerns get put aside for these most important days of the year.

Post attractive worship schedules inside and out. Somewhere near the doors could be put baskets of handouts and prayer books for the Triduum (for example, prayers to take home and booklets with the stations of the cross to use individually in church). These too have to be kept orderly and attractive, and handsome decoration—such as a bundle of willows—can draw the eye to these things.

See to it that the church gets a good cleaning inside and out. No decoration is as important as this cleaning. When the parish gathers on Thursday evening, the cleanliness and even the freshly cleaned smell of floors, woodwork and windows, and especially a well-kept outdoors, can reflect the holiness of the Passover. (Getting the parish landscape into reasonably good shape is excellent Lenten work.)

This spring cleaning might take place in stages, with some tasks happening any time during Lent, others scheduled for immediately before Palm Sunday and still others needing to wait until Holy Thursday morning. A job board posted in a vestibule might be the place to advertise for volunteers, although some tasks must be reserved to insured professionals.

Although the eucharistic hall is kept stripped and simple, with bunting and garlands we can ornament the parking lot, the parish sign, the front doors and other entryways as an urgent summons to the neighborhood: Come into this holy house, for the angel of death is abroad in our land. Choose life and not death. Come under the protection of the Lamb of God.

Some parishes ask folks to dress in special ways for the Triduum. In this way our clothing becomes a strong part of the worship environment and a sign of our unity, too.

For example, some parishes have the good tradition of dressing in bright colors for Easter, a reminder of the dignity of baptism; many Southerners keep this custom with vigor. Some parishes dress in the colors of mourning on Good Friday and during the day on Holy Saturday. You might explain the significance of red vesture and request that people dress in red and other colors that signify self-sacrifice and royal honor.

Perhaps dress for these days is more formal than usual, but still comfortable enough to permit staying together in worship and dressy enough to suggest that these days are different from all others. Such customs are popular where they are kept, perhaps because it is a form of participation in worship.

Give priority to the requirements of the rituals before concerning yourself with decoration. These next pages offer suggestions about elements that are required and would get first attention (for instance, footwashing vessels) and elements that can be lovely but are secondary (for instance, processional banners). If the primary elements are well taken care of, secondary elements can be added gradually over the years.

It's not helpful to use something one year and leave it out the next; that takes the feeling of tradition out of the parish celebration and can even make parishioners feel like guinea pigs. If something seems worth using every year, that's a good way to know if something is worth using the first time.

Certain ritual items may be ornamented with flowers. For instance, a wreath of fresh flowers might go on the processional cross; a cluster of pussy willows might be tied to processional candles. Rose petals might go into the water used for the washing of feet. But any floral ornamentation shouldn't obscure the item. Sometimes it's better to leave an item unadorned;

for example, the cross on Good Friday. Some of the possibilities will be covered later when we walk through the Triduum rituals.

When will the body of the church be decorated for the Easter season?
Maybe this isn't a question that troubles you, but the answer isn't simple. The question hinges on our attitude toward the Triduum—are we willing to lose some of the Triduum by spending several of its hours getting ready for something else? This question is discussed beginning on page 121, in the chapter about Eastertime.

The practice of stripping the eucharistic hall for the Triduum might leave liturgical artists with a few questions: Why should the imagination leap up at the wealth of decorations at Christmas but be left dry at the Paschal Triduum? Aren't these days also filled with traditional visual expressions that can be shared with the parish? Isn't it our responsibility to open up the visual language of the Triduum, and isn't this work a vital way to build parish zeal for these holiest of holy days?

There's plenty of room in the church complex for the rich visual imagery of the Triduum. You can display some outside the church and maybe in the vestibules, and perhaps also in the place the parish meets for fasting meals and for the Easter breakfast after the Vigil. You can decorate the parish hall and library. The windows of the parish school also ought to communicate that this is no ordinary time. You will need to decorate the eucharistic chapel (or create one if you don't have one). And you can take some time during Lent to introduce households to paschal traditions in the home.

This is hard and necessary work, and it goes hand-in-glove with the stripping and simplification of the main body of the church.

Make sure lights are working and are aimed properly. Check sound and ventilation systems too! (Who hasn't experienced worship sabotaged by a malfunctioning amplifier?) Someone might be in charge of electrical devices to make sure that microphones are on, outdoor lights are working, and indoor lighting is used to establish a reverent atmosphere.

Days beforehand, have a nighttime rehearsal to fit interior lighting with the rituals. (The goal is reverence, not drama.) The many candles at the Vigil will create a burst of smoke when they are blown out. Some churches seal certain vents and windows during winter—are they now unsealed? During the Triduum, keep a log to suggest improvements for next year.

A focus for prayer: Many parishes have a strong tradition of keeping watch in church or in a separate chapel throughout these days. This focus for prayer can receive elaboration and is discussed beginning on page 94.

A month or so before Easter, sit down with the florist and explain what you're after: flowering plants, cut flower arrangements, and special items such as boutonnieres, wreaths, candle-rings and cut branches. Because the date of Easter varies from year to year, the availability of plant materials also varies. One year hyacinths are easy to find and cheap, another year they're hard to find and expensive. You can waste money by trying to duplicate orders each year. It's better to decide on the relative quantity of plants and colors but not be fixed on specific kinds of flowers. Then you can let the florist match your general expectations to a budget.

Be specific if you don't want something, such as autumnal-looking yellow mums, or if you want something special, such as blooming forsythia shrubs that eventually can be planted outside. Instead of a messy mixture of hot and cool colors, it's better to specify a particular "palette," of perhaps pastels—lavenders, pinks, blues and white—or hot colors—oranges, yellows, hot pinks and reds.

Stipulate that you want "spring flowers," especially in any cut-flower arrangements. Many florists take this request as their cue to avoid the commonplace materials seen throughout the year.

Advance notice enables the florist to prepare special ornamentation, such as a ring of rubrum lilies for the paschal candlestand or crowns of stephanotis for the confirmed. The florist also might connect you with suppliers of certain materials, such as olive branches, red anemones or particular shades of ribbon.

Tulips and daffodils fade in a few days. If cared for (and in good shape to begin with), azaleas and hydrangeas can last four weeks—although they cost more than tulips. Tell the florist that you want flowers that will last beyond Easter Sunday. That information might help the florist decide to send you plants that still have many buds to open.

If you have the room, you might get the flowers delivered at once on Holy Thursday morning rather than have a second delivery Holy Saturday. (Why expect anyone to work during the Triduum?) Ask the florist to leave the plants wrapped up. They'll take up less space and are easier to move.

For more about Easter flowers, see page 149.

Enter into the prayer yourself. You won't be able to do that if you're overwhelmed with last-minute preparations or with worry, which is particularly destructive to the spirit and gets communicated to others.

Before the Triduum begins, the physical objects that are used for worship—from the vessels for the holy oils to the follower that goes on top of the paschal candle—should be gathered somewhere. Find a spot that can be secured and that doesn't have a lot of traffic.

Perhaps one person should be responsible for all these things; or perhaps one person could be in charge of everything made out of fabric, another in charge of books and a third in charge of everything else.

Make checklists. Even a mind like a steel trap tends to get unsprung at the Triduum. Accurate checklists, especially if they are reviewed and edited immediately after the Triduum, can be helpful later in the year to remind us of things we need to purchase or have made or repaired for next year. (LTP's *The Sacristy Manual,* by G. Thomas Ryan, includes a thorough section

of checklists for seasons and feasts, which can be used to help form your parish's lists.)

During the year you might just bump into what you need at a price you can afford—a wicker basket of certain dimensions, an exquisite glass vessel with a convenient stopper, a particular shade of fabric. The most

cost-effective way to acquire items used at worship is to have an accessible budget so that you can make spur-of-the-moment purchases when you happen to find something; available funds allow you to keep an eye open for items all year long. The least efficient and sometimes most expensive way is to go searching for something days (or hours) before you need it.

A checklist also can help you discuss the formation of a budget with the people who need to be involved.

A well-celebrated Triduum will have us making the most of various parish facilities. All sorts of issues will arise—the usefulness of the font, the quality of the church's sound system, issues related to nighttime safety, and most importantly, how well parish ministries coordinate. The preparations for next Triduum would best begin a few weeks after this Triduum: Note carefully what worked and what didn't, and what deserves attention throughout the year in order to be well-prepared by next Easter.

Bear in mind that the many aspects of the Triduum liturgies are probably the best barometer for long-range concerns in the building and renovation of churches. As an environment and art minister, you might have a role in parish long-range planning, and your experience with the Triduum can be brought to bear on the eventual renovation of your parish buildings to make them more suitable for participation in the liturgy.

LTP's video *This Is the Night* shows St. Pius V Parish in Pasadena, Texas, celebrating the Lenten scrutinies and the Easter Vigil in their wonderfully renovated church. This video could be an eye-opener.

BOOKS

Texts for the rites of the Triduum come from several sources. Many, of course, come from the sacramentary and the *Rite of Christian Initiation of Adults* (*RCIA*) (and, perhaps, the *Rite of Baptism* of infants). Choices have to made among the many options. Some texts need to be written "in these or similar words" (which is the direction the church's books give when a few fresh words can be composed by someone gifted in writing).

Reading publicly from a sacramentary and the *RCIA* during the Triduum can mean clumsy page turns or awkward searches for the chosen texts. Adapted texts would need to be taped into a book.

Presiding at the liturgy of the Triduum can benefit from a home-made "presider's book" in which all the texts, music and instructions are put in the right order under one cover. Everything's there; nothing extraneous is added.

The church's texts would be copied and pasted up to make new pages. Adapted texts would be typed and added to the book. If possible, texts and instructions would be kept on file in a computer and run out in large, bold type; 16-point Palatino (or Optima) bold is useful for spoken texts. Use a smaller size italic for instructions.

One of the great advantages of preparing such a book is that the presider also can use it at rehearsals to jot down reminders. Especially at the Easter Vigil, there's something reassuring about having all the texts and instructions under one cover. Don't underestimate the value of this reassurance.

The book can be a loose-leaf ring-binder covered in beautiful fabric. Clear vinyl, top-loading sheet protectors make it easier to insert pages, but for some people these are more difficult to read because of glare. For a covering, choose a fabric that doesn't soil easily and that isn't too stiff (so it doesn't buckle when the book is opened). Dacron padding or sizing can be placed underneath the fabric when constructing the cover. The stitch needs to be loose enough to accommodate stretching.

As always, the lectionary should be beautiful and worthy of the liturgy. It is never dignified to read from loose sheets or from missalettes.

On Good Friday, each gospel reader should get a book with a complete copy of the Passion according to St. John, not just their own part. (A highlighting pen is good for marking parts.) These books must be handsome but should be readily distinguishable from each other.

On Good Friday, if the deacon or a reader announces the petitions or intercessions and the presider offers the collects, both people should have all the texts with their parts marked. The texts should be gathered into handsome books.

The liturgy of the hours, the preparation rites for the elect, and any blessings or devotions would also require attractive books for the presider, deacon, cantors and readers.

At the Easter Vigil there could be a special book with the text and music of the Exsultet. A spectacular alternative is to create a cloth scroll that is gradually unrolled from the ambo as the Exsultet is chanted. The text on this scroll could be illustrated, with illustrations upside-down to the cantor but right side-up to the congregation.

Vesture

Three vestment colors come into play during the Triduum: purple, red and white. (These colors also might be used together in any ornamentation outdoors.) The vestment scheme is a bit complicated:

Holy Thursday

Mass of the Lord's Supper	*white Mass vesture*
liturgy of the hours	*purple cope, dalmatic, stole*

Good Friday

Celebration of the Lord's Passion	*red Mass vesture*
liturgy of the hours and other rites	*red cope, dalmatic, stole*

Holy Saturday

liturgy of the hours	*purple cope, dalmatic, stole*
preparation rites of the elect	*purple cope, dalmatic, stole*

Easter Vigil

white Mass vesture (perhaps a white cope for the service of light, liturgy of the word and liturgy of baptism)

Easter Sunday

Mass	*white Mass vesture*
liturgy of the hours and other rites	*white cope, dalmatic, stole*

If the parish has a certain set of vestments worn only during the Easter season, or a set of gold or silver ones worn on high holidays, it's probably best if they make their first appearance at the Easter Vigil, not on Holy Thursday. (Easter white is discussed on page 134.) For the Mass of the Lord's Supper it may be fitting to use white vesture trimmed abundantly in red, which makes a connection between this liturgy and what is to follow.

Red is the color of Good Friday. The vesture certainly should not have Pentecost symbols. Many prefer a deep and solemn red for Palm Sunday and Good Friday. In the Byzantine tradition, a very dark and bloody red (a color as close to brown or purple as it is to red) may be worn on somber occasions. The church's use of red on Good Friday evokes blood, sacrifice and royal splendor.

We tend to think of almost any color except red at the Easter festival, but many of our forebears thought red was the most significant color of the Christian Passover and used it abundantly in decorations. In many places red is considered the best color for Easter eggs; it is an emblem of mortality, which falls away to reveal the white and gold of resurrection.

Purple communicates "Lent," and Lent is past. Instead of wearing purple at the liturgy of the hours on Holy Thursday night and on Holy Saturday, some parishes use red.

Purple does have strong popular associations with the Easter festival and, like red, is a regal color. Also, like red, the color is associated with blood and sacrifice.

Some parishes simplify the church's scheme in a pattern that makes sense:
There is a special set of vestments just for Palm Sunday and the Triduum.
The predominant color is a deep, bloody red, although white, black, purple and gray might be used in the ornamentation. This vesture is worn at all services during the hours of the paschal fast, from Holy Thursday night until just before the Easter Vigil. Then the Easter white set begins to be worn at the Vigil.

Using a cope for the liturgy of the hours and for the preparatory rites adds a sense of solemnity. In addition, if the presider at the Vigil begins the liturgy wearing the cope, it can be removed for the baptisms. Afterwards, the presider can don a new alb, a white stole and a chasuble.

Holy Thursday Evening

The sacramentary tells us that "the tabernacle should be entirely empty" before the beginning of the Triduum. This rubric implies that the tabernacle doors are left open, the veil is removed, and the vigil lamp is extinguished and taken away. If the tabernacle is in the eucharistic hall and not in its own chapel, it is not illuminated.

The sacramentary also says that at the end of the evening, the place of worship is cleared so that it is entirely bare. Gone also is the cross, which must be covered if it cannot be removed. By custom, most everything removable is taken away; the font and holy water stoops are empty. Tomorrow and the next day, if anything is needed (such as a chair or music stand), it is carried in for the time it is used and removed afterward.

A logical time to strip the eucharistic hall is when it is cleaned earlier in the week. That's when all Lenten decorations are removed. On Holy Thursday evening, the gathering parish should be able to see at a glance that Lent is completed and that the long-awaited Passover is now here.

Holy Thursday is about more than the Last Supper or the priesthood. The liturgy's entrance antiphon sets before us the mystery of the Christian Passover: "We should glory in the cross of our Lord Jesus Christ, for he is our salvation, our life and our resurrection; through him we are saved and made free."

The antiphon tells us a lot about the atmosphere tonight. We are making our entrance into the entire Three Days. Bells can ring throughout this gathering and then be silenced after all are assembled.

When people come into church on Holy Thursday night, the building itself can seem to reflect our trembling and awe. Be sure the space is sparkling clean. Subdue the lighting. Gather the people with gentle singing. Ornament the doors with palm, olive and willow branches, with bunting, with *farolitos* (luminaries) and outdoor lanterns. Votive candles in their small glass cups can be put into larger glass bowls that are placed into macrame hangers and hung outdoors from tree branches.

First Things

It seems fitting to add solemnity to the entrance procession with candles, strips of fabric on poles and handfuls of flowers. Bearing many flowers and candles into a barren church sets the pattern for these days, when the things of worship are carried into our midst for the time they are used and then are carried out afterward.

Flowers this night can be any spring flowers (although it would be good not to use Easter lilies; that way the lilies can be seen, and smelled, for the first time at the Vigil). Several pots of a single kind of flower could be arranged in large, shallow baskets and carried in during the entrance procession. Hyacinths are wonderfully aromatic and might be placed somewhere that people can stick their noses into them.

For the entrance, one parish gathers at the church doors, where a banner is unfurled bearing an image of the paschal lamb. Everyone enters singing Psalm 122, "I rejoiced when I heard them say, Let us go up to the house of the Lord." They march into the Triduum behind an enormous branch of flowering plum.

At another parish, ministers carry in important physical requisites of the Triduum, including the new (unlit) paschal candle (carried horizontally this night), the veiled cross, and even the baptismal robes. These are carried in and then taken reverently to appropriate sites around the church building, some things to the vestibule, some to closets and cabinets. This is done in a way that doesn't create clutter and yet announces that these things are the beloved sacramental materials that the parish community uses to keep the Passover. It is a powerful image of ingathering and of the unity of these days and can convey the sense that these things belong to us and don't appear by surprise out of a sacristy cupboard.

The mood of the entrance is not merry: It is *awesome*. Here in our holy house gathers the church—the living and the dead joining hands so that, in the words of Psalm 22, "they may proclaim to a people yet to be born the justice God has shown."

Although the entrance antiphon mentions the cross, that's not a reason to emphasize the cross in the entrance. The chants and prayers of the

church throughout these three days repeatedly mention the cross and resurrection. Tonight's antiphon is not unique in this. In the course of our three-day liturgy, the showing and veneration of the cross will happen in its proper time.

Some parishes use the processional cross as usual tonight during the entrance and during the transfer of the eucharistic bread, then leave it in the chapel through tomorrow. That way those keeping watch there have a

cross on which to meditate. If the processional cross is the one venerated on Good Friday, it can be carried from the chapel back into the midst of the assembly at that time.

Some parishes do not use a processional cross tonight and make sure any other crosses are removed or hidden before tonight's liturgy. (That way the space isn't disrupted by this activity once the Triduum begins.) This pattern makes special sense in parishes that have put away the cross throughout Lent in order to welcome it more devotedly on Good Friday.

See pages 67 and 98 for discussions of the cross and of the veneration on Good Friday.

In many parishes the oil of the sick, the oil of catechumens and the sacred chrism are welcomed this night as the "Easter gifts" of the bishop. During the entrance rite the oils and the chrism are carried in, placed on the altar and honored with incense. After a few words, they are carried to where they will be stored throughout the year.

Older ambries are usually too small to hold large, handsome vessels. If that is so, a new ambry is needed. (An ambry should be able to be locked, like a tabernacle. An ambry that isn't used should be removed.) Perhaps in the meantime, a pedestal (or three— one for each vessel) is set up to hold the oils and chrism. Perhaps in an older church, a side altar becomes the year-round place for them.

Tonight the ambry (or wherever the oils go) can be ornamented. Lit candles will make the oils sparkle, and a few olive branches and forsythia or lilacs (which are northern relatives of the olive) can be woven into a wreath. (The olive family is known for the intense fragrance of its flowers.) Perhaps the candles and branches are carried up in the entrance procession and then carried to the ambry.

If the ambry is not within the sight of the assembly, perhaps this decoration could be kept up throughout the Triduum and on into the Fifty Days of Easter.

WASHING FEET, COLLECTING GIFTS

Footwashing requires attractive and portable chairs. These go in place when they are needed and are removed later. Metal chairs are too noisy (and usually too ugly) for this purpose. Sturdy wooden benches are perfect.

Water basins and pitchers also are needed, as are ample towels. (Plain beach towels work well.) Beautiful pottery is not difficult to find, although pottery shatters easily and is heavy. Unbreakable vessels may be more versatile. East African copper kettles or Native American gourd vessels may be splendid for this purpose.

At the beginning of the ritual, towels, basins and pitchers are brought out of the sacristy by several people. (There's a "procession" going on here that deserves a dignified pace and perhaps even processional candles and banners to accompany it.)

Use warm water. Some parishes put scented soap and even flowers into the water. Both feet are washed, not just one. Full, broad and slow gestures are needed, which require rehearsal. The splash of water adds to the atmosphere of the rite. Even if only a few people attend to the fullness of

the gestures, the reverence is contagious. What is going on should be sensed by everyone in the church.

Some parishes invite everyone to take part in the washing of the feet. (This invitation is given throughout Lent and doesn't come as a surprise on Holy Thursday evening.) A dozen three- or four-chair stations or long benches facilitate parishioners coming forward and washing someone's feet, then sitting down, removing their shoes and having their own feet washed.

Afterward, the presider, deacon and communion ministers may need to wash their hands, so a lavabo bowl, another pitcher of water and towels may be needed.

On this night during the preparation of the gifts our Lenten alms are collected for the poor. This collection is one of the important and characteristic rituals of this night and deserves full attention. It may take the form of more than the gathering of money. In many places hampers are provided for clothing, food and other gifts.

The hampers are gathered near the altar, although if the quantity of alms is large, perhaps the hampers are placed in an aisle or in another spot where they are visible but do not block traffic. Even if the procession with gifts for the poor involves only a collection of money, this rite is another of the Triduum's processions requiring a noble and dignified pace as well as incense, candles, flowers and the other elements of a procession. Some of this might be left by the gifts throughout the eucharist.

Lenten alms are part of the "worship environment" of this night. They are sacramental signs of the presence of God: "Where charity and love are found, God is there." Obviously, for this collection of alms to happen as it should, the parish must come tonight prepared. This preparation is one of the necessary tasks of Lent.

BREAD

Naturally enough, in some parishes on this night the eucharistic bread is home-baked. The Triduum calls forth the things we would like to do all year long. On this night we consecrate enough bread for tonight and also for tomorrow's liturgy. Reserving home-baked bread overnight requires airtight containers. (It certainly would be peculiar to place on the altar home-baked bread for tonight and wafers for tomorrow.) Check to make sure that the large vessel for Good Friday's communion bread fits easily in the tabernacle or the special repository.

The transfer of the eucharist is a practical action but also a beloved rite invested with good memories and great devotion. The procession to the tabernacle chapel can involve everyone in the assembly. Everyone can march inside the church or march outside and circle the church. People can carry flowers that will be strewn around the tabernacle when the procession is complete. In small assemblies people can carry candles that eventually are placed in large pots of sand.

It was customary to carry a canopy over the eucharistic bread as it was carried in procession. The canopy (four poles holding aloft a great square of fabric) was an image of the tent of God's presence. (This strong image is discussed on page 256. The tabernacle veil employs the same imagery.) The processional canopy marked a focal point, something valuable in a procession. That function also can be carried out with tall candles or banners; four of these surrounding a focal point in a procession can be a noble sight.

There's no reason a canopy (or the four banners or tall candles) can't be used in several of the processions during the Passover. Why not use the canopy over the chrism during the entrance procession, over the lectionary

during the gospel procession, over the jugs of water during the preparation of the footwashing, over the gifts for the poor during the preparation of the altar, over the eucharistic bread during the transfer—and at all the other processions tomorrow and the next day as well?

It's not likely that you will have an old canopy (baldachin) that is still in good shape, although some of its hardware and decoration might be salvageable. Like any liturgical accoutrement, the canopy should complement the style of the church. The four poles should be good-looking and create a canopy that is higher than the largest item to be carried under it. The poles can be topped with beautiful finials. With floor stands to hold the poles, perhaps the canopy could remain in place first over the chrism, then over the gifts for the poor, then over the tabernacle throughout the night.

The width of the cloth should be narrower than the width of the aisles it is carried in. A square cloth might be more attractive than a rectangle. Metal grommets can be fastened to any sturdy fabric. Stiff cloth such as tent fabric will not drape well.

A Paschal Chapel

According to the norms for church design, throughout the year the tabernacle belongs in its own chapel. Some churches have one. Most don't. According to the rubrics for Holy Thursday, the eucharist is transferred to the chapel, so if you don't have one, you need to create one somewhere.

Especially on Holy Thursday night, many in the parish will want to keep watch communally. In fact, keeping watch—together as a parish—is an important part of the Triduum. Is the parish to be divided into those who can fit in the chapel and those who sit in the church? That can be a problem with small chapels. In some places the custom of visiting seven churches is kept with vigor. Can the tabernacle chapel accommodate parishioners as well as visitors?

One parish has a eucharistic chapel that fits about 30. It proved too small for the number of people who wanted to keep watch together.

There developed the understanding that those who keep watch would sit in the main body of the church. When coming and going, people briefly visit the tabernacle chapel but do not remain there long. The chapel is stripped of chairs, and a large, padded carpet is put down to permit kneeling.

The chapel is filled with hanging votive lamps, baskets of flowers, and an arrangement of strong paschal imagery: a crown of thorns and other emblems of the passion, bitter herbs, palms and olive branches, a crock of myrrh, a winding shroud, a laurel wreath and a basket of red-dyed eggs set

into a platter of sprouting grain. The entry to the chapel is hallmarked by a swag of red fabric suspended from two wreaths hung high.

The church itself is kept in a hushed and reverent atmosphere. On Holy Thursday night, midway down the main aisle, a large image of Gethsemane is surrounded with candles as a focus for prayer. The image is removed Good Friday morning and replaced with an image of Calvary, which is removed before the Celebration of the Lord's Passion.

After the Passion, the holy cross goes into the chapel. It remains there until the Easter Vigil. An image of the entombment of Christ is kept in the main aisle of the church from after the passion liturgy until an hour or so before the Vigil.

In this way the people who come and go in prayer make a kind of pilgrimage through the church, to the chapel, and then back again. This arrangement will work in many parishes, but it means two special areas are prepared:

> 1. A small chapel of intense visual beauty is arranged to be visited briefly by people coming and going. The chapel holds the tabernacle and then the holy cross. The chapel can be kept simple, but it also can contain a rich array of iconography befitting the Triduum.

> 2. In the body of the church, a simple but changing focus of prayer may be kept up between services but not during them.

One parish prepares a paschal chapel in its baptistry, near the entrance to the church. (The font is empty but gets filled Holy Saturday afternoon.) Perhaps a bride's room, an unused sacristy or a deep alcove far from the altar is suitable. Parishes with spacious gathering areas or very large vestibules might be able to create a chapel there.

Another parish creates a large "chapel" in the school gym. The gym is made as attractive as a gym can be (which isn't saying much), but its chairs are fairly attractive and sturdy, the site is accessible to disabled persons, and it's located right next to the school cafeteria, where parish fasting suppers and the Easter breakfast take place. (A classroom is used for childcare.) Fabric hangings, beautiful images, the lovely light of candles and the fragrance of flowers do much to transform the gym into a holy place. The chairs are arranged in two sets of parallel rows facing each other, with the tabernacle in the middle.

The gym is where the eucharist is carried in procession on Holy Thursday night. Night Prayer concludes adoration there. Morning, Midday and Night Prayer are held there on Good Friday. Morning, Midday and Evening Prayer are held there on Holy Saturday, and everyone first gathers there for the Easter Vigil before processing out to the fire and then on into the church.

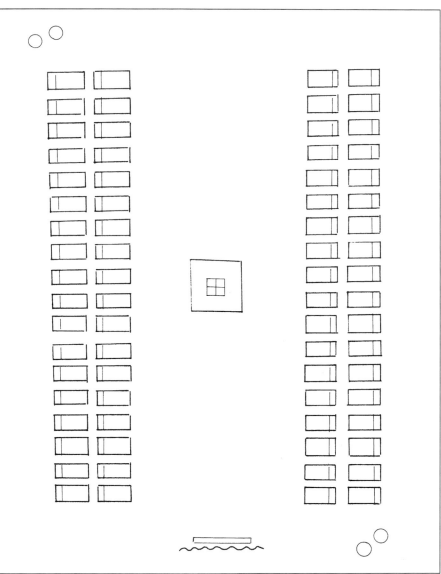

No matter where the paschal chapel goes, you will need to draw the eye to it, and the best ways to do that are through candles and other illumination along with bunting and other noble decoration.

Especially if the location of the chapel or the custom of keeping watch is unfamiliar, you might need to invite people to pray there and direct them to where it is. Some parishes have the ministers of hospitality offer these invitations, a gracious gesture. Sometimes signs are necessary, and these should be attractive.

Another sign at the door can be helpful:

SILENCE
is requested
for the sake of those
remaining in prayer.

The sacramentary says that the tabernacle chapel is "suitably decorated." What's suitable? Several decades ago parishes would compete with one another in building elaborate displays of flowers, candles and fabric surrounding the reposed eucharistic bread. But some felt that these displays were incompatible with the mood of the Triduum. In those churches where the tabernacle was in the main body of the church, such displays were indeed inappropriate come Good Friday morning. Over the years, this practice stopped in most places.

Something got lost, though, something sensual, enthusiastic, affectionate and human. But beautiful textiles, fragrant flowers, flickering candles and abundant incense all can be used more fully in all the processional rituals of the Triduum, including the transfer of the eucharist. Perhaps the difference between our own day and the displays of the past is that now we might include these "decorations" in the procession (carried with rehearsed choreography) and might surround the tabernacle (and, tomorrow, the cross) with these signs of glory. That way, instead of a static display we have a "work of the people," a liturgical activity.

What if there is simply no safe, accessible place to set up a chapel? Then use the regular tabernacle on Holy Thursday evening. However, if the tabernacle is so close to the altar that it competes for attention (if it's located on an old side altar only a few feet from the main altar, in a niche in the sanctuary, or still right behind the altar, for example), then a pedestal in the main aisle might be the right spot for the tabernacle of repose.

The advantages here are that it's not hidden from people who come and go; it's intimate, approachable, even touchable; and it leaves the area around the altar stripped and simple.

The trouble with setting the tabernacle or any other focus of prayer in a central spot is that it will need to be taken down before the Good Friday service. You do not want to create a focus of prayer that competes with the liturgy.

What's important is that parish members gather to keep watch between the principal services. Throughout these days the Body of Christ keeps vigil. Whether everyone gathers in the chapel or remains in the body of the church, perhaps soft singing, instrumental music or appropriate recorded music can be used to build the atmosphere. Keep lighting safe but subdued. Quality books of prayer and poetry, such as LTP's *A Triduum Sourcebook*, could be available to help people pray and meditate.

The parish may own a statue of the sorrowful Mother or other images of the Passion. Perhaps these images are present in the church in wall art, windows or mosaics. These things could be given honor simply by keeping burning candles near them. If they happen to be scattered around the church, the effect of the candles might be lovely or might be too busy—experiment to find out.

Good Friday

Good Friday's moods run the spectrum—triumph and desolation, grief and gentle assurance. The moods of the day are not one or another but all held in balance. The day's color, red, tells us something of this manifold imagery: Red is at once festive and solemn, bright and somber.

The simplicity of the worship environment this day does not mean that a thoroughly spartan approach is the goal. Remember, the eucharistic hall itself is kept simple to emphasize the rituals. Things are carried in when used and then carried out afterward. But the things we use in the rituals should be beautiful, and some can even be luxurious.

GOSPEL

Today and on Palm Sunday the Passion is proclaimed without candles or incense. This stripped-down visual format brings something unique to the most sacred gospel readings of the year—unless, of course, the ordinary Sunday format for proclaiming the gospel is without these visuals.

In keeping with the tradition, the gospel procession today might occur in complete silence. However, the use of more than one reader also adds a traditional dimension to the proclamation. Readers who aren't deacons or presbyters might also wear albs, the proper vesture of anyone who is baptized. (Albs, too, add a certain simplicity.) Red capes also are proper vesture for readers and cantors.

Part of the worship environment at this time is the assembly standing to hear the gospel, even if the gospel is long.

CROSS

The veneration of the cross has its origins in the Christian East. In contrast to other rites, perhaps there's something extravagant about the veneration that's like the arrival of a monarch. There must be nothing hokey here, but there could be something sensual and majestic in the spirit of this rite.

That seems a fitting response to the appearance of the cross of Jesus Christ—which for us is also the tree of life, Noah's ark, Isaac's sacrificial pyre, the burning bush, Moses' staff, the ark of the covenant. In two crossed planks of wood, these sacred things are sacramentally brought before us.

Which cross to use? The question here really is not whether to use a cross or a crucifix, or how big it should be. The question is: How can the parish venerate the main cross in the church? That's what the Good Friday liturgy calls for.

Maybe you've never given this much thought. But think about the value of venerating the main cross and not a substitute: Shouldn't parishioners come to expect that on Good Friday they are able to show special affection for the cross that graces their church throughout the year?

Substituting another cross, one used only on Good Friday, makes it necessary to hide the main cross. That's usually far from satisfying. Parishioners are justified in wondering why the main cross is hidden, of all days, on Good Friday.

In some parishes the main cross is reconstructed so that it is possible to take it down for the veneration. In many new or renovated churches, the processional cross is the only cross in the church, and it is kept in a floor standard. (*Environment and Art in Catholic Worship,* 88, expresses a preference for this arrangement.) The processional cross is the one venerated on Good Friday.

Venerating this main cross is more important than whether or not it has a corpus (an image of Jesus' body) or is made out of wood. However, because the cross is used each year for this liturgical action, the liturgy itself suggests that this cross be made out of wood and that it be without a corpus. In the liturgy we are invited to "behold the wood of the cross on which hung the Savior of the world." These words tell us about the sacramental mystery of this ritual in which ordinary wood becomes for us the cross of Christ.

Even if the main cross has a corpus, isn't made out of wood and can't be taken down—say, in a grand old church with an enormous bronze crucifix—it still can be venerated on Good Friday. One way to do that is to veil it on Holy Thursday or even when Lent begins. On Good Friday the cross can be unveiled and the assembly can come up in procession as close to it as possible. If the cross is too high to be touched or kissed, each person can kneel for a moment beneath it in worship.

What's lost here is the ability to kiss or otherwise touch the cross; which is important but secondary to the honor given to the main cross. The parish may decide that this loss is too serious, and so an alternative cross is used. In that case, this alternative can be brought into the church on Good Friday. The main cross would need to be hidden so that there aren't two crosses competing for attention. This screening needs to be done in a way that complements the church interior and that doesn't call even more attention to the cross (which is just what the old-fashioned veiling often did).

If the parish uses a special cross for the veneration, that cross might go in a place of honor throughout the Easter season, even perhaps in front of the screen that hides the main cross from view. That way the "Good Friday cross" becomes the parish's "main cross" for a season.

The sacramentary offers two possible forms for the showing of the cross. In one form, the veiled cross is unveiled in three stages in front of the assembly. (Notice that it isn't carried through the church and unveiled in three different locations.) In the other form the (unveiled) cross is carried through the assembly, and at three places along the route the cross is hoisted high. If the unveiling option is chosen, the veil might be a regal red or even a mixture of royal colors.

Purple and black once were customary, although it's best if the veil is compatible with the red vesture.

The church's preferred form for the showing of the cross is not the unveiling but the carrying of the cross through the assembly, with the same three stops (at the doors, in the center of the church and in the front) that will be made with the paschal candle during the Easter Vigil.

The sacramentary says that the cross is accompanied by "two ministers with lighted candles." However, four candle-bearers squared off around the cross can look handsome. The candles might be ornamented with spring flowers, and the showing of the cross might include the noble elements used in other processions during the Triduum—flowers, banners, incense, even a canopy.

It's usually best not to ornament the cross itself, for instance, by putting red drapery on it or putting a crown of thorns in its center. The reason? It's very hard to do that without calling too much attention to the ornamentation.

That being said, it's also hard to imagine how we can be content to welcome the cross in a lifeless or pedestrian manner. Why wouldn't this be an occasion for the vibrant use of color, aromas, sights and sounds appropriate to the entrance of the holy cross? Even the quality of the servers' footwear enters into this ritual! This is neither a gaudy, jolly event nor a cold military exercise, but it can be one imbued with joy, trembling and tears.

The place the cross goes during the veneration deserves embellishment. Perhaps a beautiful handmade carpet defines it. Freshly cut herbs could be strewn on the carpet—fresh laurel (bay) leaves, myrtle and rosemary are ancient and bitterly fragrant signs of triumph. The carpet, the herbs and

anything else used to receive the cross get put in place after the intercessory prayers and before the cross is brought in. You might want to anoint the cross with aromatic oil of balsam or cedar when you clean it in preparation for this rite.

The cross is never leaned on anything, especially the altar. It's not dignified. In some parishes the cross is held by hand throughout the veneration. If done well, this conveys affection. It's also much better to have ministers hold the cross than to stick it upright in a base because the base would likely have to be massive and too obtrusive to keep the cross from being pushed over by the people venerating it. If the cross is held, ministers need to be physically able to carry out this task. Pairs of ministers might alternate in this work. Their faces and posture, and even their clothing, can foster reverence.

In many places the cross is placed flat on the ground. Perhaps the horizontal crossbeam rests on large, brocade pillows—a good liturgical use of the art of embroidery. (Two pillows on either end of the beam keep the cross from teetering.) A bowl of burning incense might be set behind the cross.

Putting the cross on the ground in this manner invites people to prostrate themselves in the act of veneration. The bowing to the ground and the rising up is a powerful gesture of "passover." It's possible to do this well even in parishes with many elderly people as long as there are responsible ushers to assist. Parish ministers of care may be happy to help.

We venerate one cross, not several (which is why the rubrics say to hide any others if they happen to be permanently fixed in the church). Venerating alternatives to this one cross misses the point of the liturgy. We're not here to venerate *a* cross but *the* cross. In sacramental mystery we have just announced that a particular cross is the holy wood on which hung our salvation.

Yes, the national rubrics permit the use of multiple crosses when "the number of people is very large." But what's very large? The assembly in a baseball stadium, maybe, but it seems not in a cathedral: *The Ceremonial of Bishops* makes no provision for the use of multiple crosses.

Don't expect people to climb steps to get to the cross. The steps around altars are often incredibly easy to slip on.

You don't need to explain to people how to venerate the cross. But you can make it possible for people to perform certain traditional gestures: prostration, kneeling, kissing, embracing. Such gestures are made possible by a large padded carpet under the cross and by able ushers standing by, but not by kneelers, which will act like barriers to such gestures.

It's much better to spread a large padded carpet than to use something smaller, such as pillows or little kneeling pads. Test what you're going to have people kneel on.

After the veneration, the cross may stay where it was venerated and remain there through the rest of Good Friday and through Holy Saturday. Or the cross may be put into the eucharistic chapel (the tabernacle there is now empty). If the cross is the main cross of the church, it can be returned to its usual place (that's what the sacramentary says), although it seems better to keep it where people can continue to offer it their affection this day and the next.

The Holy Sabbath

The second day of the Paschal Triduum is the sabbath. Rome's 1988 *Circular Letter* suggested that an image of the entombment of Jesus and the Mother of sorrows may have a place near the cross throughout the paschal sabbath.

In Byzantine churches the holy shroud is honored on this sabbath, much as we in the Roman rite honor the holy cross on Good Friday. An ordinary piece of cloth is venerated as the winding shroud of Christ. On this sabbath the church wraps itself in this cloth. In some parishes this day, people are anointed with myrrh, the fragrant burial oil that is in fact used as chrism, the robe of immortality we wear in the Spirit.

The sabbath means a cessation from work, even our work in church. (That's why the day is customarily "aliturgical," without liturgy, because liturgy means "the work of the people.") Together we participate in God's rest after the work of creation. We share in the sleep of Jesus, who in preparation for a new "first day" returned to the primordial chaos in the oblivion of death.

This sabbath repose calls into question the timing of the Easter cleaning and decorating of churches. See page 127, where the question of when to put up the Easter decorations is discussed.

Easter Vigil

On no other night of the year is it more important to coordinate environment and art with the music and the rituals. Look over Gabe Huck's *The Three Days* (Liturgy Training Publications, 1992) and LTP's annual *Sourcebook for Sundays and Seasons* for the fundamentals. When parish ministers settle on the ritual patterns of this night, we parish decorators must square those patterns with our plans.

DARKNESS

The proper environment for beginning worship this night is darkness. That's why the rubrics specify with strong language that the Vigil cannot commence until well after the sun has set and darkness has fallen. (And that time is not the same every Easter!) It really does help to make sure all the lights on the parish property are kept off before the Vigil (even parking lot lights) and that entrances are lit as minimally as can be done safely.

That means adjusting automatic timers and taping over switches that might accidently be turned on. Areas of bright light keep eyes from adjusting to the darkness; it can be safer to have almost everything dim than to have bright areas and dark ones.

Something *not* to do is to have people enter a well-lit church and then turn the lights off a few moments before beginning. What kind of an "environment for worship" is that? Allow this night's holy darkness some room in the life of the church, if only to sharpen our anticipation of the light.

This night especially the assembly needs ushers. They direct people to their seats, distribute candles and hymnals or song sheets, and tell people where child care is provided, where to put baskets of Easter foods, where the elect and their godparents have gathered before the Vigil and where these people are to sit during the Vigil. And all of this happens quietly, without commotion, for the sake of those who are keeping watch in prayer.

Even if your ushers don't wear badges of insignia, maybe this night they could wear albs. Or they might need some visual sign that they are there to help: boutonnieres, for example.

FIRE

In Latin, the word for the Easter fire is *rogus*, a bonfire. You can't have a bonfire indoors. Don't even think about it. (A substitute indoor fire means

it will need to be quenched, which is not appropriate. We don't extinguish the light of Christ!) Some people create brief indoor fires out of alcohol or some other quickly burning, relatively odorless fuel. That smacks of a magic show.

If it's pouring rain this night, a gale is blowing or there is some other reason you can't have an outdoor fire (some city churches do not have a proper site), skip the fire and go directly to the lighting of the paschal candle.

Some parishes have a spot specially constructed for this fire. The site can be used at other times of the year, for instance, to burn palms to make ashes. The eves of the Birth of St. John, of All Saints and of Christmas are other nights for a holy bonfire.

You may need to inform the fire marshal of your plans or get a permit. That's not something to do the week before. Some thick blankets should be handy nearby in case of an accident. Of course, the church's fire extinguishers would be charged and accessible, but don't leave one in plain sight next to the fire.

If you need to build a temporary site, you probably shouldn't use a barbecue grill; most (but not all) look like you're having a picnic. A metalworker can design a vessel for the fire, although a horse trough put right-side up on top of an upside down one will also work well. Attractive, large stone or brick pots are available at some garden centers. (Concrete or clay vessels might burst from heat.) Several layers of brick under the vessel would insulate grass from the heat. Heat kills trees; don't build a fire under them.

For a fire built right on the ground, you might lay down a tarp and cover it with eight inches of sand to protect the ground from heat: This is a job for the Scouts! Bricks or stone blocks can ring the sand.

The area might be marked by fluttering flags; it certainly requires a good spring cleaning. Banners circling the site could be used in the procession into church or could be left in place as outdoor decoration throughout the Easter season (as long as the fabric is weatherproof). The flags can be an array of colors, or they might include images related to fire and light: for example, the first day of creation, the rainbow, the near-sacrifice of Isaac on a pyre, the fiery furnace, dawn, tongues of fire, the phoenix.

As people gather, the materials for the fire should already be in place (because last-minute fussing is not the right atmosphere for mystery). If for some reason you need to carry the fire materials into the midst of the gathering, make it a noble procession and not a perfunctory task. Don't be too quick to disassemble the site after the Vigil. Churchgoers on Easter Sunday morning should be able to see the ashes and wonder what they missed.

What to burn? The handiest materials are evergreen wreaths saved from Christmas. (They need to be bone dry.) A stack of them will create a great vortex of flame, but evergreens burn down in minutes.

If your fire will flare up into a merry blaze, the least amount of wind can send flames flying. A fire is a dangerous thing, especially when first lit. Especially if you're trying something new this year, anticipate what might happen, even if that takes a full dress rehearsal a week beforehand. A breezy night might mean modifying your plans and using less fuel or figuring out a good way to keep the assembly farther away from the fire.

For safety's sake it might be good to build some sort of open cordon around the fire. A series of rope loops can be attractive.

Building a slow and steady fire from large logs of wood requires proper technique, including the right kindling-to-wood ratio and the right construction to allow air to circulate through it.

The fire is customarily struck from flint. Technically, any flint lighter does that, but starting a fire the old-fashioned way lends its image of a lively spark from dead stone. That will not be visible to most people unless you elevate the site. All the small-scale struggle with starting a fire in this way might leave some of us wondering what's going on, but it also builds anticipation as the activity moves from tiny sparks and smoldering tinder (and the huffing and puffing to coax the fire along) to small flames in the kindling and finally to a brilliant, hot blaze. Such signs of the Spirit!

Some parishes have the fire already burning outdoors when people arrive. At least that way, most everyone sees the fire up close. What's lost is the transition from darkness to light, but that image occurs later as the paschal candle is carried into the dark church. What's also lost is the kindling of the fire as a public ritual, and that's a tremendous loss.

In figuring out how to have a fire in your own situation, it can be hard to balance all that's important about the images here. Is it the passover into light? Is it the slow struggle to kindle a fire? Is it the fire's growing warmth and power? What images have priority?

The most important image is the procession behind the paschal candle. That way the candle is a pillar of fire that leads us into the promised land. Having an outdoor procession to begin the Vigil may require that every-one first gathers in the church, the gym or the hall, and then walks outside to the fire. But in temperate climates, people can assemble outside right away. After the fire is kindled, the paschal candle is lit and the procession moves toward and then into the church.

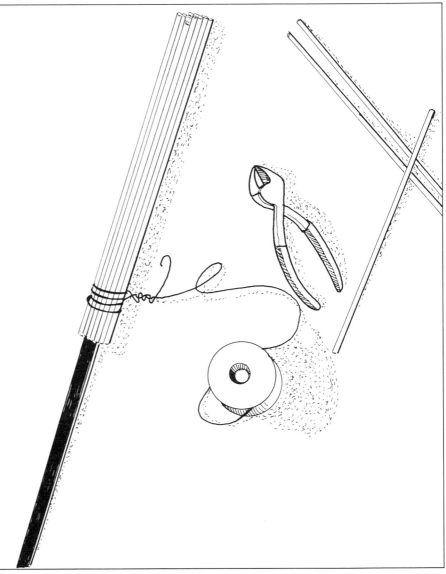

Lighting the paschal candle from a bonfire requires special tools to transfer the flame; what works well is a bundle of small wooden dowels wired to a long metal wand, or simply a long thin wooden dowel. (A large fire will melt a wax taper faster than it can be lit!) Lighting charcoal from the fire for the censer requires long barbecue tongs.

Church doors are the gates of Jerusalem, the gates of heaven. If the doorways were ornamented in royal red and purple on Palm Sunday, now they can be hung with royal blue and gold or any festive colors.

The sacramentary says that in the procession with the paschal candle, the second of the three acclamations, "Christ our light," takes place at the church doors; that's where everyone's candles are lit. No matter how you proceed to light people's candles, it's best to figure out a way in which as many people as possible can light their candles directly from the paschal candle and not from acolytes appointed to this task. Efficiency isn't what we're after here. There's something important about the candle being lowered and about our reaching out for the flame.

It might be easier to carry the paschal candle outside if it's fitted with an attractive wind guard. After the candle has been burning for a while, it can be hard to move without spilling the pool of wax that has formed. Keep that in mind. What might be useful is a heatproof glass candle follower that permits the flame to be seen, that functions well as a follower, that acts as a wind guard and that keeps the pool of wax from spilling when the candle is carried in procession.

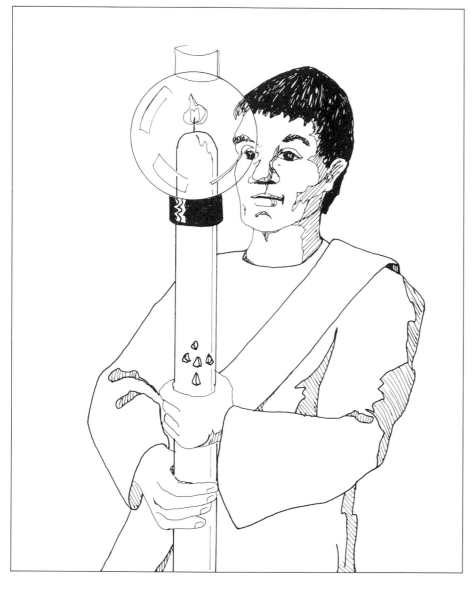

The procession with the candle can include banners and flowers. The censer-bearer leads the procession; the paschal candle is second in line. Any banners eventually would be laid aside once we're inside so that everyone can hold candles during the Exsultet. (The banners can be used again later for the gospel procession.)

The paschal candle needs to be big enough to last the entire year, but not so big that it can't be carried. This is a generalization, but the beauty, size and authenticity of the paschal candle is often a barometer of the parish's year-round care for the liturgy. The good news here is that, judging from what manufacturers are creating, more and more parishes are using splendid candles. Some parishes make their own candle; if you've never done this, know that it is not easy. Absolutely critical is the ratio of the wick to the candle's diameter.

What's the condition of the candle stand? Many parishes are using larger candles than in previous years and some may have jerry-rigged their old stands to accommodate a thicker candle. Such stands are neither as sturdy nor as handsome as they ought to be. Some parishes have a second stand made so that the candle can be used in processions—that second stand might go near the font this night so that someone doesn't have to hold the candle throughout the baptisms. (It's hard to hold for that length of time.)

Ornamentations. Some people prefer a simple but massive wax pillar free of ornamentation. And some people want an ornamented candle. The style can depend on the church interior, not on personal preference.

Certain decorations on the candle are traditional: the alpha and omega, the numerals of the current year, and five grains of incense set into the shape of a cross (the grains sometimes are surrounded by wax in the form of a nail). Those ornaments make the candle a kind of consecration of time, an announcement of the *hodie,* the timeless "today" of the paschal mystery. ("Christ the Lord is ris'n *today!*")

Decorations that never belong on paschal candles are representations of the things that are elsewhere in church, such as baptismal water. What's the sense of that? Some manufacturers even have paschal candles decorated with drawings of little paschal candles!

Wax ornamentation is usually more handsome than paint or decals, and it's safer, too. When paint or decal ornaments get burned as the candle melts down, they can burst into flame, sometimes explosively.

Don't blow out the candle tonight! The candle burns all through Easter Eve and on through the next day until evening. This is a strong tradition. (Can your candle can be left burning safely?)

On Easter Eve we sing, "May the Morning Star which never sets find this flame still burning." That sentiment reminds us of the ancient expectation that what we keep vigil for this night is not Jesus' resurrection but our own resurrection when Lord Jesus appears in glory. Tonight is a sacramental foretaste of the end of the world, and that mystery also lends a certain meaning to the Easter fire. By leaving the candle burning, at least it keeps vigil until dawn, even if we've called it quits.

If this is impossible, give the impression that the candle burns continuously by extinguishing it only after everyone has left and lighting it again before anyone arrives. Keep this pattern throughout the Easter season.

The stand for the candle goes near the ambo. At the Vigil the candle's light shines on the Exsultet and on the holy scriptures. Then the candle is carried to the font to be plunged into the water and held high during the baptisms. Some parishes first place the candle in the midst of the assembly, where a special lectern is put for the singing of the Exsultet. Afterward, the lectern is removed and the candle is placed near the ambo for the liturgy of the word.

Some parishes save the lighting of the people's candles for the baptismal rites and skip the lighting during the procession. The area around the ambo is lit with many candles in candlesticks for the Exsultet and for the liturgy of the word. (These parishes then use psalm refrains that are simple

enough not to require everyone's singing from participation booklets.) That way, the liturgy of the word becomes a proper vigil in expectation of the light, and the baptismal rites become the time of full illumination—a splendid image.

It's particularly lovely to ornament the paschal candle stand with a ring of flowers and to have pots of flowering plants nearby. A ring of flowers is easy enough for most florists to make, but you may want something that you can keep spruced up with fresh flowers throughout the Easter season. For more about the paschal candle and the decoration around it, see page 132.

WORD

The Exsultet and the liturgy of the word that follows sometimes are embellished with elements that become the seasonal decorations for Eastertime. That's a useful way to think about almost all the Easter decorations: With the right design, they can make their appearance tonight and then remain with us throughout the Fifty Days as evidence of Easter.

Perhaps as each reader walks up to the ambo, someone could carry up a basket of flowers and put it in an appointed spot. Banners (or some other decoration) might be carried in and hung in place or unfurled at the beginning of each reading, or they might be carried by someone who accompanies the reader and then stands alongside the ambo as the reading is proclaimed. After the reading the banner is then hung somewhere or placed in a stand. This works only if it does not appear contrived or theatrical. Rehearsing this is necessary.

Of course, the artistry of these decorations needs to be marvelous and any figural images must be elemental and within the tradition (so that people don't wonder, "What's that?").

In one parish a paper-cutting artist created splendid, four-foot tagboard medallions depicting the earth, Noah's dove, a ram, the paschal lamb, and Lady Wisdom—images that correspond to the Jewish scriptures proclaimed in this parish this night. During each reading a server holds one of the medallions aloft on a pole and then, after the reading, hangs it in its appointed place over the assembly.

This activity establishes dignified times of silence as the reader slowly walks to the ambo and also slowly departs. The psalm then breaks the silence. After the psalm everyone stands for the prayer after the reading (the rising up is good for the body), and then everyone sits and settles down as the next reader stands and walks slowly to the ambo.

"Embellishing" the proclamation of scripture with visual elements is difficult (but not impossible) to do without distracting from the proclamation or without unfairly focusing on one or another aspect of a reading. If the readers are excellent, if the gestures are gracious and well-paced, if the psalms are inviting to sing, if the silence after each reading is observed reverently, you have the foundation for the use of visuals in celebration of the readings.

GLORY!

According to the *Ceremonial of Bishops*, flowers are banned at worship from Ash Wednesday until the Gloria of the Easter Vigil, at which time bells are rung and the altar candles are lit from the flame of the paschal candle. (Any candle lighting from now until Pentecost means the gracious

gesture of first going to the paschal candle to receive a share of its flame and then using that fire to light the other candles.)

At this time also, according to custom, the statues and other sacred images in the church are unveiled. What's possible here is a worshipful procession of people lighting candles and bringing up flowers and removing the veils, with all this activity accompanied by exultant singing and the ringing of bells—a transfiguration!

Of course, removing drapery as part of the liturgy is potentially awkward, but it also can be wonderfully exuberant. Perhaps after the veils are removed, the statues could be surrounded with candles and flowers. (In one parish the youth group performs this task with style.) Perhaps at this time the images also can be crowned with flowers, a simple and traditional act: *Glory to God in the highest and peace to God's people on earth!*

The Gloria reminds many of us of Christmas, but its origins are paschal, and so it became the Sunday song of the church, a song we "gave up" with the alleluia throughout Lent. The church's current ritual here is to sing the Gloria after the last reading from the Jewish scriptures and before the reading from Paul's Letter to the Romans. That means that the Gloria is sung within minutes of the alleluia. Many parishes find it difficult to observe these two strong moments so close together.

If the Gloria is omitted, sung at the sprinkling rite or sung during communion, the alleluia of the gospel procession might include the bells, the flowers and the unveiling.

The proclamation of the gospel can always be celebrated with incense, and tonight it would be used in abundance. According to rubrics, in the presence of the paschal candle other candles are not carried for the gospel.

If the parish has been using flowers, banners and even a canopy to mark other processions during the Triduum, use them also during the gospel procession, which tonight deserves a slow and royal pace, a long route, and an alleluia that's not jolly but exalting. See page 140 for a discussion of the maypole, which can make a fine tall standard to carry this night at the head of this procession. With a sturdy stand, it can have a place in the church's house throughout the Easter season.

Some parishes use the holy cross at the head of the gospel procession, the same cross venerated on Friday, and this is the moment they return it to its usual place throughout the year.

Strangely, the rubrics never call for the cross to be carried in any of the processions this night; but perhaps it might be used now, during the procession with gifts or during the recessional—or not at all. Whether or not

it is carried in processions, you might decorate the cross with a wreath of fresh flowers.

WATER

The rites of initiation can follow one of several patterns, depending on the physical arrangements in the building and on the people being initiated—adults, children or infants. LTP's *The Three Days* and *Sourcebook for Sundays and Seasons* can help the parish determine what is called for, but nothing substitutes for a thorough grasp of the rites.

Even though your ministry is focused on the physical environment for worship, you need a working knowledge of these rites. If your parish has a good, working font that will be used at the Easter Vigil, you might be responsible for making sure it's clean, filled, not leaking and perhaps appropriately decorated. What's appropriate? You certainly don't want anything that interferes with movement or that blocks people's sight. The Eastertime decoration of the baptistry is discussed on page 135.

In many parishes the font gets surrounded by too many plants. Sometimes that's done to hide the flaws in a temporary (or even a permanent) font. Sometimes it's done to emphasize the imagery of life or of paradise. Still, if somehow the plants catch the eye as much as or more than the water, something's askew.

In LTP's *A Place for Baptism,* Regina Kuehn writes of the baptistry and its physical requirements. Ideally, you try to adapt the parish's existing font to tonight's requirements—even if the font's size and location are not ideal—rather than creating a completely new site for baptism. For parishes without an adequate font, Kuehn offers excellent material on building and furbishing a temporary one.

Baptism, especially of infants and children, requires reasonably warm water. Chilly water can evoke a shocked, comical or even pained response from the one being baptized. If you have a font with abundant water but are without the means to warm it safely, rather than drawing directly from the chilly water in the font you might use some handsome vessels filled with warm water to pour over the baptized.

In parishes where the font is in a separate baptistry and no one is being baptized this night, a large vessel of water is sometimes put somewhere up front to be blessed and used for the sprinkling of the people during the renewal of baptismal promises. However, it seems better to bless the water in the font no matter where it's located (even if that means the ministers disappear for a few minutes from the assembly) than to create an alternative

source of water. (Wireless microphones may make it possible for all to hear the prayer, even if not everyone see.)

In some parishes—and this is very strange—that have a font in view and that even have baptisms this night, another vessel of water is put up front and kept there throughout the Easter season. This water is used to sprinkle the people—and the practice makes no sense! The best practice is to dunk the water bucket into the font for the sprinkling rite and afterward to pour the remaining water back into the font. That takes a little bit more walking around, but so what? At least the connection between baptism and the sprinkling is made clear.

Are both the bucket and sprinkler attractive? Most of the ones sold by church suppliers are hideous. Many ice buckets are better looking. There's really no good reason to use anything other than a nice bundle of green branches for a sprinkler. (Wrap the stems with green florist's tape.)

In Latin, "sprinkler" is *aspergillum,* and asparagus got its name because it was used for this purpose (When mature, the plant's foliage is feathery). Arborvitae, juniper and cedar all will work fine, but so would a bundle of cherry, plum or peach blossoms—even if the petals get dispersed with the water.

Make the processions in the rites of initiation as dignified as possible. The procession to the font, the movement from the font to the changing room, and the movement from the changing room to the place of confirmation all require a slow, deliberate pace. The paschal candle leads the procession to the font and then from the changing room to the place of confirmation. Banners and the other processional items used earlier in the Triduum can have a place here too.

If the distance between altar and font is short, take the long way around. The procession is important; the journey is from time into eternity. That's why during the passage to the font we call upon the saints as if we were marching into the kingdom.

The movement of each of the baptized and their godparents from the font to the changing room would benefit from some processional banner to establish a dignified pace, especially if the distance is more than a few yards. This "procession" should not interrupt the other baptisms.

In ancient times, the procession from the font to the place of confirmation was absolutely awesome: Baptisms took place in private because the elect entered the water naked. Then after they were vested, they carried torches and entered the assembly, which was keeping vigil in darkness. So the arrival of the newly baptized was marked by the entire church's passover from darkness into light.

Perhaps in this procession the candle-bearing newly baptized could each be accompanied by a processional banner or some other tall ornament to accentuate their position in the procession. That will only happen well enough, though, if their candles are tall and handsome. If a canopy was used earlier in the Triduum (see page 93), and if it can accommodate the number of the newly baptized, perhaps it could be used as they come back into the assembly.

When the newly baptized arrive at the place of confirmation, any candidates to be received into the church join them. They too would be wearing white robes (throughout the Vigil) and will receive candles lit from the paschal candle. The newly baptized and the newly received are now candidates for confirmation. (The word "candidate" literally means "someone in a white robe.")

The baptismal robes and candles have to be glorious. Anything skimpy here will appear especially cheap in contrast to the ministers' vestments and the paschal candle. The robes should be at least as fine as the presider's alb. ("Alb" is short for "white robe" and is the garment of all who are baptized.) A fine pattern for making your own baptismal albs can be found in *The Three Days*.

Some parishes have the elect wear dark gray or brown clothing before and during the baptisms, or at least some sort of clothing that is in contrast to the baptismal robes. It's never appropriate to be baptized already wearing the baptismal garment.

The candles might even be smaller versions of the paschal candle; these will look especially fine if they're as tall as possible. When held, they might stand head-height, suggesting the image of tongues of fire during the anointing with chrism. The candles help foreheads shine.

The candles might need followers and handsome wax guards (bobeches). Pretty paper cones are sold by some candle companies or can easily be crafted by hand. The candles surely will need a place to be put after confirmation so that they can remain burning throughout the eucharist. (It doesn't seem right to blow out the baptismal candles in front of the assembly.) Perhaps the candles can go near the candidates' seats, perhaps fastened to the pews or chairs.

An ancient custom is to crown the newly confirmed with a wreath of flowers or of laurel or myrtle twigs. In the donning of baptismal garments or the receiving of the lit candle, the fewer words of explanation, the better. The effectiveness of these rites is communicated not by words but by deliberate, gracious and well-rehearsed gestures and by the beauty and fullness of the ritual items.

CHRISM

The vessel of chrism should be exquisite. A stoppered pitcher is a logical shape for it. Chrism should be given the same respect as the eucharistic elements—it is, after all, a consecrated sign of the Spirit. On Holy Thursday the vessel of chrism would be placed in the ambry; but if it must go in some other place, that spot should be beautiful. A candle-lit pedestal might be the right spot.

Chrism is more than oil. It is perfumed oil, and the aroma should be strong enough for the assembly to notice.

TABLE

A gracious and traditional gesture during the presentation of gifts and the preparation of the altar is to clothe the altar and light the candles from the paschal candle. Until this time the altar would be bare, with no candles or flowers nearby.

The eucharist this night, of all nights, calls for home-baked bread and flavorful wine. Communion vessels ought to be the parish's most festive. Of course, what this liturgy calls for are many of the elements we hope to have all year long.

After the prayer after communion, many parishes have the blessing of Easter foods. This is also part of all morning Masses, too. It's amazing how much these Easter baskets add to the visual loveliness of the church; you'll need to determine the right spot for people to put them as they arrive.

Many parishes conclude the Vigil with a party. Easter communion breaks the paschal fast, and now the breakfast continues. The guests of honor are the newly baptized. Where will this breakfast take place? It's a great site for decorations of the sillier sort, and even for a visit from the Easter bunny.

Easter Sunday

See the chapter about Eastertime, beginning on page 121, for a discussion of the worship environment through the Easter season.

Large crowds mean that ushers, custodians, sacristans and parish decorators may have their hands full in the busy times between Masses. Janitorial staff and volunteers might be on hand Easter morning. The environment for worship includes clean restrooms, orderly entryways and vestibules, and tidy pews or other seating.

The ordinary things of the worship environment might be well placed at other times of the year but on this morning become a hindrance to traffic. This potential trouble can be frustrating to decorators who add flowers and other visuals to the assembly's place, to vestibules and to doorways, where people can see them up close but also where a crowd can crush them. Balance the practical concerns with the splendid hospitality offered by decorations placed close to the people.

The outdoor decorations (page 140) might be especially festive on Easter Sunday and throughout the Octave. They are like church bells announcing the good news to the world.

If your ministry is broad enough to include parish education about the prayer and imagery of the season, Easter Sunday is too much of an opportunity to miss. At least the bulletin can be used well to provide some lively introductions to the festival and to the keeping of the Easter season. And you will want to advertise your ministry, too, by informing the parish about how they can participate in it.

A gracious gesture this day is to have some security staff on hand so that you can leave the church open throughout the day. We are, after all, still within the Triduum; why should church doors be locked on this holiest day of the year?

People could be invited to return any time in the afternoon with family and friends—to show off the beauty of their parish home, to enjoy the decorations, to breathe in the fragrance of the flowers and to offer thanks to God. You would need to be sure that the church is tidy, the paschal candle is left burning (and other candles if possible), enough lights are left on to provide safety and atmosphere, and perhaps even a tape of appropriate recorded music is playing.

The best element to provide is liturgical prayer. Easter Sunday Evening Prayer closes the Triduum. It is one of the principal liturgies of the Triduum, but not very many parishes have caught on.

Who would come? Actually, it's interesting to note just how many households are looking for some late afternoon activity in the spirit of the day. Conservatories, zoos, public gardens and movie houses are packed. Strangely, many parishes that ordinarily have Sunday evening Masses do not do so Easter Sunday as a courtesy to their exhausted staffs. But there might be many people in search of worship.

At heart, this Evening Prayer is a return to the font to contemplate the mystery celebrated there. The prayer is a meeting with the risen Christ, who breathes on us the gift of peace. The service, like the others in the Triduum, emphasizes movement and can include items used at the other processions of the Triduum. The atmosphere of the prayer is gentle, almost informal.

The good thing is that Easter Sunday Evening Prayer doesn't require much in terms of environment—all is already in place, except perhaps incense pots.

Other parish activities can be coupled with Evening Prayer, such as a supper especially for those who could use a hot meal and good company, an egg hunt or Easter caroling. Those events also need their decoration.

Eastertime

A Sense of the Season

The eight weeks after the Triduum are a season of "mystagogy," which means "the learning of mystery." But here, mystery doesn't mean a puzzle to figure out—it means a new life to experience. We "learn mystery," a lifelong task, by entering into it and by living it.

Mysterion *is the Greek word for "sacrament."* Sacraments are not something the church does to us. They are something that the whole church does, head and members—Christ and us. In other words, sacraments are forms of liturgy, "works of the people." They are liturgical signs that point us toward God's reign, and so they are filled with layer upon layer of imagery.

No wonder the Easter season overflows with sacramental imagery, and that the caretaking of that imagery is one responsibility of environment and art ministers. Eastertime will keep us busy.

The season lasts 50 days, from Easter Sunday until Pentecost. Why 50? Seven is a sign of fullness—there are seven days in a week. Seven weeks signifies "fully full." And when one more day is added—to make 50—we have a sign of the "fullest" fullness. God is so gracious to us!

That's where we have been rocketed by the Christian Passover—into the fullest fullness. And so we keep Eastertime by "playing heaven," by learning how to live with both feet planted firmly in the reign of God.

The word "neophyte" means "newly planted." Anything freshly planted requires intense care to keep it from drying up or from going into transplant shock. A time of settling in and sending down roots is necessary. So "neophyte" is the name that we give to those newly initiated at the Vigil.

The Easter season is essential to the neophytes and to all who are renewing their baptism, especially the newly confirmed and those brought to the table to make their first eucharist. They are signs of Christ dead and buried and risen among us. They are the loveliest of the signs of the season.

On Easter Eve we sang that tonight heaven is wedded to earth. If the Triduum is like a wedding, the Easter season is like a honeymoon. Some of it is romance, some is fresh discovery, and some is intense brooding and even storminess.

These 50 days are one-seventh of the year. Bishop Athanasius called them the "Great Sunday." As the Lord's Day is to the week, the Easter season is to the year. It can be a time of rest, renewal and recreation that leaves us created anew.

In the northern hemisphere Eastertime falls in spring, and not in muddy March but in April and in flowery May, when spring is often at its best.

But even in April and May not everything is sweetness and delight. In North America, May is the month of the greatest number of tornados and hailstorms.

April 22 is Earth Day. Its observance is strengthening, especially in schools. April 23 is St. George's Day, which we might call an earlier version of Earth Day, because George's name is Greek for "earth worker."

George is a patron of gardeners, farmers, ranchers and all who live close to the land, and his legendary battle against the dragon is an engaging sign of the paschal victory. Perhaps that is why the martyr George is also considered the patron of spring. May 15 is St. Isidore's Day. He and his wife Maria Torribia are patrons of farmers, and the U.S. Catholic Rural Life Conference sponsors celebrations and blessings of farmers and farmlands on this day. In our blessed springtime, we might take our cue from the first reading at the Easter Vigil and renew our efforts to restore this good earth to the freshness of creation.

An ancient and authentic image of the season is the sowing, sprouting, growth and eventual harvesting of grain. In the Jewish calendar, the 50 days from Passover, *Pesach,* to Pentecost, *Shavuot,* are a time of anxiety. In Mediterranean lands, barley and wheat grow ripe during these days, and a sudden squall can devastate a field. Farmers must be vigilant.

Paul uses the image of ripening grain to speak of the resurrection: Christ is the firstfruits of the dead. Christ is first, but then will come the resurrection of all who have died, like a harvest. Bishop Maximus of Turin, one of the poetic writers of the early church, spoke of the resurrection as a flowering and of the ascension as a ripening.

The harvest may not be a familiar image of the season, nor even an image that seems to fit the spring, but Eastertime itself is not all that familiar to many Christians. We still have much work to do in raising parish consciousness about the significance of the season. Amazingly, this is our most ancient season—it is even older than Lent. Its scriptures, psalms and sacramental rites are wonderfully rich and foundational to faith.

At this season we hear that the risen Christ will not be kept out by locked doors. Angels tell us to quit cloudgazing and to stand firm in our hope in Jesus' abiding presence. The Spirit bids us to spill out into the streets and share the good news.

In this romantic, revealing and sometimes stormy season, the wounds of Christ paradoxically become signs of resurrection. A stranger is fully recognized as a beloved friend. Our good shepherd leads us into a verdant pasture. Our wonderful gardener plants us in paradise.

Overview

In the weeks after Easter Sunday, some may wonder why the Easter decorations are still up. It's not enough to bark, "Because it's still Easter!" Parish decorators need to offer sound catechesis about the Fifty Days. Especially helpful is sharing ways that Eastertime can be kept in the home. That way we share convincing reasons for sustaining the season at church.

Sometimes, too, people are not accustomed to the very notion of decorating for Easter. Flowers, yes, at least for Easter Sunday, but beyond that, it might not be clear to some of us why the church has extra color and imagery during these Fifty Days. We may need a number of years to get into our souls that these days have their own sounds, sights and aromas.

Eastertime brings with it familiar observances: We might be coaching Little League, celebrating Mother's Day, having a picnic, cleaning windows, planting geraniums and chatting with neighbors whom we have barely seen all winter. Eastertime brings the sound of children playing outside after supper, the scent of lily-of-the-valley, more than the usual number of first communions and weddings, and end-of-the-school-year functions to attend.

Perhaps one of our tasks is to help others recognize these familiar activities for what they can be—encounters with the risen Christ and bestowals of the Holy Spirit.

The Fifty Days require a worship environment that stays mostly the same from week to week, if only to help us learn the presence of the season. Of course there are special days and events within Eastertime, such as Ascension Day, but any additional decorations shouldn't replace or overwhelm the seasonal decor.

Eastertime is splendidly rich in sensory images. There's a lot to work with. Lent is a kind of fasting from these, a time when we veil and otherwise put away the things of earth. So Easter is a feast where the things of earth are recognized as signs of the Spirit.

Not everyone will agree, but in this season it's probably better to err on the side of excess than of paucity, on the side of elaboration than of reserve. The church complex can reflect that these Fifty Days are no ordinary time, that Easter is our *laetissimum spatium,* our "most joyful season."

Environment and Art in Catholic Worship, 100, speaks of seasonal decorations creating "an atmosphere and a mood." During Eastertime this liturgical climate is "Hallelujah." But this climate is never one-dimensional. At

times hallelujah is the praise we offer at the sight of an apple tree in bloom, the praise we offer when witnessing a wedding, or the praise we offer over the graves of the dead.

Three things deserve special attention throughout the season: the cross, the paschal candle and the baptismal font. At the very least, they are kept clean and well lit. You might use flowers and other decoration to give them intensified notice, but any decoration should not overwhelm these things and especially should not overwhelm the ambo or altar.

The cross and paschal candle in Eastertime are discussed beginning on page 132; the font is discussed beginning on page 135.

Where else might you focus efforts this season?

1. Preserve the good things you began during Lent. Put clutter away. From week to week, put things away unless they are being used. Make sure the church and the outdoors are kept clean.

2. Maintain fresh flowers in certain sites around the church. (See the advice beginning on page 149.)

3. Make a special effort to decorate outdoors so that the parish's joy in this season is shared with the neighborhood. (See page 140.)

4. A certain number of seasonal decorations can go in the area over and around the assembly's place. (See page 128.)

5. Keep any shrines in good shape. (See page 136.) If you had a "paschal chapel" for the Triduum (page 94), it might be kept up during the Easter season.

The ordinary elements of worship deserve extraordinary attention. From Ash Wednesday through Pentecost is a time of parish renewal and a time to call forth the best in liturgical practice. Because of the images in the scripture readings, the Easter season demands good and real eucharistic bread and wine; real candles; abundant incense, water and oil; and excellence in the ritual use of these elements.

The Fifty Days are perfect for starting or reviving proper and graceful liturgical practice, such as a time of silence after the readings, using home-baked bread, sharing communion from the cup, or having parish fellowship after Mass.

LTP publishes *Preaching about the Mass* to help us do a job that often isn't done: Helping the parish understand the Mass. This book can guide a parish in using the Sundays of the Easter season as eucharistic mystagogy. Parish decorators know the need for the learning of this mystery.

Many Eastertime elements can be related in certain ways to the Triduum. Like the paschal candle, perhaps they make their first appearance during the rites of the Triduum. For instance, fabric hangings representing the readings of the Vigil (that were carried in during the Vigil) could be left in place throughout the Easter season. Or, certain elements offering evidence of what transpired during the Triduum can remain: For example, photos and a bit of biography about the neophytes can go in the vestibule.

Decorations can express the unity of the paschal seasons of Lent, Triduum and Eastertime. Materials noted by their absence during Lent would receive prominence during Eastertime. A pot of bare, thorny branches could go near the font during Lent, and fresh, flowering branches could be kept there through Eastertime. One cross and one cross only could get special attention throughout these days (pages 67 and 130). A triumphal arch (page 55) could grace the outdoors from Palm Sunday to Pentecost.

Should the Easter decorations be more abundant than those for Christmas? Easter is a greater festival than Christmas, not because it is higher on some scale but because Easter contains within its mystery the fullness of all the year's mysteries.

Perhaps the Eastertime worship environment gets more attention than any other. At the least, it shouldn't take a back seat to Christmastime. (Which is why we need at times to examine the year as a whole.) But comparing the two seasons may be counterproductive, because our goal really isn't to make one look greater than the other but rather to make our places for worship decorous, "fitting."

Decorations for Easter and for Christmas can reflect each other. For instance, the same locations on the parish campus and in the church building could be decorated for both seasons in complementary ways.

When should the Easter decorations be put up? Maybe you have never asked this question because the parish has always done this work on Holy Saturday so that everything would be in place for the Vigil.

However, this decorating interrupts the paschal sabbath, which is the second of the three days of the Triduum. The sabbath lasts from sunset on Good Friday to sunset on Holy Saturday, and the observance of a sabbath rest at least means not spending the day running errands.

There are other arguments against decorating the church on Holy Saturday. One is the sense that the Triduum is not a preparation for Easter but rather is our Easter. The Triduum is the sacred time for which we have been preparing all during Lent. We waste the Triduum if we spend it getting ready for something else. We also might be interrupting the people who are keeping prayerful watch in church. And it's their right to be there.

Another argument is that the decorations of the Easter season might not create the right atmosphere for the Vigil. Certainly not everything that would be appropriate during Eastertime is appropriate that night. For instance, it might be wonderful to have all sorts of candles twinkling in church during Eastertime, but not at the Vigil (at least not beforehand).

One way to keep from interrupting the paschal sabbath is to make some of the Easter decorating an integral part of the Vigil. Flowers and banners might be brought in during the course of the rites. (This takes well-rehearsed choreography and cannot appear melodramatic.) Appropriate times for this are the Gloria, the Alleluia and the preparation of the altar and gifts.

Decorating also might take place when the Vigil is over. After all, some cleanup needs to happen after the Vigil, and this task can be joined to decorating, to continued rejoicing and to "breaking the fast."

Any work that must happen earlier on Holy Saturday or on Good Friday night should be done with respect for the round-the-clock prayer vigil. And even if your parish isn't doing that, the Church is, at least in spirit. Perhaps this work might even be regarded as a way of keeping watch, as a kind of prayer in action. Especially if that is so, no parishioner would be excluded from this activity.

It might be wise to get any heavier work done late at night on Good Friday rather than on Saturday morning, so that bodies have a chance to recuperate with a good night's sleep. Why enter into the Vigil already exhausted? Also, with planning and forethought, many Easter decorations could be made as ready as possible before the Triduum begins and hidden away until needed.

THE ASSEMBLY'S PLACE

In celebration of the resurrection and ascension of Christ and the descent of the Holy Spirit, it seems especially appropriate to make use of elements that draw the eye upward. Color can be added to the open space found over the assembly in many church buildings. Decoration in this area might catch our attention when we first enter, but in most buildings it doesn't demand notice once we are seated.

Simple swaths of fabric arcing from wall to ceiling can convey exultation. That's a lot more interesting than merely hanging banners flat against walls. Especially in spring, sheer fabrics hung so that they allow light to pass through seem more appropriate than heavy, opaque fabrics.

You might wish to consider adding figural images to fabric hangings. Silk-screening is especially lovely on translucent materials. Of course plain fabric can be beautiful and sufficient for the purpose of creating a festive atmosphere, and a banner is never to be turned into a billboard to drive home a point. But the use of figural elements on fabric might help us grow more familiar with the imagery of the season. Eastertime probably needs these appeals to the imagination.

Popular Easter images that lend themselves to treatment in fabric are the rainbow and Noah's dove. Maybe they are used too often and have become hackneyed, but they certainly are authentic to the season. Apart from the neophytes themselves, it's difficult to imagine stronger signs of creation, of the new creation, of covenant and of christening. The elemental images from the story of Noah's flood keep recurring throughout the scriptures.

Rainbows are formed from the interplay of light and water. They are mythological signs of the union of heaven and earth. Genesis tells us that their purpose is to remind us of God's covenant with the whole of creation.

The dove calls to mind the lovers in the Song of Songs as well as the Spirit, who descended on Jesus at his baptism. The story of Jonah, whose name means "dove" in Hebrew, adds a rich layer to this image. The olive branch also has become a sign of anointing, of christening, of the peace and forgiveness of the risen Christ: "Christ" and "Messiah" mean "anointed."

An Easter rainbow in church might appear less hackneyed if the image is something other than a spectrum of intense colors applied to a banner. Not that this is always bad, but the rainbow could be hinted at rather than depicted realistically. For instance, sheer pastel fabrics of various colors can rise from several spots in the church to a common point over the assembly. A series of flags can be held in place with wall standards. A dozen or so wide ribbons can be hung from a horizontal ceiling beam and attached at the bottom to a wreath of flowers.

The colors need not complete a spectrum but merely suggest it. The use of color here would need to complement and not conflict with the vestments and other fabrics in the church.

Clouds, rain and lightning might be incorporated into the decoration rather playfully. One parish silk-screened impressionistic clouds onto bolts of diaphanous blue fabric. Another had cascades of glass beads drifting through Indian saris (ordinarily six yards long) in shades of blue, lavender and apricot; the saris were loosely stretched diagonally high over the assembly's place. Perhaps a collection of prisms could be positioned to catch sunlight, suggesting rain. Perhaps the image of a dove—beautifully designed and in scale with the space—could be suspended over the assembly.

The Exodus, of course, is a key paschal story. Eastertime may be likened to the journey from Egypt to Mount Sinai, from liberation to the receiving of the law. Eastertime has also been likened to the crossing of the Jordan and the entrance into the promised land.

Other paschal images are the seven days of creation; Abraham and Isaac; Esther, Judith and Jonah; Daniel rescued from the lions' den; the three youths in the fiery furnace; and Susanna's trial. Toward Pentecost come the tales of the tower of Babel, the fire and wind on Sinai, and the faithfulness of Ruth and Naomi. These scriptures might have pride of place throughout Eastertime.

Are any of these images found in windows, mosaics or other permanent art in the church? A hanging lamp might be a noble, not too assertive way to draw the eye to an image. At the very least, in a homily or in an article in the bulletin remind everyone of the presence of the parish's art.

The book of Revelation, the letters of Peter and the first letter of John provide strong baptismal imagery, and much of this returns in November and during Advent. You might plan the Easter environment with an eye to returning or adapting some of its elements during November. For instance, the placement of decorations might be similar, although the color palette changes. Easter imagery also returns strongly in August. Perhaps something of the Easter decorations can be used in celebration of the Transfiguration of the Lord and the Assumption of Mary, her "passover" into glory.

It's rather untraditional to show Christ rising from the tomb. Yes, artists try, but those who try forget an old discipline: The gospels do not speak of the moment of the rising of Jesus. This has been interpreted as a call to reverence for this moment. If the rising of Jesus from death is depicted as an event, even an extraordinary one, its transcendent mystery can be compromised. Something can get lost of the affirmation that Christ is risen and that we are risen in Christ.

The Byzantine icon called *Anastasis,* "Resurrection," sticks to this discipline. Jesus is not shown departing the tomb; instead, the scene shows him among the dead. The cross lies flat and Jesus stands on it. The powers of hell are crushed underneath the cross. Adam and Eve are rising from their graves, and Jesus is taking them by the hand to pull them out. Amazing! Here the departure from the tomb is not that of Jesus but of all humanity.

The icon gives visual expression to the Easter acclamation:

> Christ is risen from the dead,
> trampling down death by death;
> and to those in the tomb
> Christ bestows life.

During Eastertime the church reads from the gospel of John. This gospel overflows with paschal images—the good shepherd; the door to the sheepfold; the way, the truth and the life; the vine and its branches. Other traditional depictions of the risen Christ are often allegorical—a phoenix, a pelican, a shepherd, a gardener, the Sacred Heart. At worship the shining paschal candle is a sign of the Risen One. Other depictions, if any, might be placed at a distance from the candle to avoid the redundancy of symbols.

Here's a clever banner that employs imagery from Revelation: Designed to be visible from both sides, five panels of very sheer fabric are placed one in front of the other. One-by one-inch strips of wood separate each panel and are bolted and glued together to hold the five panels in place. The banner is hung from eyehooks screwed into these strips.

The center panel has the image of a paschal lamb applied to it. Moving out from the center, the next two panels are applied with identical images of

the holy city, with the lamb visible through the city's open gates. The outermost panels are applied with identical images of palm branches that form a kind of halo around the city.

This multilayered form of hanging might be used to show Jonah in the whale, Judith in Holofernes' tent, Daniel in the lions' den, the three children in the fiery furnace.

We aren't all that accustomed to using wreaths and garlands at Easter, but their use is traditional. As at Christmas, they signify triumph and eternity. Some customary materials for these at Easter are boxwood (which stays a good green even after it dries), pussy willow and laurel. Studding them with flowers and ribbons might help them look appropriate to the season.

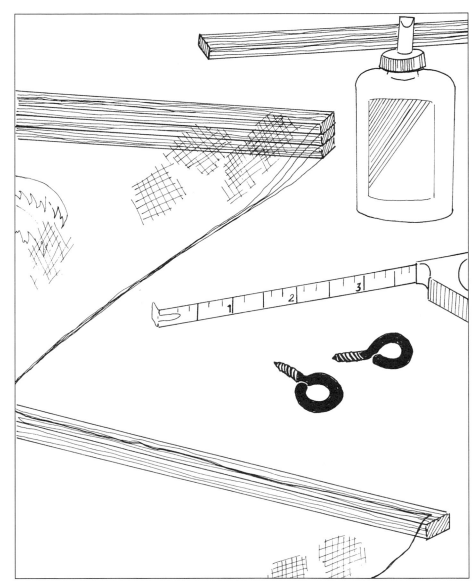

In some places, paper garlands and chains of paper flowers mark holy days. Some of these paper decorations are wonderful folk arts, and, as with other kinds of decoration, will appear appropriate in some buildings but not in others. A way to keep garlands more in scale with a large area is simply to use two or three in parallel swags.

ALTAR, AMBO AND CHAIR

The altar cloth might be especially full and festive throughout the season. Ordinarily the altar cloth (and the area around the altar) is not a good place for figural images. But some altars are embellished with carvings, inlaid mosaics or other sacred images. The paschal lamb is a common motif. Some parishes have the pelican carved into their stone altars. (According to legend, the pelican feeds its young on its own blood, and so it became a sign of Christ's paschal sacrifice.) During Eastertime the parish can surround this carving with a wreath of flowers.

The paschal candle goes next to the ambo during the Easter season. It's light illuminates the pages of scripture. During the rest of the year, the candle goes in the baptistry.

The candle is lit for all liturgical rites during the Fifty Days. Take special care that it is lit at times when a visitor is presiding, such as at a wedding.

The candle is a sign of the light of Christ and the Spirit's fire. There is a good custom of never extinguishing the candle publicly, because that would be too much of an "anti-sign." As much as possible, the candle is burning while people assemble and stays burning until people have left.

The area around the candle (near the ambo) is good for flowers as long as they permit people's free movement and don't overwhelm the site. Putting other smaller candles around the paschal candle suggests the sharing of the light. One parish leaves the candles of the newly baptized around the paschal candle. These candles are large enough to burn on Sundays through the Easter season and then to be taken home at Pentecost.

The cross would receive special attention during this season. The one venerated on Good Friday is the one to honor now. (For more on this, see page 67.) Keep candles burning near it and some flowers nearby. Be sure this cross doesn't compete for attention with another cross, especially the principal cross in the church. This principal cross is the best one to venerate on Good Friday and to honor throughout the Easter season.

The holy cross is our tree of life. Flowering branches seem especially suited to honoring it. Another sign of affection for the holy cross is a victory

wreath, ordinarily a ring of aromatic bay or myrtle leaves. A crown of thorns can be woven from fresh, leafless hawthorn.

In many parishes a white shroud is hung on the cross. To some people's eyes this is beautiful, but to others it is cliché. Recognize that this cloth is not mere ornament but represents the burial shroud of the Lord. If used, it should be handsome.

Some parishes have a special Easter cross set up somewhere, even out-doors. (For a discussion of this practice, see page 68.) But indoors or out, it's not good to use the cross as mere decoration.

The area near the altar often receives the bulk of the Easter flowers. See if you can find sites for flowers other than front-and-center. The ambo and the altar should not be banked with decoration. Remember: It should be possible to walk around the altar to honor it with incense.

VESSELS AND VESTURE

Some parishes have a set of vessels that are used now and perhaps also during the Christmas season. Some parishes use a particular set between Ash Wednesday and Pentecost and at no other times. Perhaps a certain variety of incense is used for this season; manufacturers have a wide range of flower-scented incense—rose, lilac, jasmine. Some of the aromas are splendid, and some smell like cheap bath oil. Choose carefully.

Water-base flower essences might be added to the baptismal font. Natural essences, such as lily of the valley or violet, can be easier on the nose than more exotic compounds. There are, of course, people who are allergic to certain substances, which is why good ventilation is essential in any public building.

The use of a particular set of vessels or kind of incense is a subtle distinction between seasons likely to go unnoticed by most parishioners. That's fine. What would not be fine is to interrupt worship to call attention to such distinctions. The subtlety would be lost and would make the elements too important.

The bulletin might mention that certain vessels or certain vesture are being used, and it's good to mention who donated these things, who the artists were and what materials were used.

Easter is a season for white vesture. The color calls to mind the image of the saints in white robes gathered around the Lamb (Revelation 7:9). This passage offers a good rationale for baptismal robes and wedding garments; they are the glory we'll wear in heaven at the wedding supper of the Lamb.

Many southerners in particular have the grand Easter tradition of decking themselves in white from head to toe—a celebration of heaven on earth. The alb (literally, "white") is the baptismal garment; all the baptized can wear albs whenever they worship.

During these days of white vesture, we might be sensitive to the various shades of white being used in church. Are they compatible? Manufacturers have come up with an amazing array of "white" vestments, from grays to yellows to mixtures of shades that seem to change depending on the light. Of course, the various fabrics in church—the hangings, the vestments, the altar linens—should all be compatible. But that doesn't necessarily mean they match.

Some parishes use gold or silver vestments during the Easter Octave and on Ascension Day. It's good to give visual distinction to certain days, but it's also good to preserve the unity of the Fifty Days. One way to do that is to use the same vesture on all the Sundays of the season, except, of course, on Pentecost.

Some parishes also make a practice of wearing the "Easter set" at all funerals and at most baptisms and weddings throughout the year. The festivals of the Transfiguration, the Assumption and All Saints might especially be occasions for a reprise of the paschal white.

Eastertime lends itself more than other seasons to the use of light materials rather than heavy ones, of pastels rather than deep colors. After all, it's spring! However, judging from what vestment manufacturers produce, most of us are not inclined to consider the use of airier, lighter fabrics and colors. For example, on white vesture it's common to see gold, scarlet or royal blue trimming but not yellow, pink, aqua or peach.

We could argue that aqua and peach are the colors of golf pants, not colors for liturgical use; but we could also argue that royal blue and scarlet

are the colors of bowling jackets. Perhaps we think that lighter materials and pastel colors convey a lightweight approach to mystery. But do heavy, deeply colored materials convey mystery any more appropriately?

We need to determine what looks best, what complements the other elements in the building—and that just might be deep and heavy or light and pastel. The use of the right colors and textures will accomplish much in gracing the atmosphere for Easter worship. But color alone doesn't bear the weight of mystery.

FONT

Keep the font clean and full throughout the season (if not all year long). Be concerned for safety. Water is inviting and dangerous to small children.

The biblical expression "living water" means moving water. Parishes that have no circulating system for the font often add a small water fountain or bubbler for Eastertime. The stirring water is a sign of the Creator Spirit. It calls to mind many of the images in the gospel of John, notably the healing pool of Bethesda (John 5:1–9).

Adding electrical equipment to a font is potentially deadly; the equipment needs to be designed for this purpose, and plugging it into a ground-fault outlet is essential. Many fountains and circulators are ugly, and any materials used to mask this ugliness (plants, stones) shouldn't make the font unusable for baptism. One parish hides the water pump in a stone fish that sits under the water.

The font ought to convey a wealth of meanings, and the chief among these are womb (a place of birth), tomb (a place of burial) and bath. Those images can get lost or confused when a baptismal font looks too much like a garden fountain.

That's not to say that flowers, candles and other decoration should not grace the font. They certainly should. The names of two lovely often-blue flowers, cinerarias and hydrangeas, have an appropriateness to baptism: Cineraria means "rising from the ashes" and hydrangea means "water vessel."

If there's a good spot, perhaps an array of scriptural imagery can grace the baptistry, especially during these Fifty Days: the wind rushing over the primordial water, the great flood, the passover through the sea, the crossing of the Jordan, the cleansing of Naaman, Jonah's journey in the belly of the fish and the entombment of Lord Jesus in the belly of the earth.

A resurrection garden: After the reforms of the 1950s and 1960s, but before it became common to baptize at the Easter Vigil, some parishes

would create a kind of Easter garden with running water. The water was blessed and used to sprinkle the assembly.

Oddly enough, this practice sometimes is still kept up even in parishes that have renovated their fonts and now use them for baptism at the Vigil. In some churches the font itself gets "landscaped" at Easter with rocks and plants.

What's going on here? There's a lovely custom from Christian antiquity of building a "resurrection garden" complete with empty tomb, and that might have a place in a parish shrine. Perhaps it can go in the same relatively private location that the Bethlehem scene was placed, but the custom shouldn't get jumbled up with the font.

Although nativity or Easter scenes have at times become so delightfully elaborate that they have included running water, you might just leave the water out if it's likely to get confused with the blessed waters of baptism.

The ambry (the place where the holy oils and sacred chrism go) might receive ornamentation during Eastertime. Fragrant flowers are perfect there. A bundle of olive branches will stay looking good even after it dries. Any fragrant herb or flower seems appropriate close to the chrism.

Especially if the oils are in glass vessels and the ambry is transparent, the place might be ornamented with a cluster of votive lights or, better, one or even several hanging oil lamps. The flickering flames will highlight the oils and the glass. One parish keeps something they call their "Spirit-mobile" suspended over the ambry throughout the Fifty Days. The mobile is made of seven suspended lamps.

Throughout the Easter season an image of the descent of the Spirit on Pentecost could be kept near the ambry. Two images to complement this are the tower of Babel and the giving of the law on Sinai.

SHRINES

The Catholic practice of devoting the month of May to Mary is beloved by many in the church. A problem arises when the practice gets disconnected from Eastertime or takes precedence over the season. Something's askew in parish life, for instance, when the parish school puts more energy into May crowning than into Ascension Day or Pentecost, or when the May shrine is fancier than the Easter decorations.

Some people argue that May crowning grabs the human heart more than, say, the festival of Pentecost. But is that really true? Generations ago the liturgical seasons and festivals overflowed with hearty celebration.

Devotional practices (such as May crowning) entered Catholic life as substitutes for the liturgy. As schoolchildren, we were taught (and often still are being taught) about May crowning. Are we being taught the practices of Eastertime? Nothing is gained by reorienting priorities heavy-handedly, because we are involved here with human affections, and those take generations to form.

This Maytime devotion to the Blessed Mother has an interesting pedigree.
It falls in the same "evolutionary line" as other civic and pre-Christian religious devotions to the burgeoning life of the spring season. A common denominator was the "mystical marriage" imagined as the source of the new life of spring, the same archetypal imagery that gave us maypoles.

The mystical marriage is an image found in the scriptures: God is Israel's spouse. Wisdom is the beloved. Jesus is the groom and the church is the bride. Jerusalem is bejewelled for its marriage to the Lamb.

In Christian lore, the Virgin Mary is compared to a bride, to a dove, to the church, to holy Wisdom, to the Spirit. (Much of this imagery comes into play at Pentecost.) The contrast between women and men is not the focus here. The images are of desire, courtship, loving union, cooperation, fidelity, and the birth and upbringing of children.

The spirit of the liturgy can shape Maytime devotion to Mary and give it fertile ground in which to grow. We can schedule Marian devotions to coincide perhaps with the Pentecost novena (the days between Ascension Day and Pentecost) or with the feast of the Visit of the Virgin Mary and Elizabeth, May 31. Or May Day might be the annual occasion for the crowning of an image of the Blessed Virgin, because May 1 always falls during the Easter season (unlike May 31).

Perhaps Mary's shrine is decorated not for May but for the whole of Eastertime (which includes many or some years all of the days of May). Perhaps the strong Eastertime image of the *Regina caeli,* the "Queen of heaven" (the Marian antiphon of the Easter season), becomes foundational to this shrine and also to crowning the image of Mary.

Mary is named the mother of the church. This title has two echoes in scripture: When he was dying on the cross (John 19:26–27), Jesus told his mother and the beloved disciple that they were now mother and child to each other. The last mention of Mary in the scriptures, Acts 1:14, tells us that she was present with the other disciples praying together in the upper room. That mention is one reason artists have shown Mary at events that flank this passage: the ascension of Jesus, the election of Matthias and the descent of the Holy Spirit.

Some of this art, including the Byzantine icons of the Ascension and Pentecost, can be included in the shrine. The Ascension icon shows Mary with arms uplifted in the posture of supplication. Here she is an image of a Christian's lifelong expectation of Christ. The Pentecost icon sometimes shows Mary at the head of the gathering of the apostles. Beneath this gathering is a small figure called "Kosmos," a personification of all creation, which is being renewed by the Creator Spirit.

Especially if the shrine is a proper devotional space—private enough to foster meditative prayer and mostly out of the line of sight of the liturgy—the old-fashioned bunting, candles and flowers of a May shrine could have a place throughout the Easter season. Especially fitting are spring flowers that can be gathered from backyards and brought to the shrine—tulips, violets, lily-of-the-valley, spirea, peonies. Encourage this devotion.

For Mary's shrine, one parish created a handsome scroll with the words and the music of the chant *Regina caeli*. The music is illuminated with floral designs and animals. Another parish includes a goose egg on which is painted an icon of the harrowing of hell.

Another parish uses the shrine as a place to gather many of the smaller scale folk arts of Easter: a carved balsa bird of paradise, finely woven ringlets of palm fronds, an inlaid enamel icon of St. George slaying the dragon, and batik-dyed Easter eggs. A basket of freshly sprouted wheat grain forms a living carpet for the eggs.

One parish's neighborhood is filled with roses during Eastertime, and so they are used abundantly in church as signs of the season. Mary's shrine receives a tapestry embroidered with roses, and one of the parishioners crowns Mary's statue each morning with fresh roses.

Flower crowns and wreaths of flowers are not only traditional for Mary's statue but for all the sacred images found in the church during Eastertime. Flowers are a kind of festive counterpart to the Lenten veiling of images. You might want to put some effort into keeping burning candles and fresh flowers near the church's sacred images throughout the Fifty Days.

SEASONAL CORNERS

Some parishes devote a corner of the church to making known some of the prayer intentions and concerns of the community, to teaching ways of observing the season at hand and making any home prayer resources available, and to opening up some of the folk arts and other images of the season. Lent is obviously an important time for much of this, and any good efforts begun during Lent should continue through the Fifty Days.

Perhaps the good work of charitable organizations can be advertised, especially those organizations that receive parish alms. This almsgiving is renewed and intensified during the paschal season so that it can continue more vigorously all year long.

You can post pictures of the happenings of the Triduum. You can help the parish become better acquainted with the neophytes, with the newly confirmed and with those who have made their first communion. The same is true for the newly married and the soon-to-be-wed. Some of this could be presented in the manner of a community bulletin board, but some could also be presented as a request for prayer and remembrance. The display must be dignified and beautiful.

Something important that might happen in such a corner or in a parish library is the opening up of the visual imagery of the season. This "mystagogy" is sparked by the parish's experience of the sacraments during the Triduum.

Some people say that "faith is caught, not taught." There's truth in that, because faith is a gift of the Spirit. What needs to be taught is not faith but the language of faith. Without it we remain religiously illiterate. One aspect of Easter mystagogy is the teaching of this language, and parish environment and art ministers deserve an important role in opening up for others the signs and symbols—the language—of faith.

Three very different books that many have found helpful in opening up this language are Jean Danielou's *The Bible and the Liturgy,* Romano Guardini's *Sacred Signs,* and Balthasar Fischer's *Signs, Words & Gestures.* The first two books are scholarly (but readable) and the last book is for young students and includes beautiful block prints by Helen Siegl. They're all out of print, however, which is a scandal to anyone who values liturgical

imagery. But sometimes you can find them in used bookstores or in rectory or seminary libraries.

VESTIBULES, DOORWAYS, OUTDOORS

More than any other season, Eastertime seems to need the public witness of outdoor decorations. You might disagree, but sometimes what works well outdoors, in addition to colorful bunting, flags or other signs of festivity, is a beautifully designed banner that simply says "Christ is risen," "The Easter season" or "The fifty days of Easter."

That's a blunt bit of advertising and catechesis that would not have a place inside the church. But outdoors it serves as something of a shout, a declaration and a witness not to the parish but of the parish.

There is, of course, the cross on the top of the steeple or in some other location that marks the building for a holy purpose. You might see if you can decorate this cross for the Easter season. You might be able to circle the cross with flowers or bright flags and keep it illuminated in the evenings.

A maypole makes a wonderful Eastertime decoration outdoors, and it can be used as a processional pole as long as there's a stand for it at the beginning and at the end of the route.

Indoors, be careful where you locate a maypole (or any portable banner): It can either compete too much with the processional cross and paschal candle or can emphasize and grace them beautifully. A strong and colorful vertical element such as a maypole might have a place near the font during the Easter season.

In the medieval imagination, during spring the Maylady married the Maylord, and their love gave birth to the fruitfulness of spring. The marriage is represented by a maypole (originally a tree trunk with a wreath of flowers at its top). Many towns in Europe still set up maypoles. They look a lot like suspended Advent wreaths because the maypoles' wreaths are so prominent. In some places they're given a more clearly Christian cast by being enormous crosses ornamented with a crown of flowers.

The lord and lady of spring might strike us as too fanciful or even too heathen an image, but imagery of love and marriage fills the scriptures. Maypoles can be a grand sign of the paschal wedding of heaven and earth.

Wind is one of the pentecostal signs of the Holy Spirit. Flags, windsocks, ribbons and lanterns swinging outdoors in the wind seem right for celebrating the Fifty Days. But wind and sunlight are enemies of outdoor decorations unless these decorations are designed correctly and constructed from appropriate materials.

Most polyester and nylon fabrics are not particularly attractive, but many of them are useful outdoors. Decorations that are exposed to the elements need to move with and not resist the wind, and that movement is facilitated by swivel hooks, by plastic sleeves on flagpoles that permit the fabric to spin freely around the pole, and by holes cut into banners to let some air pass through.

One parish uses well-crafted, commercially available windsocks in the shapes of daffodils and irises to decorate the light fixtures in the parking lot. In another place, an array of rather simple, single-color windsocks are hung from aluminum poles set into ten-foot-long metal pipes hammered into the ground. Distributors of these sorts of things may give a discount if you buy in quantity. Another parish commissioned a flag company to create an outdoor banner with an Easter greeting emblazoned on it.

Every door on parish property can have a wreath. Or, a single, large wreath can be hung outside in a prominent location. Many people are getting accustomed to using wreaths at home throughout the year, probably because the circular shape happens to look good on a door. The wreath is a sacred sign that shares the same significance as other ritual circles—including the crown and the wedding ring.

Craft stores offer wreaths made from an abundance of materials, and for Easter the ones made out of birch or willow branches or ficus

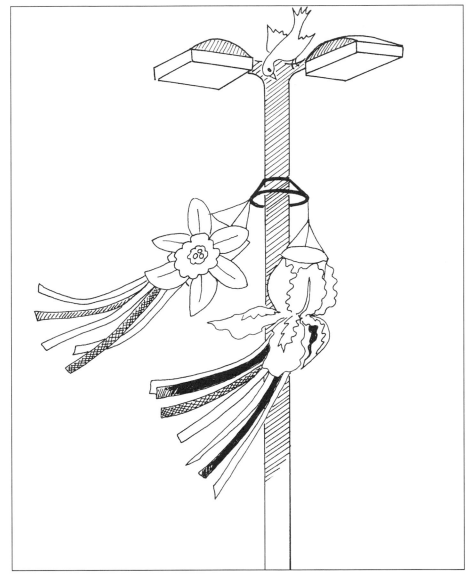

roots are often handsome. Pussy willows also make a wonderful wreath, and, while this may sound hard-nosed, it's best if the wreath isn't "domesticated" with pretty ribbons and other craft-store additions. The beauty of the material from which the wreath is constructed and the circular shape is more important than any ornamentation.

You might not want to lose the traditional image of the victory wreath made out of fragrant laurel. One parish uses living wreaths made from variegated ivy, and a parishioner waters these daily through the season.

Garlands and a triumphal arch (page 55) are customary accompaniments to wreaths in outdoor ornamentation. If large and full, these can be beautiful, although to some people's way of thinking they might appear triumphalistic and cliché. A simple fabric archway over the main doors can be handsome. These kinds of classic "triumphant" materials might be reserved for communal festivals, such as Easter, but would not be used in celebrations of individuals, such as the installation of a bishop.

The Ascension of the Lord

An eagle often steals its prey from another. Our Savior did something like that in the ascension. The Savior snatched humanity from the jaws of death. The Savior soared into the heavens with the human race held fast in his talons.

—Maximus of Turin † c.408

We miss the point of this celebration if we think the day is about a departure. The festival, and every Christian festival, is about the everlasting presence of the risen Christ.

Any festival needs its special signs. Today's signs are added to those of Eastertime, joy upon joy. The second reading at Mass, Ephesians 1:17–23, tells us that Christ fills the universe. Celestial signs seem right this day—the earth, sun, moon and stars, or the wheeling spiral of a galaxy. Images of blaring trumpets and clapping hands are from Psalm 47. From Acts we have the holy sign of the cloud, perhaps the strongest image for this day.

In former times the paschal candle was extinguished on this day, and there was something satisfying about watching a curl of smoke rising from the smoldering wick. But snuffing out a flame is a terrible image. According to the liturgy, the paschal candle stays burning brightly until Pentecost. One of our "clouds" today surely might be an abundance of incense, and a bowl of burning incense would look well-placed near the paschal candle. Perhaps the candle could be surrounded with a cloud of crabapple or locust blossoms.

Ascension is often a day for an all-school liturgy, and in some places students participate in a balloon launch. That's a fun activity that catches the imagination, and it gets all eyes gazing into the skies—but what is the message here? That Jesus is gone? That heaven is up there somewhere? That it's fine to litter the earth with bits of plastic?

By all means, organize outdoor activities for Ascension Day. Perhaps the day's liturgy can end with everyone tossing a grain or two of incense on a bed of burning charcoal outside. That will turn our eyes upward.

An old custom for the day is to march in procession around the parish boundary or just around the parish property. The paschal candle might be carried at the head of the procession. That's a way of putting into motion those words of Paul that the "fullness of Christ fills all in all."

Pentecost

What day is today?
Red Pentecost Day!
With acacia and peonies
    earth smells like
    heaven.
Let's take to the streets,
    get out in the sun!
Even the dead need light
    on Pentecost Day.

– from a Hungarian rhyme

For centuries Pentecost was one of the premier days of the year for decorations. Customary at Pentecost were branches of fresh foliage, bundles of green grasses and reeds, and a large number of familiar flowers— roses, poppies, peonies and irises.

At this season people feasted on the first pickings of their gardens— asparagus, peas, lettuces and herbs, rhubarb and strawberries. With pastures lush and with flocks and herds giving birth, the abundance of dairy products transformed winter's fast into summer's great feast.

These signs of the season came to be interpreted as emblems of the life-giving Spirit, as reminders of God's covenant with all creation.

On the Jewish calendar, Shavuot, the feast of "Weeks," falls 50 days —seven weeks—after Passover.

(*Shavuot* is also called Pentecost, from the Greek word for 50.) The days between Passover and *Shavuot* are the time of the grain harvest in many Mediterranean lands. This most important harvest of the year must be successful, though even a good crop of grain is extremely vulnerable just before it is gathered in.

When grain ripens, it grows brittle and is easily broken by wind, easily rotted by rain. The 50 days in Jewish lore are a time of pensiveness, of holding one's breath until the harvest has been safely brought into storage.

Even in more northerly climates we know the anxieties of spring. When will the fields dry out so that we can plant? When will the rains come so that the seed will sprout? A hailstorm can wreck an orchard, a cold snap can kill newly hatched chicks, and a dust storm can asphyxiate a herd.

Pentecost became a celebration of the end of anxiety—a feast of fulfillment. Some of its customary images are dishes prepared from milk and honey as signs of our arrival in the "promised land" of the settled days of summer. Cheesecake was just about invented as a Pentecost delicacy.

Another Hebrew title for Pentecost is Yom ha-Bikkurim, *"the day of firstfruits."* A firstfruit is an offering to God of the first of each harvest. Throughout the Fifty Days, an offering of barley was made to God, and at Pentecost the offering changed to the first sheaves of ripe wheat.

In Jewish and Christian folklore, Pentecost is associated with ripe, red strawberries, golden apricots and cherries—the first of the summer fruits. This is just about the time of year these fruits grow ripe in the warmer places of North America, and markets everywhere have them in abundance. Even in southern Canada, June brings serviceberries, which at one time were a principal source of vitamins in the Native American diet.

The Pentecost custom of filling homes and houses of worship with lush greenery was kept by Jews and Christian alike. The custom still lives on in central and eastern Europe. There is great mystery in a simple green branch or a stalk of green grass.

Not that many weeks ago the earth seemed lifeless, but in time the ground softened, the buds swelled and blossomed, and the Passover arrived. Now that the season is complete, the days have gotten long and warm, trees are green, and the earth has grown fruitful.

The branches and bundles of green grasses may remind us of phrases from the Pentecost sequence—*"dulce refrigerium,"* "sweet refreshment," and *"in aestu temperies,"* "mildness in the heat." These are attributes of the Holy Spirit.

City folks sometimes substituted paper roses and green foliage for the real thing. The art of cut paper added a lovely dimension to Pentecost and sometimes was combined with real greenery and flowers. Paper birds, flowers, garlands and other ornaments would be used to festoon whole small trees cut and brought inside. In past generations, Christmas wasn't the only season for decorated trees.

Many Byzantine churches use small birches and poplars in their decoration, especially of the front doors. Some Jewish synagogues spread their floors with sweet-smelling hay and decorate the ark of the scriptures with tree branches. We might try something along those lines—the customs have too much history to fall into disuse.

The story of the covenant on Sinai, where God came down in fire and wind, became the principal focus of the festival of **Shavuot.** The covenant completes the Passover. The Israelites kept vigil while Moses received the tablets of the law; thus keeping vigil throughout the night became a Jewish custom for *Shavuot.* It also became a custom for Christians at Pentecost so that Eastertime would end the way it began, with a nighttime vigil.

We Christians add the story of the descent of the Holy Spirit to the other stories we celebrate at Pentecost, the stories we have received as a legacy from the Jewish celebration. With special delight we contrast the story in Acts of the Spirit's gift of the understanding of languages with the disruption of languages on the tower of Babel. Pentecost can be for us a kind of festival of the nations—like Epiphany, the herald of a world at peace.

Parish environment and art ministers have a holy duty to use their talents to help "create" the festival. Without this work, the day can be lost. Pentecost is thoroughly ignored by the media and by society in general, yet it is one of the greatest days on the Christian calendar, ranking alongside Easter, Christmas and Epiphany.

It's really not enough just to shift the color of vestments to red for this day. There's extra work required, not only to have a splendid eucharist this day but to have a splendid day—a festival filled with its traditional signs of celebration, signs that we see, hear, touch, smell and taste. There's work required to get our blood flowing and our imaginations engaged.

When we keep such a festival, it begins to keep us—forming our souls, guiding our hearts.

Parish schools can host an international fair in the days that precede Pentecost. Some of this opening up of the parish's ethnic heritage can be put on display in a shrine or in a seasonal corner (where it's easy to visit but doesn't compete with the liturgy).

In some languages, "to make a Pentecost" means "to go on a picnic," because that's what most everyone does to celebrate the day. Pentecost is a premier day for the annual parish picnic. That, too, can have an international atmosphere if people are invited to bring ethnic dishes to share potluck-style. The event deserves abundant decoration, of course.

Effective Pentecost decorations would be the Eastertime ones adapted to the hot colors of the day. Pastels could be replaced with scarlets, fuchsias,

oranges and hot pinks. The visuals this day would mark the completion of Eastertime and not some independent festival.

Notice that the story in the second chapter of Acts doesn't mention the appearance of a dove; that's an image unique to Jesus' baptism. But it's hard to imagine Pentecost without this borrowed image. Iconographically, the Spirit-dove sometimes is transfigured at Pentecost into a firebird with blazing feathers. The phoenix is an amazing legend found nearly throughout the world, and Christians see in the story a sign of the resurrection.

Red is the liturgical color of the day and it could appear just about everywhere. So be sure that the shades of color in the vesture and throughout the church are complementary.

A fine tradition is to request that everyone dress in reds and other hot colors on Pentecost. Dressing up for the day becomes a popular practice once begun, and (appropriately) parishioners themselves become the day's decorations.

Asking a florist for arrangements "heavy on the red" is sure to get you carnations. But such hothouse flowers are too tame in comparison to the abundant blooms of fields and gardens at this time of year—daisies, larkspur, poppies, irises, peonies and roses. A good Pentecost tradition in rural or suburban areas is to have parishioners bring flowers to church the day before, with a crew on hand to arrange them.

Perhaps branches could be hung with paper-cuttings (50 roses?); a mobile of flickering votive candles set up in the same spot the Advent wreath goes; bundles of green wheat and other fresh grasses tied to the ends of pews. A brunch of cheesecake might make delicious after-worship fellowship, and fresh strawberries could be handed out as people depart.

The day also might need its share of fire and wind, something that disrupts us and that gives us a rush. Like the disciples spilling out into the streets of Jerusalem, Pentecost requires its outdoor expressions.

Streamers, pinwheels, windsocks and mylar balloons might festoon the parking lot. The youth group might tuck Pentecost greetings (or a table prayer) in the form of red paper "tongues of fire" under car windshield wipers. It once was customary to toss rose petals on the assembly as they departed the church. Outdoor luminaries, hanging lanterns and (why not?) red and white Christmas lights might be used to celebrate the vigil. Fireworks displays are a wonderful Pentecost custom.

The principal pentecostal fire has been shining in church throughout these Fifty Days: The paschal candle remains by the ambo today, but perhaps it could be surrounded by a dozen or even 49 smaller candles. At the end of worship, the candle is carried to the font, where it stays throughout the year.

Easter Flowers

> The Lord of all things lives anew:
> And all his works are rising too.
> The Lord is ris'n, as all things tell:
> Good Christian, see you rise as well.
> —from the collection of carols *Piae Cantiones*

More than any other season, Easter is a time of flowers. The Lenten liturgy discouraged their use at worship; perhaps the Easter liturgy almost demands them.

Come up with a plan (and budget) for flowers that can be maintained throughout the Fifty Days. An explosion of flowers for Easter Sunday is exuberant, but if it can't be maintained, you wind up communicating that Easter is over once the flowers are dead. Your plan might require scaling back the order for Easter Sunday so that you can afford flowers for the rest of the season.

If the flowers will make less of a display than in years past, you can compensate with other forms of decoration.

Some parishes make use of backyard blossoms: Forsythia can be used one week, flowering plum the next, apple and pear blossoms the next, and so on as various plants come into bloom throughout the spring. The use of indigenous materials can help foster a sense of the progression of the season and its building toward Pentecost.

Heavy branches need heavy containers. Urn-shaped waterproof concrete vessels are good. You can use lighter vessels if you first put the branches in them and then add pebbles as ballast. Sand also works as long as it's salt-free. A few drops of chlorine bleach in the water keeps it fresh.

Most backyard flowers are especially short-lived but often make up for that by being fragrant and splendid. The parish church might just be the only place some people can stick their noses into a bouquet of lilacs—surely a sign of heaven on earth.

Some parishes decorate indoors with containers of landscape plants, with the intention of planting them outside later. This can work if you don't leave the plants indoors more than a week or so. Because most churches are too dark and too warm for outdoor plants, their growth turns leggy and pale, which weakens the plants and can kill them.

The upkeep of flowers (and of the other elements in the worship environment) might be a task for every Friday afternoon or Saturday morning. Earlier in the week you would anticipate what will need replacement and would then put in your order or make plans to cut your own flowers. Keep in mind that it is a lot easier to work with flowers in bud, ready to pop, rather than flowers already fully bloomed. Buds are much less fragile than open flowers.

Some flowering plants are long-lived and some won't last a week. Cut-flower arrangements and most potted spring bulbs (daffodils, tulips, hyacinths) rarely stay in good shape through two weekends. But azaleas, kalanchoes, hydrangeas, cyclamens, mums and some others might stay attractive for three or four weeks in a cool church.

Chrysanthemums will last a long time. Although they are autumn flowers and most varieties just don't conjure up an image of springtime, some of the daisy-type mums (with a single row of petals and a prominent yellow center in each flower) have been bred to look appropriate in spring. Some varieties have a wonderful fragrance ('Queen Anne', for instance).

Bright light but not blazing sunshine, a cool and humid environment, and evenly moist soil go a long way in keeping potted plants looking good. However, some flowering plants will last indoors only if they have direct sunlight (geraniums, lisianthus and potted roses). Some have an especially hard time reviving after being allowed to go dry (azaleas, cinerarias and hydrangeas), but nearly all plants are killed if allowed to stand in water. Roots need oxygen and will drown in too much water.

Another factor in the longevity of flowering plants is how far blossomed out they are when they arrive from the florist, who probably thinks that you

want a good show for one Sunday and therefore sends materials in full flower. Explain that you want some of the flowers to last as long as possible.

Some potted flowers (lilies, hydrangeas, azaleas, mums) can be planted outside permanently if the varieties are hardy in your climate and if their time indoors didn't ruin them. Many of the azalea and mum varieties that florists grow are only hardy in the Deep South. Easter lilies can't be grown where the soil freezes deeply, but pink, yellow and orange lilies are very hardy.

Ribbons and fancy wrappings can catch the eye even more than the flowers, which is misplaced emphasis—and these also can add to the cost. Some parishes have the florist send the flowers without wrappings, and then they put them in straw-colored "hat baskets" that get reused from year to year. Even more handsome are terra-cotta pots.

Potted flowers look better if they are clustered rather than evenly spaced in rows; they aren't cabbages. To create attractive groupings, a massive pot or basket can be filled with a number of individual smaller pots of one kind of flower. Easter lilies can look splendid arranged like that. Individual plants can be repotted in the large pot or basket, although it's not always necessary to unpot the plants in order to fit them together in a larger pot.

Of course, you can order large pots with several plants in each, but clustering them yourself is easy and much cheaper than having a florist do it.

At certain sites in the church (for instance, around the paschal candle), you might have several different groupings of flowers. For instance, you might have one big basket of seven 'Stargazer' lilies, a medium basket of three white azaleas, and a small basket of five blue primroses. The grouping of plants of the same variety looks better than mixing everything up.

Each variety usually drops its petals at about the same time. If varieties are mixed up, you'll need to take the whole thing apart and rearrange the grouping from week to week.

To get some height into your arrangements, use branches of flowering shrubs or even small trees set into pots of water. Pussy willows are versatile for this purpose because they don't need water. (In fact, water makes them drop their buds.)

Peacock feathers can be used to add height. They are a traditional Easter decoration especially in some Mediterranean countries. The peacock was regarded in biblical times as a sign of immortality, and the bird became a favorite image to carve on tombs. The royal blue feathers are certainly festive and can look wonderful tucked among lilies or other white or pink flowers.

The use of plant stands, small tables or other devices for adding height to clusters of potted flowers often detracts from the flowers. Just as the pots

should be attractive, so too should be any device for holding the pots. Masking ugly plant stands with cloth or Spanish moss usually draws even more attention to them. Good-looking pedestals, even very short ones, are often attractive for this purpose. They can be an expensive though worthwhile investment.

Some people use potted palms or other green plants to add height to arrangements. Sometimes that looks fine, but often the greenery is too dominant. It's not a good idea to use lots of flowers on Easter Sunday and then replace them with long-lived houseplants. Houseplants just don't convey the notion of festivity and certainly don't convey the imagery of spring.

Figure out a way to get flowers into the assembly's place. Too often we put flowers at a distance instead of putting them where they can be enjoyed up close. You might put flowers on windowsills or in baskets hung on the walls.

Of course, setting single pots of flowers here and there throughout the church will look busy. By choosing a few sites and grouping the pots, you create an arrangement more in scale with the space. For example, say that you have large columns in the assembly's area and you want to use them for flowers. It's probably better to put a few pots into some sort of large, lightweight container, such as a plastic-lined basket, than to arrange the pots individually around the column.

Be sure that the font, the oils, the cross and the paschal candle receive flowers or fragrant herbs throughout the season. These sites might be the priority spots for flowers and greens, and these can take some unusual forms. For instance, the processional cross might receive a wreath of ivy each Sunday of the season, or a bouquet of tulips might be tied to its standard. The font might be graced with floating gerbera daisies and candles. Another site for flowers might be the seating area of the newly baptized.

Vestibules and entryways are excellent sites for flowers. Float one in each holy water stoop. Place a bouquet where people receive worship folders or bulletins. Poke them into the buttonholes of all the liturgical ministers, especially the ministers of hospitality. Even if it means taking some of the flowers from near the altar and ambo, get them where they can be enjoyed up close.

Summer Ordinary Time

A Sense of the Season

In ecclesiastical jargon, the word "ordinary" can mean "ordered"—in other words, "counted." Thus, each week of Ordinary Time is sequentially numbered to help us organize our books of readings and prayers.

Ordinary Time is not a liturgical season, at least not in the way that Eastertime and the others are seasons. Notice how we title the Sundays. We say the Second Sunday *of* Easter or the Fourth Sunday *of* Advent. But we say the Eleventh (or Twentieth or Thirty-third) Sunday *in* Ordinary Time. Not exactly an attention-getter, but it's deliberate.

Lent and Eastertime, Advent and Christmastime each have their own particular images, so their Sundays have something to belong to (which is why we can say "of"). But Ordinary Time is not a source for images of the paschal mystery.

However, that being said, summer and fall *are* ripe with imagery—and so is the Lord's Day, and so are the festival days, and so are mornings and noontimes and evenings and nights. These are what bring substance and significance to these "counted" weeks of the year.

The days between Pentecost and the First Sunday of Advent span over half the year. Many people admit that they can't get a handle on this long stretch of green-vestment weeks. What do these weeks look like? What is their liturgical atmosphere?

The weeks between Eastertime and Advent "look like" June, July, August, September, October or November. The weeks may look like the longest days of the year, when linden trees fill the night air with a heavenly aroma and when fireflies make their graceful arcs of light on the lawn. Or the weeks may look like a farmer's market overflowing with corn and tomatoes, with bunches of cosmos, tarragon and dill, with *ristras* of garlic and dried peppers—a market where city folks can celebrate their rural roots.

Or the weeks may look like school letting out for summer vacation and then reconvening as summer wanes, or like a trip to the beach, to the amusement park, to the zoo. And they may look like the Fourth of July fireworks, like Halloween trick-or-treating, like visiting the folks on Thanksgiving.

Eventually, before Advent, the earth is transfigured into winter, the antithesis of Passover—the foliage of trees gets glorious before falling, geraniums turn into frosted slime, summer birds depart, and perhaps the first snow falls. No wonder that in November the church's heart opens itself up to remembering of the dead.

The readings and prayers we keep so well-organized in our books bring to individual days certain images. There may even be links among the Sundays in Ordinary Time because of the sequential reading of the year's gospel or of one of the letters of Paul.

Perhaps this is a summer Sunday on which we hear about the prophet Elijah or Jeremiah. Perhaps for the next several Sundays we will hear Jesus' teaching about the bread of life. Perhaps this is our once-every-three-years encounter with the tale of Abraham bargaining with God for the lives of the townspeople of Sodom and Gomorrah.

These are powerful parables, and good summer ones, too, even if they never were intended to be signs of the season. The threat of fire and brimstone, a tale of Elijah's thirst or a lesson about manna in the wilderness are being told to us in an atmosphere of long days, of often uncomfortable warmth, of sudden thunderstorms and of fields ripe for the harvest.

On summer Sundays we hear of the mustard seed growing into a great bush, of a storm on a lake, of a sower who went out to sow, of Peter walking on the water with Jesus. Our Lord tells us, "Come to me, all you who are weary." When the weather is warm, we might be more disposed to accept the invitation.

For parish decorators it can be helpful to imagine summer as roughly divided into two spans. Each span has a different atmosphere. One we might call by the old name of "Midsummer," not really the middle of summer but the weeks right after Pentecost that surround the solstice. The other span would correspond to late July, August and early September.

The first span, Midsummer, like June is "bustin' out all over" with solemnities. We ease out of the paschal season with two white-vestment Sundays: Holy Trinity and the Body and Blood of Christ. At the end of June, closer to the solstice, we celebrate the Birth of John the Baptist (June 24) and also the festival of the apostles Peter and Paul (June 29).

Social, civic and business calendars are packed: There are graduations, weddings, Father's Day, Canada Day, Independence Day, and a spate of parades, parties and picnics before things quickly quiet down for the summer.

As spring peaks and summer commences, the world can seem as perfect as it gets—warm but not wilting, ripe but not rotting. The air can be fragrant with honeysuckles, magnolias and roses. At Midsummer the wheat ripens across the Great Plains—an awe-inspiring sight, and, with its ancient ceremonies, a vital image for the church festivals of June and July.

We are halfway around the year from Christmas. The parable of the solstice returns in reverse. Now the sun is at its highest, but the moon is at its lowest, and a full moon low in the summer sky takes on an amber cast

called a "honeymoon." Christians have seen in the longest days of the year something of a foretaste of the kingdom's eternal day, of the marriage between heaven and earth. Perhaps in these days we have the year's most romantic images of our entrance into the reign of God.

The second half of summer (at least before school starts up again) is more mellow than the first. These are favorite days for vacations, and most parish organizations take a summer hiatus. Maybe these are the most ordinary weeks of Ordinary Time, but they also are the most filled with images of fruitfulness.

Our planting now bears produce. Now is the time of ripe peaches and zucchini and tomatoes, often in greater quantities than we know what to do with, the time of fragrant basil and cilantro and airy bouquets of dill. Gladioluses, those mainstays of florists throughout the year, finally are in season along with zinnias and sunflowers and Queen Anne's lace.

The heat and humidity can bring with it a tropical atmosphere, an opulence and color unique in all the year. Winter seems at its most distant and the earth can seem its most hospitable. City streets can reflect this liveliness. When we're without air-conditioning, sleep comes with difficulty at this time of year and many folks vacate their homes to sit outside on stoops and porches late into the night.

The church has its celebrations that reflect late-summer fruitfulness and carnality—the Transfiguration of the Lord (August 6), the Assumption (August 15) and the Birth (September 8) of Mary, and the feast of the Holy Cross (September 14). In various times and places, these days were once marked with blessings of flowers, herbs, produce and livestock. They were like Labor Days, summoning forth our blessings on what "earth has given and human hands have made."

In *To Dance with God,* writing about Assumption Day, Gertrud Nelson reminds us of the linguistic connection between "mother" and "matter." Late summer can seem the most material, maternal days of the year, when mother earth offers the most food to those who are hungry and the least harm to those who are homeless.

But not everything is abundance in the festivals of late summer. There is death here, too, and the shedding of blood: Mary's death, the murder of Deacon Lawrence on a fiery gridiron (August 10), the flaying of Bartholomew (August 24) and the beheading of John the Baptist (August 29). At this time of year the Jewish calendar includes a remembrance of the destruction of the Temple. Not too far beneath these images lies another image: the often oppressive heat of late summer, a spark to violence and a danger to the heart.

Though it is mostly lost to us, this late summer period was once a time of fasting. In some places the 40 days—a "quarantine"—between Transfiguration (August 6) and Holy Cross (September 14) became like a mirror to Lent, a low-key time of introspection to make us ready for the change of seasons.

The fasting occurred amid the hard work of gathering and putting up the produce, which would not last long once it was ripe. There was a need for all hands on deck to get the work done, and there was no time to lose on preparing anything but the simplest of meals. In the doldrums of August we might just need a rallying cry for the season soon to arrive, the autumnal "new year" of so many human endeavors.

Overview

By the solemnity of the Holy Trinity (the Sunday after Pentecost), the Easter decor should be gone. This is not fussiness but instead shows respect for the parish, which has kept the Fifty Days that are now over.

As the weather warms up, parishes tend to scatter. Especially as the school year ends and summer sets in, people often have a bustle of competing responsibilities. Vacations, social events, home repairs and just plain laziness take their toll on the liturgical ministries.

If you happen to be reading this in winter or early spring, keep this annual flagging of energy in mind; it has claimed many a good intention. Either you can scale back your plans from the start, which can result in lukewarm and unsatisfying accomplishment, or you can get things done far enough ahead.

Another way to keep the worship environment during Ordinary Time from getting short shrift is to build on (or maintain) what was done in past summers: You don't need to keep reinventing the wheel.

You might give priority to three considerations during summer Ordinary Time:

1. Figure out a way to maintain housekeeping tasks throughout the season. Perhaps a small crew or a few households could be responsible for seasonal flowers gracing each Sunday and feast, for regularly cleaning the candles and the altar covering, and for caring especially for the area around the baptismal font and the entrances to the church.

2. Summer is a popular time of year for renovation and maintenance projects. This is also the season during which we may just find the time to get certain tasks accomplished, especially those that never seem to get finished throughout the year. What sort of goals have you set for yourself this summer?

3. Don't treat Ordinary Time as a homogenous block. Because Ordinary Time is not a season, it does not need a look all its own. So there's no point in having certain visuals stay the same from Pentecost to Advent.

On the one hand, these weeks seem to be the most appropriate time of year for plainness, which can offer visual refreshment. On the other hand, during no time of year should the worship environment be ignored. We might (but don't need to) introduce some visuals that are used each summer.

Bringing something of the summer into our communal praise can be an act of thanksgiving and a petitionary prayer for all that the season represents.

The purpose of this decoration is to create what *Environment and Art in Catholic Worship* calls a climate of hospitality and an invitation into mystery.

Certain festival days offer natural "hinges" within Ordinary Time. Perhaps the time can be divided roughly as follows: from Pentecost to Transfiguration, from Transfiguration to Holy Cross, from Holy Cross to All Saints and from All Saints to Advent.

How would these divisions affect the worship environment? Perhaps the vesture changes: It stays green, but the shade of green and the trim colors might "ripen"—perhaps with yellows, golds, oranges, purples—as summer turns into autumn. The successive ingathering of the harvest is an image that unites these weeks. This image is discussed beginning on page 176.

That gradual "ripening" also might be reflected in the choice of flowers and other elements, which can offer a sense of progression. For instance, the variety of incense might change. June's incense can smell of roses and mock orange, September's of heliotrope and jasmine. (Other elements are discussed as the various locations throughout the church are covered.)

Dividing Ordinary Time in this way would be done loosely and certainly would not involve dramatic shifts. Otherwise, we end up creating significance where none is warranted. What we shouldn't do is give each month, a span of weeks or even any single Sunday a thoroughly distinct visual treatment. We don't want to create the impression that a month or a block of weeks constituted some sort of liturgical season.

The feast days of summer warrant special decoration, but these days also can lend their imagery to the overall appearance of the worship environment throughout these weeks. For instance, Assumption Day would be celebrated with white vesture, and Mary's shrine might be ornamented with herbs and garden produce. But any other visuals in the church would remain up through the weeks of late summer and could reflect the fruitfulness of the earth, a common denominator during this time of year.

THE ASSEMBLY'S PLACE

The scale of the space is a challenge. To look good, materials need to be proportional to the area, and the assembly's place is the largest in the church. Of course, large materials are more expensive than small ones. Does the budget accommodate Ordinary Time?

This is often the space for banners, and during summer these might be simple fabric panels in shades that complement the vesture. Or, there might be figural images suggested in the banners. Botanical or geometric designs can work well.

Fabric stores often have handmade and hand-colored fabrics from various corners of the globe. Keep an eye open for this kind of artistry. Although many of these fabrics are not permanent press and some aren't even colorfast, all they may need is some hemming and ironing to be turned into magnificent hangings.

Some biblical images that have a special place during these weeks are the grain harvest, the sea, mountains and the summer sun. Often enough on summer Sundays, we hear in the gospel that the harvest needs laborers, that wheat and weeds will be allowed to grow together, that the kingdom is like a pearl of great price or like a dragnet thrown into a lake, or that Jesus was in a boat, by the seashore or on a hillside.

Such graphic images probably work better if they are suggested rather than depicted literally. For instance, hangings might employ the colors of earth and water or be evocative of sails, nets, hills or flocks. Or perhaps they might be hung so that they can billow in the breezes coming through the windows.

One parish created summer banners out of cotton fabric printed with a bold Maori design of fishes. Another used a Japanese silkscreen print of waves. Another created a series of traditionally designed quilts featuring stylized, summertime patterns: scythes, wheat, seashells, the sun, moon and stars. Designs were fundamental, simple, handsome—and didn't thump a viewer on the head with too straightforward an image.

The goal of such imagery isn't to illustrate the gospel of any particular Sunday; each Sunday wouldn't have its own decoration. Instead, certain figural designs may have a place throughout a span of weeks; they would "illustrate" (which means "to make bright") not specific gospel passages but our very worship during these weeks. That the images allude to scriptural passages is secondary to the atmosphere they create for worship.

Of course, depending on your own neck of the woods, some images will resonate better with the community than others. Perhaps the local mountains are snowclad or covered in rosebay. Perhaps your parish's peaks and valleys are formed by skyscrapers.

Maybe yours is a farming community in the corn belt, in a blueberry-growing region or in a ranching state. Maybe you're near a seaside or mountain resort, in a harbor town or in a port on a river, or in a city with one or several summer festivals.

What allusions to the scriptures and the prayers can be seen through the parish windows?

The area over the assembly or some other place in the church might be graced throughout the summer by a handsome and noble image of the sun. That image is present in the *Benedictus,* Zechariah's praise at the birth of his son John, which is the song sung by the church each morning. The image of the sun is also present in the readings of the feast of the Transfiguration of the Lord and of the solemnity of the Assumption of Mary.

An interesting bit of folklore connects the image of the sun to John: According to the prophet Malachi, Elijah is to return to usher in the days of the Messiah. (Elijah is remembered in the the Byzantine church on July 20, an important feast on their calendar.) Jesus had said, "If you are willing to accept it, John the Baptist is Elijah who is to come" (Matthew 11:14).

In Greek the name Elijah is *Elias.* The sun is *elios.* Ancient Christian writers recognized the poetic connection of the sun with both the prophet who ascended into heaven in a fiery chariot and John the Baptist who, like Elijah, made the desert his home.

Summer is flanked by the birth (June 24) and martyrdom (August 29) of John. In folklore he is considered the "patron," along with Mary, of

the summer season. His image and some of his symbols might grace the baptistry or some other spot throughout the year and especially during this season.

Besides Mary and John, another patron of summertime is the angel Uriel. The angel is mentioned in the apocryphal second book of Esdras. Uriel is translated "fire" or "lion" of God. A lion with a golden mane is an image of summer's heat, and in scripture the animal is almost always associated with the desert because a lion, like John, is a voice crying in the wilderness.

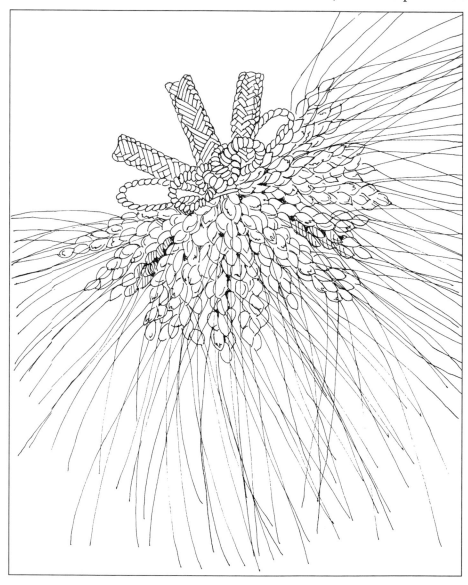

Much of this is part of the folklore of the Mediterranean, where summers are rainless and hot. The summertime drying up of vegetation, which also occurs throughout much of the American Southwest, has become a paschal emblem of death and burial. Assumption Day, August 15, and Holy Cross Day, September 14, are like turning points in expectation of the rains and the resurrection of the land in autumn.

Those of us unacquainted with agriculture tend to identify the time of harvest exclusively with autumn. In reality, though, the "amber waves of grain" are a phenomenon of June and July in the Great Plains of the United States; a Ukrainian proverb warns the farmer not to put the sickle to the crop until SS. Peter and Paul Day (June 29); and the Celts had an August 1 festival, Lammas ("loaf-Mass"), in thanksgiving for the first bread made from the summer harvest. At one time these days were occasions for a wealth of splendid folk arts involving the use of straw and grain in the making of crowns, scepters and crosses.

"Corn dollies" sound cute, and some craft stores have kits for making dolls from husks of maize. However, a real corn dolly isn't a human figure but an intricately woven bunch of rye, wheat or oats. ("Corn" here means grain, and "dolly" means an effigy.) Made into an amazing array of geometrical shapes, these may have a place hung on walls circling the pews or in a mobile hung high over the assembly.

The corn dolly has an interesting lineage. In ancient times the grain harvest was invested with ceremonials of life-or-death importance. One of these rituals was the enthronement of the grain: The first (or final) bundle of grain was brought home with pomp and then honored at a communal meal. This bundle eventually became the seed-source for the next year's planting, and so in some places was called the "grandmother" as the forebear of the continued life of the community.

A great circle of sheaves of grain makes a splendid ornament for the assembly's place (or perhaps for the outdoors). This wreath is called a "harvest crown." One enormous wreath can be splendid but may be too difficult to make or to find. Three or more wreaths can be overlapped a bit; they don't have to be the same size or even made of the same materials. Perhaps they're made of the principal grains on which civilization depends—rice, maize and wheat.

None of this imagery is distant from the gospels, but it may be far from our lives. This detachment is unfortunate, because human society continues to depend on these most important harvests of the year. As custodians of scriptural imagery, perhaps one gift we can offer our parishes is some insight into what matters most in human affairs.

ALTAR, AMBO AND CHAIR

Many parishes are in the good habit of having someone be responsible for decorating the church each weekend with one or two splendid bouquets of seasonal cut flowers. In June these might include white madonna lilies and blue delphiniums. In July there might be spikes of cattails and purple loosestrife. In August there might be buckets of sunflowers and gladioluses.

Many florists have slim pickings during summer, which seems surprising, but some have access to a variety of flowers, including those grown in gardens and fields. Check around. You might gather your own from roadsides (although permission from the landowner is always necessary) or even begin a churchyard garden with a patch or two reserved for growing materials for cutting.

In late summer many American roadsides are filled with goldenrod, white boltonia and purple asters. It is simply not true that these cause hayfever (ragweed is the culprit), although they bloom at the same time as ragweed. Marigolds, dahlias, and zinnias are Mexican and Central American natives that have been bred into garden favorites. These often hot-colored flowers have mythical associations with the sun.

What flowers are "classic" to your area? What folklore is associated with them? What summer flowers are "immigrants" from other continents? Don't overlook the ornamental value of grasses, herbs and vegetables. Corn tassels, gourd vines and ripe peppers can make a wonderful bouquet.

Some parishes rely on houseplants to provide visual interest in summer. That sometimes works just fine, but often the plants become part of the clutter in churches. Most houseplants do not offer seasonal interest, and many common varieties are not all that interesting. Some bring the atmosphere of a shopping mall or a waiting room into worship.

Like other forms of seasonal decoration, perhaps houseplants can come and go and not become regular features of the church interior. Some growers permit people to rent plants for periods of time. But remember that there is a necessary art to arranging houseplants; while some look fine by themselves, others need companions in small groupings.

Any pots or other containers should be handsome and not too prominent. Most plastic or brightly-colored ceramic pots call too much attention to themselves and can look peculiar (like white tennis shoes on someone in a suit). Some wicker, terra-cotta or dark metal containers can look fine. Rather than being machine-made, a pot or container could be handmade and bear the distinctive mark of the artist's touch.

Casters, even attractive iron ones, are too noticeable to be left in place. Any drip pans belong inside the decorative container; they're just too ugly to leave in plain view.

The church may have planters that require permanent plants. In that case, someone skilled in indoor horticulture needs to keep them in good shape. There might be an effort to marry the space to the species: for instance, a creeping fig might grow up a wall; a large ficus tree (which needs lots of sunlight to do well) could act as a support for a passionflower vine; and some plants that come into bloom at certain times of year, such as orchids, can contribute seasonal interest.

FONT

Fonts require regular cleaning and maintenance, and summer intensifies that need. Warm weather increases evaporation, as does air conditioning. Lime deposited by evaporating water needs to be removed with vinegar or a stronger acid.

Sunlight and warmth will cause microbial life to grow in the baptismal waters. If your font has no water purification system, small doses of chlorine bleach once a week will kill algae, although especially in brightly lit churches more potent chlorination may be needed. (The rule of thumb is that if you can still smell the chlorine bleach after it is diluted in the water, it's potent enough to kill algae.) But be careful: Mixing chlorine bleach with an acid (such as vinegar) or a base (such as ammonia) releases chlorine gas, a deadly substance.

One wonderful effect of large, well-made baptismal pools is that they are refreshing to behold. But they also can be inviting to small children, so take heed: It may be necessary to have an attractively designed grate placed over the water or a transparent net submerged just beneath the water.

SHRINES

It might be fitting to ornament Mary's shrine in some special way between Assumption Day and the feast of Mary's Birth (September 8) or the memorial of Our Lady of Sorrows (September 15). Are these images of Mary present in the parish's permanent art? Then they can be decorated with hanging lamps, flowers and bundles of herbs. Two other customary images that reflect the late summer festivals of Mary are Our Lady of the Harvest and the Star of the Sea.

Perhaps there can be a shrine that changes as the weeks come and go. This would be in an alcove, in a vestibule or at some other site that doesn't compete for attention with the liturgy. For instance, from the day after Pentecost until the day before Transfiguration Day, there could be a collection of images and symbols of a few of the saints of early summer—such as John the Baptist, Peter and Paul, Benedict, Kateri Tekakwitha, Mary Magdalene, James, Ann and Joachim, and Martha. Then on August 6 or thereabouts the collection changes to the saints of late summer.

The saints of the season come "clothed" in many summertime images. These images might be used to ornament vesture and hangings or could be gathered into the seasonal shrine. For example, grasshoppers, honeybees and seashells are signs of John the Baptist (June 24, August 29). Boats are reminders of the travels of Paul (June 29). Boats and fish are signs of the fishermen apostles Peter (June 29) and James (July 25). The beehive and the ship are two emblems of the church itself, where we all must work for the common good, where cooperative efforts are necessary to arrive at our destination.

Seashells also are customary signs of James: Scallop shells were carried by medieval pilgrims who traveled to the Spanish shrine of St. James in Compostela. To be carrying a "cockle shell" was like a plea for food and lodgings. Eventually the shells became emblems of hospitality to travelers.

St. Martha (July 29), like James, is also a patron of hospitality, and of course she's also the patron of cooks. By happy coincidence, on the sixteenth Sunday in Ordinary Time in Year C we hear the story of Martha and Mary. And in Year B, Jesus tells us in the gospel, "Come by yourselves to an out-of-the-way place and rest a little." This Sunday always falls in the second half of July, at the peak of the vacation season.

The scripture readings during these weeks are rich in such summertime allusions. This was not the intention of the framers of the lectionary, although the summer season may just open our eyes a bit wider to the mystical meaning of such ordinary things as fishing, farming, cooking and even napping.

Does the parish have outdoor shrines? How are these kept up throughout the year? Outdoor shrines are best if they are located in a private spot suitable for meditative prayer. Outdoor iconography needs at least an annual cleaning and would benefit from ornamentation on the image's feast day and on the parish's patronal day as well.

Seasonal iconography might be put outdoors in celebration of special events. In a coastal town where every summer brings an abundance of tourists, maybe a temporary shrine to St. Peter (a patron of fishing) could be set up on parish property. Vacation Bible school, a summer convocation of women, or any parish outreach of evangelization might take St. Mary Magdalene (July 22) as its patron and set up a shrine to her. (She is titled "apostle to the apostles" because she was first to spread the good news of resurrection.)

Perhaps a town has a music festival every July, and so a parish there might hang an outdoor banner in honor of Cecilia, the patron of musicians. A coastal town might mark August and September with an outdoor image of Jesus calming the sea, as a prayer for safety against hurricanes. Where there are many orchards, the church parking lot might be hung with banners featuring cherries, peaches and plums—and twin icons of Adam and Eve in paradise.

SEASONAL CORNERS

In some larger parishes most every summer weekend brings weddings. How does the parish inform itself about the weddings and other sacramental rites celebrated in its name? Maybe a bulletin board in the vestibule can be devoted to helping parishioners get to know the names and faces of newlywed and engaged couples and their families. That kind of sharing of information can be done beautifully, in a dignified manner, and as an invitation to prayer for the sake of all who are married in the parish church.

Often in summer there are all sorts of community activities advertised on parish bulletin boards. The upkeep of these boards—as well as any book racks, gift display cases, lost-and-found cabinets, or market day and fundraiser advertisements—requires a dedicated and discriminating soul. Sometimes these things form a visitor's first impression of a parish church. With orderliness and beauty, these things can function well and won't disfigure our entryways.

VESTIBULES, DOORWAYS, OUTDOORS

Church-sponsored processions and carnivals and other outdoor activities all demand the ministry of beauty. An annual summer fundraiser is like a parish feast day and would benefit from abundant outdoor ornamentation, especially of an image of the parish patron—although this may be the tail wagging the dog. To set things more in perspective, why wouldn't the parish's patronal day be celebrated each year with an outdoor carnival?

One gift to the parish of the ministers of liturgical art might be a renewed appreciation for the festivals of the liturgical year (including the parish's patronal day and the anniversary of the dedication of the church) and the links between these festivals and the other facets of parish life (such as social and fundraising events). The parish social calendar should be set in sync with the liturgical year.

Parishes have a responsibility in their neighborhood to become models for manifesting a respect for trees and other plants. So how's the church landscaping? It's something of a scandal that so many churches put so little effort into their landscapes. In contrast, some parishes put a priority on this. Even the parking lots are shaded by trees.

The garden is one of the first and strongest scriptural metaphors for communion with God. Some parishes have "Lady gardens" (featuring plants associated in folklore with Mary), Bible gardens (featuring plants mentioned in the scriptures) or fragrance gardens. Perhaps plants can be chosen that will become the source of material for indoor decoration. Not coincidentally, many of the skills of garden design are allied to the skills necessary in the design of seasonal liturgical art.

Some parishes have renovated or rebuilt their worship spaces so that courtyard gardens are clearly visible from within. There may be a visual or even an actual link between outdoor fountains and the baptismal font. Sometimes windows are located or trees are planted so that sunlight and shadows can better enter into the interior atmosphere. The intention is that the changing seasonal conditions outdoors become part of the seasonal environment indoors.

That wonderful effort might follow the same principles as any decoration in that it ought not compete too forcefully for attention during the liturgical rites. Caring for such a "liturgical garden" would be a year-round ministry. On the one hand, the garden requires a design and plant materials that appear pleasing throughout the year; on the other hand, there would be some shifting seasonal interest that never dominates the whole. (That sounds like the intended aesthetics of a Japanese garden.)

Throughout the summer, an urban parish especially might make an effort to ornament its grounds with light and color, simply as a way to beautify the neighborhood and to reflect some of its vitality.

Summer Festivals

All-powerful God,
we appeal to your tender care
that even as you temper the winds and rains
to nurture the fruits of the earth
you will also send upon them
    the gentle shower of your blessing.

Fill the hearts of your people with gratitude,
that from the earth's fertility
the hungry may be filled with good things
and the poor and needy
    proclaim the glory of your name.

—from the Assumption Day Blessing of Produce
in *Catholic Household Blessings and Prayers*

The Birth of John the Baptist (June 24), the solemnity of Peter and Paul (June 29) and the national days of Canada and the United States (July 1 and 4) fall within a two-week period soon after the summer solstice. These days, though unrelated, share much of the same imagery and form a kind of "holiday season" that ushers in the summer.

MIDSUMMER

The Birth of John was once celebrated with many of the same customs as Christmas: with wreaths, bonfires and caroling from door to door. John had said that he must decrease and Jesus must increase. John's birth comes just as the days begin to grow shorter. An old name for St. John's Day is Midsummer because it falls midway between the spring and autumn equinoxes.

Fire and water are twin signs of the Baptist. The old Roman Ritual had a blessing of bonfires in honor of John, and at one time or another nearly every town throughout the Middle East, North Africa and Europe had its Midsummer fire. Surely every parish can celebrate June 24 (and its holy eve) with outdoor candles, lanterns, luminaries and (why not?) Christmas lights. (After all, it is the summer nativity.)

A lovely tradition for these days, common to such diverse places as Puerto Rico, Holland, Poland, Lebanon and Egypt, is the floating of fire on water in the form of oil lamps or candles fixed into seashells, wreaths of twigs or

other tiny boat-like lanterns. In the mid-July Obon festival of the dead, the Japanese float small lanterns on rivers so that the current carries them away. The effect is awe-inspiring and matches in spirit the traditions of Midsummer night.

Of course, fireworks are an ancient way to celebrate the solstice. The custom stays with us still: In the time of the American revolution, Catholic and Lutheran settlers celebrated St. John's Night with bonfires; the tradition was observed and borrowed by the founders of the United States, who ordered that Independence Day be observed with "illuminations."

There are few stronger images of the turning of the year than Fourth of July evening in an American city neighborhood—the air stinks of gunpowder mixed into the evening haze and flashes of light drive away the brief night and maybe even echo the passing of the solstice. Is it more than coincidence that for Southerners in the United States the other great fireworks festival is Christmas?

The association of Midsummer with one's founders comes from ancient times. The church's celebration of Peter and Paul replaced an ancient commemoration of Romulus and Remus, the founders of Rome. The apostles were understood as the new founders of Rome, but the festival was observed not just in Rome but in all Catholic and Orthodox churches. (Which demonstrates the antiquity of the day.)

Not surprisingly, many Christians in seacoast or port cities have special affection for St. John's Day and for SS. Peter and Paul Day. The wheat harvest is a particular emblem of these festivals as a reflection of the saints who began the harvest of God's reign.

The maypole is a traditionally northern European decoration for Midsummer that might have a place outdoors throughout late June and

early July. Mai means "greenery," and the Midsummer maypole (distinct from the May Day pole) has a curious configuration that represents the passing of the solstice. Basically it's a large cross. Two wreaths are suspended from each end of the horizontal beam and greenery is wrapped around the beams using bright ribbons.

As the decorated evergreen is to Christmas, so this maypole is to Midsummer—an emblem of the tree of life, a foretaste of paradise and a sign of the cross.

In many places Midsummer comes clad in the red, white and blue of poppies, daisies and bachelor buttons—collectively known as "cornflowers" because they grow alongside fields of grain. Poppies (the kind associated with Memorial Day because they bloom so abundantly on graves or on any disturbed soil) in some places are called Peter's flowers. Paul's flowers, naturally enough, are bachelor's buttons. John's flowers are daisies, "day's eyes," emblems of the summer sun. The maypole can hold two wreaths of ripe grain, boxwood or yew, and might be ornamented with red, white and blue flowers and ribbons.

Missouri primroses, tawny daylilies (an Asian native) and black-eyed Susans turn the sides of many North American roadways golden in early summer. Yellow hypericum (from Hyperion, the mythical father of the sun) is called "St. John's wort" because it was used, along with green rushes, cattails and oak leaves, to decorate doorways at this season. Purple heliotrope (meaning "turning toward the sun") is a fragrant southern annual. Throughout tropical America, royal poinciana (or "flamboyant tree") comes into extravagant red bloom. What's in flower in your own neighborhood?

PATRONS OF HOSPITALITY

Halfway through summer come the days we remember Saints Mary Magdalene (July 22), James (July 25), Ann and Joachim (July 26) and Martha (July 29). That's an unusually rich gathering of disciples in a small corner of the year. Some denominational calendars observe July 29 as the memorial of Martha and her sister Mary and brother Lazarus. That helps to keep us from confusing Mary of Bethany with Mary of Magdala.

These saints have become identified as patrons of travelers and pilgrims and also of anyone who offers hospitality to guests. Some parishes host a blessing of vacationers and summer visitors at this time of year. On page 167 we touched on the images of these days; statues and pictures of these saints might be gathered into a shrine for the summer.

THE LATE SUMMER FORTY DAYS

At the end of summer comes one of the year's several "quarantines" (meaning "40 days"), the one between Transfiguration (August 6) and Holy Cross (September 14). This period includes Mary's most important festival, the Assumption, on August 15.

The late summer fruitfulness of the earth is a theme that unifies these days. This image is reflected in certain traditions: blessing fruit on Transfiguration Day, hosting an outdoor barbecue on St. Lawrence's Day, blessing flowers and herbs on Assumption Day, blessing flocks and herds on St. Bartholomew's Day and on the feast of the Birth of Mary, and surrounding the cross with herbs and flowers on Holy Cross Day.

These customs suggest that there now should be a movement toward the colors and ornamentation of autumn. But, of course, there is a big difference between August and November—the difference between the atmospheres created, say, by sheaves of green corn and by sheaves of frosted, brown corn.

Perhaps in August and September the green vesture and other fabrics can be ornamented in purples, yellows and golds. A wreath of strawflowers, gomphrena, statice or dried herbs can be hung around the cross. Icons of the transfiguration of the Lord, the dormition of Mary or the exaltation of the cross can be honored with flowers and candles in a shrine, in a vestibule or perhaps in a center aisle. These too could be surrounded with fragrant herbs and flowers.

Take advantage of the abundance of roadside and farmers' markets. Any herbs, fruits or vegetables used to ornament the church for a weekend would best be sent home with someone instead of being left to spoil. At this time of year many field and garden flowers are the kinds that dry naturally. So instead of putting these kinds in water, they can be bundled with raffia and hung on a wall or arranged in a pot of dry sand. (Some materials need to dry upside down if they are to stay looking good for many weeks.)

Mary's shrine can be decorated with baskets of nectarines or eggplants and bunches of dill, fennel, Queen Anne's lace and sunflowers. The psalm for Assumption Day speaks of the queen arrayed in gold: Gold, yellow, rose, deep blue and other rich, royal colors can be used as bunting. A late summer counterpart to (or substitute for) a "May shrine" may be appropriate from August 15 to September 15.

Some parishes try to move away from the nonliturgical devotion that puts emphasis on May and October and instead move toward a liturgical piety that puts emphasis on Advent, Christmastime and these weeks of late summer as Marian "seasons."

August 15 is the anniversary of the end of the Second World War.
Assumption Day was given new emphasis after the war as a festival that
offers honor to all creation, especially the human body. War too often
demonstrates that flesh is destined for destruction; on Assumption Day we
celebrate that our flesh is destined for glory. Mary is our pattern and
our promise.

Over the centuries the Assumption became an occasion to bless God for
the earth, the sea, the sky and all created things. The day and its octave are
perfect for an outdoor procession with Mary's image carried out of the
church and through the streets.

August 15 is a festival of Mary's death, burial and resurrection—her
passover. Regrettably, we tend to ignore the day's imagery of death and
burial, which gives the festival its fullness. The Assumption Vigil is a customary occasion to enter into this imagery of a wake for Mary.

Besides the funeral, other "processional" images of the Assumption are the
wedding and the coronation. In some parishes on Assumption Eve, Mary's
image is placed flat on a bed of summer flowers and then veiled in gold;
the next morning the image is stood upright and crowned with roses. It's
hard to think of a more appropriate occasion to crown an image of Mary
than Assumption Day or during its octave.

*Holy Cross Day, September 14, can be observed with the veneration of
the parish cross, as on Good Friday (see page 96).* The color of the day is
red, again like Good Friday.

Fragrant basil (which means "royalty") is associated with Holy Cross Day;
according to legend, the herb covered the site where Helen found Jesus'
cross. Because of its rapid growth, basil is a sign of resurrection. Its leaves
emerge from the stem in a cruciform pattern, and its aroma can give something of a nostalgic quality to the feast. Basil and other herbs are traditionally used to carpet the floor under the cross this day. Or, the cross might be
set flat in a sea of September herbs and flowers.

Thorny roses and gladioluses also might be used this day and the next, the
memorial of Our Lady of Sorrows. (*Gladius* is Latin for "sword." The
shape of the leaf can remind us of Simeon's prophecy.)

In monastic tradition, September 14 marks the end of the warm season
and the beginning of the cold (as Good Friday marked the end of the cold),
so some shifts of emphasis in the worship environment could be in place
by this day or in the coming week. (In the old calendar, this was the week
of the autumn Ember Days, the fast in thanksgiving for a new season.) The
next chapter offers suggestions for the worship environment in autumn.

Autumn Ordinary Time

A Sense of the Season

Parish programs of one kind or another always recommence in September. Your ministry gets a fresh start as well. The year has few stronger beginnings than the start of the academic year. Even those with no connections to schools might get the urge to buy pencils, erasers and a box of foil stars. It's in our blood.

The first cool wave stirs spirits, lends energy and maybe gets tummies hankering for acorn squash, corn fritters or sweet potato pie. We might hang Indian corn on our front door, set up a scarecrow (even if the nearest field is miles away) or go out in search of the perfect pumpkin. Autumn is the year's fulfillment.

For the church the harvest is an intense scriptural image of the paschal mystery. Paul told us that Jesus Christ is the firstfruits of the dead. Jesus is first, but soon will come all who have died, each reaped into heaven "in proper order" (1 Corinthians 15:23). The ingathering began on Calvary, as Jesus breathed forth the life-giving Spirit, and it will be completed on the final day.

The liturgist Pius Parsch wrote:

> The autumn of the church year is devoted to preparation for the end of life and the second coming of Christ. Now we more readily see the truth: Advent is really a continuation of the church's autumn season, her preparation for the Savior's return.

Without overemphasizing the imagery, we might say that the weeks between Pentecost and Advent are a gradually intensifying ingathering, a process that echoes the harvest and that is completed in the liturgy (and in the agricultural cycle) at Christmas and Epiphany, at the turning of the year.

In the Fifty Days of Easter, our holy springtime, creation seemed transfigured. Throughout the summer we continued to rejoice in the metamorphosis brought about by warmth and sunlight. Then on August 6, at the height of the earth's productivity, we climb the holy mountain where, like Peter, we ask if we should build booths. A strange question, and the evangelists tell us, "Peter did not know what he was saying." But we do.

Peter is talking about the *sukkah,* the harvest tent. And this rickety booth has already been built. It is the transfigured body of Christ, and how we long to enter it! (See 2 Corinthians 5:1–5.)

The Blessed Virgin Mary (August 15) and John the Baptist (August 29) are the first to be gathered into this blessed booth. Its main support beam, the holy cross (September 14), will bolster the booth against the autumn storms. Then "in proper order" the angels (September 29) and saints (November 1) are harvested in. Finally at Epiphany the whole of creation is wrapped in this tent as the fullness of Christ fills all in all.

For more on the imagery of the *sukkah,* see pages 256–258.

Autumn, of course, has many faces, the last of which is Advent. Autumn really isn't a single block of time as much as it is a process. It begins robed in fruitful, summer-like September, which can have triple-digit temperatures and violent storms. But more likely, the weather is as fine as it gets this side of paradise.

The daylight decreases gradually, and this loss may go unnoticed until clocks are turned back on the last Sunday of October—just in time for Halloween and the days of the dead. Within a few days, so it seems, leaves color and fall. One morning we wake up and the garden is frosted. This transformation is a kind of anti-Passover, and some folks find it unwelcome, an emblem of despair. It is, of course, more than an image of death: It's death staring us in the face.

We might regard November 1 and 2 as a funeral for the earth itself, a remembrance of all who sleep within it, and in the words of Isaiah, a plea for the earth to open "that salvation might break forth."

Much of autumn evokes nostalgia, a lovely word that means "homecoming," our yearning to be where we belong. Christian nostalgia has a distinctive character because the home we yearn for is not in our past but in our future, within the reign of God. For us the "good old days" are still to come.

Nostalgia has an added spark in autumn that comes from the longer nights and the increasing cold. Earlier nightfalls get some of us indoors earlier, and the chilly weather certainly has us scrambling for shelter and togetherness. Add to that the bounty of markets at this season, and we have the fixings for an extended feast of reminiscing and storytelling.

Nights of remembrance are an antidote for fear, which hides in autumn's shadows. Autumn has many such antidotes—for instance, our champion Michael (the guardian of the dead), the evangelists Matthew and Luke (whose angels keep telling us not to fear), Teresa of Avila (who taught us to rely on our wits), the apostles Simon and Jude (who in folklore remind us that no cause is lost), Bishop Martin (who legend says split his cloak for the sake of Christ in disguise), Queen Margaret (who like Michael is sometimes shown battling death's dragon) and the first of the winter's "five wise bridesmaids," blessed Cecilia (who might have us whistling in the dark rather than cursing it).

The Greek church has the martyr Demetrios (October 26) to allay its fears. A patron saint of autumn, in art he looks a lot like George (spring's patron), in battle gear, victorious over death. According to custom, the olive harvest begins on October 26 and lasts all winter. For generations (including the generations that wrote the scriptures) olive oil meant food, fuel and medicine. This life-or-death harvest comes just when the need for light and sustenance are most crucial.

St. Demetrios is the goddess Demeter in mystical guise. Demeter is the embodiment of the harvest and the mother of Persephone, who, as the story goes, spends each winter like a seed under the earth as the bride of Death.

That bit of lore has too much power to disappear entirely just because the old religions are gone. It offers the consolation that the bride, come spring, will come back into the light; that tulip bulbs planted in October will rise in May; that wheat, sown in autumn, will eventually ripen into our daily bread; and that, in Christ, human flesh also has its planting, its rest, its harvesting:

> My flesh shall slumber in the ground
> Till the last trumpet's joyful sound;
> Then burst the chains with sweet surprise,
> And in my Savior's image rise.
> —from *The Psalm Singer's Amusement*, 1781

The Sunday scriptures of autumn Ordinary Time include many fine images of the season. Although they weren't intended to be emblems of fall, we can enjoy the coincidence. For instance, in the week of the autumnal equinox we may hear James' beloved words, "The harvest of justice is sown in peace." In late October, before All Saints' Day, we may hear Jeremiah's vision of the ingathering of all people from the ends of the earth.

In autumn we might sing from Psalm 126 that those who sow in tears will reap in joy, or from Psalm 146 that the Lord gives food to the hungry, justice to the oppressed and watchful protection to the wayfarer.

The autumn scriptures often admonish us to take care of one another: Amos rails against complacency and threatens those who would cheat those in need. James exhorts us not to pay mere lip service to the poor by hoping that they "keep warm and well fed." Faith must take action. The Torah demands that we don't ask payment if it puts the debtor at risk of life or health. These are necessary orders as winter looms.

Autumn Sundays bring a once-every-three-years meeting with the seven brothers and their mother, with Naaman, with Bartimaeus, with Zacchaeus, with archangel Michael and with Lady Wisdom herself. We may hear about Elijah and the widow or Jesus' parable about the persistent widow, or of the widow who gave most everything she had to the Temple. Widows and orphans had been the most dispossessed of people, and the image of the widow seems to repeat like a litany throughout the season's psalms and readings.

In September and October, owing to where we are in our reading of a gospel, Sundays include a number of familiar parables about the reign of God—the ruler who wanted to settle accounts, the ruler who invited most anyone to a wedding, the prodigal son, the rich man and Lazarus. In the Gospel of Matthew a number of parables revolve around vineyards, a strong and useful biblical image during this season of the harvest.

In November, still owing to our place in each year's gospel, the eschatology (looking at the end times) intensifies. We hear a great deal about death, judgment and readiness. With such an array of parables, we might call autumn "Kingdomtide"—and some churches have done just that.

It's just as well that we have resisted inventing new titles for our weeks. The name autumn is enough. It's a word that speaks worlds.

Overview

Good news! There's no easier time of year to use decorations, and no time of year when decorations are likely to be better accepted by a parish.

The change of weather and the coming of the beloved festivals of autumn and early winter have many of us eager to see, touch and taste the signs of the season. We almost expect to see these signs just about anywhere—in schools, bank lobbies and store windows. In church, leaving up summer's green hangings just won't do. The change of seasons almost demands a change of visuals.

Autumn overflows with sacred signs: sheaves of corn, bittersweet vines, plump gourds. These beautiful things not only are well-loved, but because they are from nature, most are suitable to liturgical decoration as long as they are placed appropriately.

A few things are in order for decorations to be accepted by the parish.

1. Some consciousness-raising may be needed to open up how images of autumn can be signs that point toward the kingdom.

2. Any signs of the season must be positioned in the church in ways appropriate to the liturgy; that is, never impeding the approach to the altar, ambo or font and never impeding the ritual.

3. Decorations should never be hackneyed or trite and must always be beautiful and in scale with their surroundings.

If this is the first or second year you are decorating for autumn (or any season), you'll need to pay special attention to these principles and how they bolster one another. For instance, a corn shock sitting near the altar or ambo may be just as fitting, liturgically and artistically speaking, as a bouquet of flowers, but in this highly visible position the corn draws attention to itself rather than focusing attention on the altar or ambo. Perhaps the corn can go in a vestibule or shrine or in some other location out of the direct line of sight of the liturgy.

Also, no matter where it goes, the shock should be enormous, with the husks on the ears of corn peeled back to reveal the ears, and perhaps with a handsome raffia string, grapevine or festive sash tying the shock together. A full and magnificent shock makes a better emblem of the season and a richer sacramental sign than a skimpy one, and the fuller the sign, the more likely it is to be well-received.

Where would we best focus our attention in autumn? Here are some suggestions:

1. Parish life moves into high gear. In entryways, vestibules and meeting halls, how are parish programs and other endeavors advertised? The beauty and grace of bulletin boards, book racks and other devices for sharing information or goods become part of the environment for worship and are often some of our first impressions when arriving for liturgy.

2. The days from All Saints to Advent are dear to the church. (See page 192.) During these November days you might make a point of ornamenting the church with almost as much attention and consistency as you would one of the liturgical seasons.

Two elements overarch these November days: remembrance of the dead and thanksgiving for the harvest. The parish's book of the dead might be displayed near the paschal candle, and harvest bounty might grace the church during all the days from All Saints to Christ the King and Thanksgiving.

3. Earlier in autumn there might be certain seasonal visuals that go up around Holy Cross Day (September 14) and stay up until Advent. (The November decorations are added to this array so that autumn builds in visual intensity.) Perhaps the Sunday green vestments (and the other fabrics in the church) are trimmed in autumnal colors; make sure that the shade of green is compatible with these colors.

The parish's own dedication anniversary is ranked as a "solemnity" for the parish. Of course, a parish can observe the actual anniversary each year, or in Ordinary Time, on a Sunday close to it. However, a parish can also observe its dedication anniversary each year on the Sunday before All Saints and in that way connect it to the early November festival days.

It might be wise during autumn, especially in November, to tie in celebrations of parish patron saints, of parish history, of ethnic heritages and of the dedication of the church building. This might be expressed visually by decorating patronal images within the church, displaying (in the parish hall?) memorabilia or hanging outdoor banners and bunting in celebration of the parish (or diocese) and its history. Any of this would be done every year at this season.

An old and wonderful way to memorialize someone or something is through a patchwork quilt. Creating such a quilt would be a particularly handsome way to gather many images into one piece. Of course, the skills needed for creating a quilt are considerable and the time required is great—many a noble quilt is built over generations. It's hard to imagine a more suitable art form for liturgical decoration, or one more at home in the autumn of the year. The location of memorial or iconographic quilts is best where their handiwork can be appreciated up close.

THE ASSEMBLY'S PLACE

Around September 14 (Holy Cross Day) or September 29 (the feast of the archangels), any summertime hangings or other seasonal materials might be reoriented toward a more decidedly autumnal atmosphere. You can add to the typical autumn colors of golds, reds, oranges and browns some less typical colors, such as rust, maroon, red-purple or forest green.

As described in the section of this book on summer, for the purposes of visuals and other liturgical elements Ordinary Time might be subdivided loosely into the periods bracketed by the great festivals of summer and autumn. The time from Transfiguration Day to Holy Cross Day is a "quarantine," a forty-day period of transition from summer doldrums into autumn busy-ness. From Holy Cross to All Saints is seven weeks. From All Saints until Advent is about four weeks.

Images on any hangings could be drawn especially from the eschatological books of Daniel and Revelation. Much of this imagery is also fitting during Eastertime and Advent—the Ancient One upon the throne, Michael the great prince who weighs the souls of the dead, the Lamb with the scroll with seven seals, the Spirit-bride, the tree of life, the new Jerusalem, the morning star, the dead rising to shine like the stars. There's a lot of heaven and hell in autumn.

It would not be too difficult to use such imagery during the Easter season and then to return it during autumn, especially in November and perhaps also during Advent. Any such "recyclable" imagery could be designed to be altered somewhat for each season. For instance, an image of Divine Wisdom might be fashioned primarily out of tans, yellows, purples, golds and greens. For spring the image might be flanked with panels of yellow and green fabrics ornamented with images of honeycombs and bees; for autumn it might be flanked with tan and gold fabrics ornamented with oak leaves, acorns and owls. In Advent, Lady Wisdom might be flanked in purples and greens ornamented with oil lamps and a crescent moon.

For that matter, the parish of Our Lady, Seat of Wisdom might have this image up throughout the entire year but ornamented with all sorts of changing seasonal imagery.

Something we would never do is use images on a banner that duplicate images used elsewhere in the liturgy or in the church's decoration. For instance, it makes no sense to depict on a banner a paschal candle, baptismal water or burning incense. A banner showing a cornucopia, gourds or other autumnal materials might have a place, but it doesn't belong near the real thing; and banner is far less satisfying than an actual horn of plenty overflowing with actual produce.

In contrast, the paschal lamb, the morning star or the new Jerusalem are images that would never be duplicated in church by an actual lamb, star or city. But bear in mind that the more literal and complicated the image, the

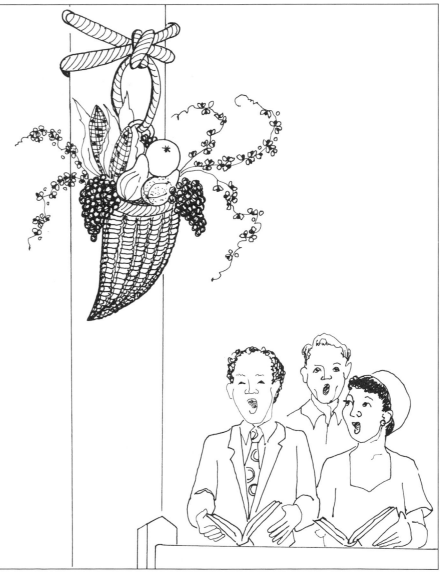

harder it is to place in church. Also, images of the saints and of God (such as Lady Wisdom) are always more than mood-setting decoration; they are often better in shrines where they can be venerated in private prayer.

Besides banners, other ornamentation for the assembly's place might include bundles of grain and dried grasses, corn shocks, baskets of flowers and produce. Some of that has a place throughout autumn but is especially appropriate during November.

Cortaderia, miscanthus, cattails, phragmites and other grasses and sedges can be absolutely wonderful. A huge pot of vermiculite or sand makes a good base for arranging grasses. Instead of tying them into bundles—which of course looks good—it's even better to arrange grasses one stalk at a time to get a full and airy effect. (Materials such as dried grasses usually don't fluff out on their own; this appearance is achieved by careful arrangement.)

You will need to gather the grasses when they are at their peak of perfection, which sometimes can be many weeks or even months before you need them. For instance, the plumy heads of the various species known as "pampas grass" open mostly in September and must be gathered then, or wind and rain will ruin them. But even if they aren't quite fully bloomed out, they will open indoors as they dry. By October many grasses may still look fine outdoors at a distance, but on close inspection they will look bedraggled.

The same is true for bittersweet vines. Gather them as soon as the seed capsules turn orange but before they open to reveal their red hearts. They will open indoors as they dry. Living vines gathered outdoors are of course more supple than dried materials and can be twisted and shaped somewhat while still alive so that they will dry into interesting shapes.

Drying any of this material needs to be a controlled process—not left to chance—because until plants are dry they can rot. You might find it best, say, to bring the grasses directly from the field into the church, arrange them while they're still somewhat green and allow them to dry in place.

Corn stalks are an exception. It's best if a frost turns the corn brown, and then, after the frost, the corn remains in the field to dry for a few days in sunny weather. Corn stalks are easiest to gather and transport on a misty day, when the foliage has rehydrated and is again supple. However, if corn is gathered when green, the foliage will dry indoors to a homely gray-green and the stalks might even decay.

Collecting decorative plant materials might be a task throughout the summer and fall. Sometimes a roadside market, a florist or some other source has a certain material for only a brief time. Take pumpkins, for instance. Because they rot so quickly in warm weather, in much of the South they appear in markets only briefly before Halloween. But even where pumpkins are available throughout October, they disappear on November 1. If you want pumpkins for November, be sure you acquire them before Halloween.

The "frost on the pumpkin" might sound poetic, but it's bad news. A freeze will wreck many natural materials, including most vegetables, so store them in a cool, dry, protected place until they're needed.

Some autumnal materials can be stored from year to year. Indian corn, for instance, lasts years. Most gourds will not, although some species dry attractively. Store natural materials in a ventilated box in a place with good air circulation and where mildew isn't a problem.

Keep in mind that stored produce, even dry, makes great eating for mice, rats and other critters. It's next to impossible to prevent a determined rodent from chowing down on these materials, although moth balls and dried blood meal may act as deterrents. (Moth balls may also help prevent mildew.) Hardware cloth (wire) cages keep out vermin and permit air circulation.

You may find that mice or squirrels have taken a fancy to these materials while they're on display in church. Although squirrels gnawing on the autumn decorations by the front doors may not be a big deal, inside these animals can cause unbelievable damage—so be warned.

ALTAR, AMBO AND CHAIR

Altar cloths sometimes are changed with the seasons. So what should autumn's altar covering look like, not only in terms of its color but of its texture, its feel? Sometimes the ambo also has a cloth covering as the "table of the word," although this is certainly far less traditional than clothing an altar.

Instead of a cloth, spiraling grapevine, bittersweet or other vines might look good spilling over the ambo and diagonally down to the floor. First attach the vine with wire or string from a single spot on the top of the ambo. Take the bottom of the vine and pull it gently as far away from the ambo as can be done without creating an obstacle to movement. Fasten this far end of the vine to the floor. A coil of grapevine (being rather solid and available in long lengths) might be the foundation to which is attached shorter pieces of purple or white beautyberry, deciduous holly, red hawthorn, orange bittersweet or other berried branches. Be sure any wiring or other means of attachment is hidden.

Seasonal flowers in autumn are plentiful. Sunflowers, turtleheads, Joe-pye weed, boltonia and asters ("Michaelmas daisies") are in season in early fall. In late fall come the chrysanthemums, and while these flowers are sold all year long, finally in autumn they are right at home (at least if their color is autumnal). Even their strange fragrance adds to the appropriateness.

Marigolds, in autumnal bronzes, oranges and yellows, are regarded in Mexico as the flowers of the dead because they bloom so abundantly in cemeteries; their foliage has an acrid aroma said to conjure remembrance. Marigolds, dahlias and many other annuals are most flowery in autumn just before the frost annihilates them. In Greece and in the Middle East, the herb basil is a cemetery plant; its fragrance, too, is said to stimulate the memory. The herb rosemary has this role in western Europe.

Especially useful in church are field flowers, grasses and seedpods that dry naturally. An amazing number of weeds are perfect for this, and their large sizes give the scale needed in church. It's much easier to arrange certain kinds of flowers before they have completely dried and then to allow the arrangement to dry in place. For instance, goldenrod can be arranged in a pot of dry sand; the flowers will gradually turn into gray, fuzzy seedheads. The flower heads of the various species of hydrangea also dry beautifully.

Of course, dried flowers are brittle and easily ruined. Some, such as goldenrod, should not be placed in drafty spots or where they can be bumped; the seedheads will blow around and stick to clothing. A cattail will stay intact for years but just about explodes into a fluffy mess when touched too hard.

Lacquer spray (such as hair spray) keeps some seeds from blowing around, although nothing protects dried flowers from rough handling. There are procedures for preserving almost any flower with special substances such as silica sand or glycerine, but the results often look artificial. To some people's way of thinking, dried roses are attractive, but to others, they just look like dead roses.

The best dried flowers for autumn would be those flowers and grasses associated with the season that also dry naturally outdoors through the action of frost, wind and sun. Gather these plants while they are still fresh and not weatherbeaten.

An arrangement of harvest plenty is easy to put together. Apples, squashes and tuberous vegetables such as sweet potatoes are available throughout the year; pumpkins, gourds and other cucurbits are available mostly in September and October. These can be grouped with dried and fresh flowers, bundles of herbs, grains and nuts.

The fungus that rots pumpkins and gourds spreads quickly if present. Pumpkins and gourds without the fungus will last all winter, so its good to locate a disease-free source. Keep them dry, cool and unpunctured.

A jack o'lantern will decay within a day or two in a heated building. You definitely need to put pumpkins and other produce on a surface that won't be marred if the vegetables rot. A decaying pumpkin (is there a more vivid image of mortality?) releases foul juices that can permanently discolor terrazzo or marble. Just in case, some plastic placed underneath any produce is good protection, but it must be hidden.

Mixing materials can be beautiful: pots of fresh mums, sheaves of wheat, bundles of gray statice and dried golden yarrow, artichokes, gray hubbard and orange acorn squashes, and small piles of filberts. Amber and red votive candles in jelly jars might be put among the materials. What really doesn't look good in such a gathering are houseplants of any kind or flowers, even mums, too gussied up with bows and wrappings.

The varied elements are sometimes arranged on draped fabric. The fabric visually unifies the mixed materials but often draws too much attention to itself. Instead of fabric, oak leaves might make a beautiful "groundcover" around produce and will hide any necessary floor protection. To get some height into the arrangement, small pedestals and upturned bushel baskets work well, as long as these don't look too contrived.

Vessels and Vesture

Autumn may seem to be the right time of year for gold vessels. Perhaps autumn is also a good time to use such things as gourd vessels from Ghana, Polish carved wooden bowls, Shaker wooden boxes or a Hopi stone pot for things like holy water and incense.

What a shame browns and russets aren't liturgical colors! Nothing seems so out of place at worship during November in North America as most green vestments. Still, there are forest greens, olive greens, teal, even khaki that borders on brown; there are any number of colors of trims and ornamentation; and the texture of autumnal vesture might somehow reflect the glory and decay all around us.

A parish might have a special set of vesture worn throughout autumn Ordinary Time. That set might make its first appearance soon after Holy Cross Day and be worn until Christ the King Sunday. Such a set also could be worn on the white-vesture festivals of the autumn season and still be within liturgical norms. Number 309 of the *General Instruction of the Roman Missal* states that on special occasions, "more noble vestments may be used, even if not the color of the day."

That sentence permits the use of antique vesture (made in the days before liturgical colors were relatively standard) and also acknowledges the principle that undergirds the use of colors—that "variety in the color of the vestments is meant to give effective, outward expression to the specific character of the mysteries of the faith being celebrated and, in the course of the year, to a sense of progress in the Christian life" (307). This "sense of progress" seems reason enough to wear special vesture during this harvest time of the year.

Some parishes may want to make a point of using their special paschal (and funeral) set of vesture for the autumn festivals and perhaps on all the Sundays of November. One parish's white Eastertime vesture is trimmed with golds and oranges and so looks especially fitting in autumn.

The key, of course, is consistency—from week to week, from year to year, and especially from presider to presider, so that everyone is clued in and follows parish practice.

FONT

After Eastertime, the paschal candle stays by the font throughout the year. Is it in good shape? Do you need another one by now? You might keep it lit on All Saints, All Souls and perhaps on all the Sundays of November. A wreath of dried flowers or a bundle of grain might be beautiful as a candle ring or hung on the candle stand.

A pedestal or bookstand placed near the candle is a good place for the parish book of the dead (page 193) or for other remembrances of the dead. The book might be put out a few weeks before All Souls so that parishioners can write in the names of the dead. The book would remain out through November, until Advent.

The font may be a good place for seasonal iconography that reflects imagery from Revelation—for instance, the Lamb of God or the new Jerusalem. The baptistry is often a better place for smaller-scale ornamentation than the area around the altar.

The story of Jonah is proclaimed in the synagogue on Yom Kippur, the Day of Atonement. The stories from that book are associated by the church with Lent, but they also can be fine images at services of reconciliation or of Christian unity at any time of the year. One parish has an icon of Jonah near the font throughout the year, and during autumn the image is ornamented with a gourd-laden vine.

SHRINES

Any decoration of images of the saints might go up for All Saints and stay up through November. Customary ornamentations are palm and willow fronds, crowns, wreaths, garlanding and bunting, along with candles and flowers. Much of the other autumnal ornamentation we have been discussing, such as baskets of gourds or a cornucopia, may look better in a shrine rather than complicating the main body of the church.

Images of angels in the church could be ornamented at least from September 29 (Michael, Gabriel and Raphael) to October 2 (Guardian Angels) and might also remain through the fall.

Biblical descriptions of the heavenly hosts are anything but flowery. Read the tenth chapter of Ezekiel. In our depictions, angels need not be Caucasian, male or even of human form; nor do they need to be militaristic, although angel guardians are figures of skill and power. God as an eagle, a strong emblem of the exodus, comes close to much angelic imagery.

Archangel Michael is a "patron" of autumn. Michael's traditional role is to battle the dragon and to guide the dead into paradise. Raphael, too, as the healer and guide in the book of Tobit, has been a beloved companion at this time of year. Gabriel is more associated with Advent, Christmas and the Annunciation, but Gabriel, whose trumpet (or ram's horn) will one day awaken the dead, is a strong image of the spirit of autumn.

We could almost call autumn a season of angels, at least in folklore, the *eschaton* of the coming of the day of the Lord. The failing light of autumn can make this day seem close at hand, the lengthening night making it easier to imagine death's dragon lurking in the shadows.

Some might shy away from such images. After all, eschatological literature is the product of people who have been pushed between a rock and a hard place. Much of the imagery is desperate and harsh, even hostile, and too much of it has been used to separate peoples rather than to unite them.

Autumn and Advent are our annual encounter with the dark, and it might be better to face it squarely rather than to ignore it or hide it behind our own lights. None of it is cute, but much of it is beautiful and thrilling. Making use of eschatological imagery, especially within a shrine, is fitting during this time of year.

Mary crushing the head of the serpent, as in the depiction of the Immaculate Conception, embodies some of this imagery. Mary's shrine could be ornamented with cherubim, with a dragon, with a scythe, with the morning star, with harvester angels.

If the shrine was decorated with produce between Assumption Day and Our Lady of Sorrows, perhaps some of that can stay in place until Advent or be slowly shifted to reflect the progression of the season. For instance, where there was a basket of peaches in September there might be apples in October and crookneck squash come November. Don't ever let such things rot and go to waste, however; let people take them from the shrine to eat.

SEASONAL CORNERS

In October you might use a seasonal corner to teach parishioners about the observance of Halloween, All Saints and All Souls. If this does not come from parish environment and art ministers, then who? We Christians have something of a duty to teach each other about Christian customs, even the ones many people don't know are signs of faith—such as how to select a fine pumpkin and carve a masterful jack o'lantern, how to make masks and costumes, or what forms the celebrations of these days take in various parts of the world.

A seasonal corner is a good place to display the folk arts of these days of the dead as well as of the other autumn festivals, and perhaps to make some of them available for purchase. One parish sets up a small shop to take orders for and sell Mexican sugar skulls and All Souls' Day bread.

The dead are very much in our thoughts during these days. Some parishes prepare and distribute homemade booklets with photos and reminiscences of those who have died in the past year.

Besides a book or scroll of names of the dead, there might be a place for memorabilia and photographs of the dead. This would be a way to remember and to honor those who have died and would also be a summons for prayer and consolation. Memorabilia might best be gathered in a shrine or vestibule or in some other visitable, private corner rather than being placed front and center in the worship space. Harvest time decorations, even jack o'lanterns, have a fitting place in this area. The dead, after all, are God's harvest.

The parish might make available booklets and other resources for remembering the dead, for planning funerals, even for writing wills. This is difficult, often uncomfortable work, but as we know, there is much good to be gained from a well-planned funeral. Funerals are family reunions that must happen at a moment's notice. That aspect alone merits attention.

Any materials for keeping Advent and Christmastime could make their appearance by All Saints. October is not too early to talk about keeping Advent as a time of expectation and about keeping Christmastime as a time of celebration. It doesn't do any good to bring up these subjects early in Advent, because by then parish households have their plans made and may even have their Christmas trees up and shining.

Materials and instructions for building Advent wreaths could be available mid-November rather than the first weekend of Advent (which is often Thanksgiving weekend).

VESTIBULES, DOORWAYS, OUTDOORS

A clump of Indian corn on the front door is a North American classic. But instead of using the ordinary bundle of three ears of corn, get extras and rebundle them into groups of five or more for ornamenting the church doors. Dried flowers and grasses can be added to the clumps.

Corn or other natural decorations can be attached to a straw or grapevine wreath. A wreath is more than a decoration. It is an emblem of royalty, of victory, of God's reign, of the wedding band we wear to remember our fidelity to Christ.

Surely All Saints, All Souls and on to Christ the King and Thanksgiving will receive attention outdoors. A simple array of autumnal colored fabrics can communicate that this is an extraordinary stretch of Ordinary Time.

One parish has a triumphal arch (page 55) for the days between Palm Sunday and Pentecost as a sacramental emblem that this building is Jerusalem, the holy city. The arch goes up again for All Saints but is now festooned with corn stalks, sheaves of wheat and gold ribbons.

November

November begins with All Saints and All Souls and concludes with Christ the King and (in the U.S.A.) Thanksgiving. The gospels in the last weeks of Ordinary Time come mostly from Jesus' warnings about the end of the world, which are presented in the synoptic accounts just before the Passion, toward the conclusion of each gospel. These feasts and scriptures point to the end times.

The Roman liturgical calendar is arranged to make sure that the "34th Week in Ordinary Time" is the final week before Advent. This is done so that the eschatological readings, psalms and chants of the final weeks of Ordinary Time are heard and sung every year. These November weeks even have their own "common psalm" in the lectionary, Psalm 122 ("I rejoiced when I heard them say, 'Let us go to the house of the Lord.'") and their own "generic" gospel acclamations, which happen to match some of those for Advent.

November isn't a liturgical season, but in some ways it behaves like one. The month is something like a flaming orange maple tree; Advent is the same tree leafless.

Ending the church year with the imagery of Doomsday makes sense. But bear in mind that this imagery is not unique to November. It would miss the mark to think that the last weeks in Ordinary Time are about endings and that Advent is about beginnings.

November, like Advent and Christmastime (and if you dig deeply enough, like every day), is a celebration of the paschal mystery: "Christ has died, Christ is risen, Christ will come again." Throughout the year we make our celebration from the images of the world around us, images that we hold dear as signs of God's reign, the things of time that become for us emblems of eternity.

In November these signs might be leaves drifting down, the departing geese honking in the heavens, the last chrysanthemums, the first snowfalls and even a grinning face carved into a pumpkin—a face set shining by our doorway to guide home the children of God, the face of death that in dank November rots away to offer the suggestion that in Christ, death itself will die.

Parish decorators would best prepare November as a whole rather than prepare each Sunday and feast separately. There might be one array of decorations that remain up from Halloween until just before Advent. There might even be a special set of vesture worn during these days and no others.

All these days are for offering thanks for the harvest, for remembering the dead and for anticipating the kingdom. This mixture might take some getting used to: We might need to uncover what there is about All Saints' and All Souls' Day that leads us to give thanks for the harvest, and what there is about Thanksgiving Day that leads us to remember the dead.

Many parishes set up a memorial for the remembrance of the dead. That might simply be a book of the names of the dead, set on a lectern near the

paschal candle in the baptistry. (The baptistry seems appropriate for this because the font, as a "tomb," is where all of us die and are buried and are raised in Christ.) The book of the names of the dead (LTP publishes a beautiful one) is a blank-page book. It can be a handsomely covered ring-binder. Unruled blank paper, perhaps in a light color other than white, is more attractive than ruled, white paper.

Some parishes have a calligrapher or graphic artist produce the pages with the names of the dead. It's better, though, if parishioners are able to write the names themselves. Those pages would stay in the book from year to year, although when the book is brought out again each autumn, people may not look for what they wrote last year and may write the same names again. That's not bad. It may be an annual ritual to stand before the book and call the dead to mind while writing down their names.

The paschal candle near the book would be lit for all services, and perhaps the book could be incensed as part of the entrance procession or during the prayers of the faithful. You might place the book on a bed of russet oak leaves and ring the candle with chrysanthemums or sheaves of wheat. The book itself and any fabric hangings or other ornamentation might be prepared in autumnal colors, although the church's liturgical colors for funerals—black, white and purple—might also have a place.

A more elaborate shrine for the dead might include photos and other memorabilia. The shrine might fit in the baptistry, but more likely a shrine such as this one will be appropriate in an alcove or chapel (not the tabernacle chapel, however)—somewhere private where people can sit and pray but not a place so out-of-the-way that it's ignored. (Yes, few parishes have suitable spots that can function as seasonal shrines—maybe that should be worked into any plans for renovating the church.) Choose a single site; it won't make sense, for example, to have a book of the dead near the font and a separate shrine for photos.

Images from Daniel or from Revelation have a special place here—for example, the dead rising to shine like the stars, Angel Michael bearing the scales of justice, or the great homecoming in the new Jerusalem "where every tear will be wiped away." Harvest bounty used to ornament the shrine of the dead brings forth the image of the dead as God's harvest gathered as the treasures of heaven.

Halloween is immensely popular in North America. It is also one of the holidays richest in visual imagery, which no doubt fosters its popularity. In much of the United States the day comes during the brief, spectacular period when foliage colors and falls and when clocks are turned back so that we lose an hour of afternoon daylight.

Strangely, on November 1 many schoolteachers (and others) take down the Halloween decorations and put up the Thanksgiving stuff. It's a very strange state of affairs that November 1 and 2 are not observed with the wonderful images of Halloween, such as skeletons, owls, gravestones, apples, nuts and jack o'lanterns. How has it happened that All Saints and All Souls can even be imagined apart from Halloween? North Americans have a great legacy (mostly from Irish immigrants) of folklore surrounding these days. Why is this legacy wasted?

Parish environment and art ministers are custodians of visual imagery. We have a special responsibility to use the imagery of All Hallows to its best advantage. We might see to it that any Halloween decorations in the parochial school, in the parish hall or in meeting rooms are not put up merely for October but instead are used in celebration of the church's festival of its ancestors and, as the preface for All Saints says, for "the festival of [the] holy city, the heavenly Jerusalem, our mother."

In the liturgy we don't emphasize our distance from the dead. We speak of communion with them in Christ. Thus the liturgy offers us an entrance into eternity, which is neither continual time nor an endless succession of days but something even more unimaginable: timelessness. To enter timelessness is to be where past, present and future dissolve into one grand now. That is where we might have communion with our ancestors and even the generations yet to be born. That's what we enter in the liturgy and what its visuals signify.

Early American gravestones offer an abundance of classic scriptural images of death and judgment that we might employ in celebrating All Hallows and November. The designs are charming, naive, often playful—angels, winged skulls, weeping willows, apple trees, palms, laurel crowns, bats, ravens, the serpent, the dragon, an hourglass, a sundial, keys, sickles, compasses, scales, even a plumb bob (to measure how straight and true we have been). The personification of death with a hooded robe and a scythe is a lot like Father Time, both getting us to our graves and eventually to Judgment Day. Keep in mind that these images were used by people for whom the scriptures were everything.

In the vestibule, an old, handsome wooden stepladder makes an interesting emblem for All Saints and All Souls. Each rung could hold a shining jack o'lantern and perhaps a collection of images of the saints, photos of the dead, as well as votive candles, autumn leaves, gourds, nuts and other signs of the harvest.

"Jacob's ladder" is a *ziggurat,* a spiral stairway, and spirals are emblems of eternity which, unlike circles, don't endlessly return to where they started. A spiralled vine festooned with berries makes a fitting decoration for November, as long as it isn't "explained." Let it speak for itself.

There are other signs of these days of the dead, customs that the major church festivals share: feasting on round or spiraled breads (doughnuts and round "soul cakes" are customary in November), victory wreaths hung on doors, lights set in windows and doorways (carved pumpkins being the festival's special lantern), and visiting cemeteries and decorating the graves.

Planting trees is an excellent and traditional way to remember the dead, and early November is a good time of year to plant throughout the South. Even in the North, many species of trees may be planted right up until the ground freezes. North or south, it's tulip bulb planting time. Spring flowering bulbs might be blessed and distributed to worshipers on All Souls' Day. It's hard to think of a lovelier emblem of the promise of resurrection.

All Souls' envelopes for memorial donations to the church are too often understood as payments for spiritual favors—an obnoxious concept. The pedigree of this custom is noble, however. Even in ancient times, donations were made to charity in remembrance of the dead, a custom that sometimes took the more direct form of the family of the dead hosting a meal for those in need. A memorial meal to benefit the poor is a way of breaking bread once more with those who have died.

In that spirit, November can be a month of almsgiving, and it surely is a natural time of year for helping others as winter looms. Perhaps in the vestibule or in the shrine for the dead, you could use some of the same decorative materials used during Lent for gathering gifts for the poor and for advertising to the parish where the gathered donations will be going.

For All Saints the parish might bless and hand out branches of autumn leaves (oak and beech tend to stay fresh longest). The statues and other images of the saints could be decked in fall foliage and crowned with chrysanthemums. This practice makes most sense in parishes that bless and distribute budding branches on Palm Sunday, flowers on Easter Sunday, green branches on Pentecost, herbs on Assumption and on Holy Cross, and evergreens at Christmas. (There are strong, natural links among these days.)

A parish really shouldn't decorate with harvest bounty for Thanksgiving if not also for All Saints. It's a mistake not to recognize how November 1 and 2 are clothed in the harvest—an intensely paschal image that the scriptures use over and over as a sign of the kingdom to come, as an emblem of resurrection.

Christ the King and Thanksgiving do not need special decorations beyond those used at All Saints. There's no need to come up with imagery or an atmosphere unique to any one of these days or the days in between. They share imagery in common. For instance, a crown is just as reflective of Christ the King as it is of All Saints. A bushel of gourds is just as suitable at Thanksgiving as it is on All Souls' Day.

If Christ the King and Thanksgiving were missing from the November calendar (as they once were), church visuals could pass gradually from the bright glory of All Saints into the misty gloom of late November.

Advent could come on the scene gradually, like leaves falling off a tree, which seems close to the spirit of the liturgy that leads to Advent.

The land slipsliding into winter makes an excellent image of the intensification of our prayer until, as Advent begins, we are ready to cry out with Isaiah, "Oh, that you would rend the heavens open and come down!"

But as it is, a parish that decorates with autumnal finery for All Saints will likely want to maintain it until Thanksgiving Day. Then most of it disappears before Advent arrives. In about five out of seven years, Thanksgiving falls in the week before the First Sunday in Advent. This means that most years we must spend the Friday and Saturday after Thanksgiving hurriedly transforming the worship environment. Keep in mind that this weekend often sees folks on the road. It might be hard to muster the troops.

Advent

A Sense of the Season

Reflect for a while on the turning of autumn into winter: We're at the tail end of the harvest season. Among people who raise crops, if the year has been good, foodstores are now plentiful. This is a natural time for some indulgence.

Especially in past generations, with farm work lighter and nights longer, people found themselves with a surplus of a precious commodity—leisure time. Winter was the chief season of the year for the folk arts, for singing and dancing, for storytelling. During winter, people were more likely than at other seasons to waltz, crochet, play cards, prepare an elaborate dessert or tell tall tales.

But not everything was fun and games. In the frozen north, farmers had to keep next year's seed safe from mice, cold, dampness—even each other, no matter how hungry they got. Elaborate rituals evolved for preserving the seed, which in some places was called "grandmother" and received the loving respect that the name implies. In some places, straw and wheat sheaves, even more than evergreens, are emblems of this time of year.

Other life-or-death rituals revolved around the supply of firewood. The old Yule log ceremonies were a wishful petition to God that the home would stay warm and safe. When roads got rutted by frost, travel became impossible; wagon wheels were brought inside and hung up to prevent them from warping. That essential, seasonal task may have been the origin of the Advent wreath.

In areas around the Mediterranean, winter is mild and wet. As in California, winter brings the most plentiful (and sometimes the only) rains of the year. The familiar Advent prayer from Isaiah is a winter image: "Let justice descend, O heavens, like dew from above; like gentle rain let the skies drop it down. Let the earth open and salvation bud forth."

The author of the Letter of James also used this image: "The farmer waits for the precious crop from the earth, being patient with it until it receives the early and the late rains. You also must be patient."

In Mediterranean lands, salad greens, barley and wheat are sown in late fall and grow through the winter. Animals are pregnant and the birthing season begins. The chilly rains bring out a flush of flowers—tulips, irises, crocuses. All these may be springtime images to northerners, but they were winter ones to the Christian poets who wrote of the newborn Christ as an early lamb, a planted seed, a rain shower, a bud just beginning to break.

Early winter also marks the final harvest of the year, the harvest of olives and their precious oil. On the old Catholic calendar the winter Ember Days were in their origins a fast in thanksgiving for this harvest; even before there was an Advent on the calendar, there were Ember Days.

This winter harvest calls to mind the words of Isaiah that tell of the Lord's Anointed who proclaims a new year of grace. In the lectionary, winter brings us the stories of Samuel and David, and also of the Lord's baptism. The evangelists compared the Holy Spirit to Noah's dove, which bore an olive branch as an emblem of reconciliation between heaven and earth.

In the northern hemisphere, during December winter settles in. Over the generations we humans have put a lot of energy into battling this season, not celebrating it.

Especially in past generations, winter brought the risk of starvation; or fuel might run out, or one of the children might get sick. Roads became icy or choked with mud, wheels stopped working, and people said farewell to folks they wouldn't see until spring.

For most of us the battle against winter is now mostly won. Thankfully, most of us have light, heat, food, transportation and antibiotics, too. But without these things in ample supply, winter can bring terrifying trouble. A hundred years ago in Britain, a strange but favorite design for Christmas cards was a robin stone dead in the snow, as if to suggest that we can expect a similar fate if we don't help each other through these weeks. An Irish carol ends, "So let's all join hands and form a chain 'till the leaves of spring-time bud again." Advent is the church linking arms to get it safely to eternity.

The decrease of daylight began in June, at the summer solstice, and the deepening darkness stirs the prayer of the church throughout autumn, not just during Advent. Lengthening nights can make Judgment Day seem nearer and more sure. The ingathering of summer's bounty becomes a sign of that great gathering on the final day, when Christ, the Lord of the Harvest, will bring us home to heaven.

Certain feasts seem to lead us gradually into Advent. On Holy Cross Day (September 14), it's as if we raise the cross of Jesus as a sign of hope to guide us through the coming darkness. At the feast of the archangels (September 29), we call upon Michael, the guardian of the dead, to come to our defense.

The old funeral sequence *Dies Irae,* "Day of Wrath," is a song of dooms-day; it's been kept in our tradition for November and the entrance into Advent. Read over the scriptures and psalms of the last days of Ordinary Time and notice how they square perfectly with the scriptures of the First Sunday of Advent. They speak of death, judgment and the end of time.

At All Saints and All Souls (November 1 and 2), when the church dares to imagine what lies beyond the grave, nature offers consolation through bright foliage, chrysanthemums and fat pumpkins. But by the start of Advent, leaves have fallen, flowers have frozen, and ungathered fruit lies rotting in the fields. With the words of Jeremiah, the church wails, "The harvest is past, the summer is ended, and still we are not saved."

The bleakness of December can have us straining for signs of hope. It's no wonder we Christians pay close attention to the passing of the weeks closest to the winter solstice, the shortest days of the year.

Christians have long been in love with nature's passovers, with any of the signs that call to mind the great passing over of Christ. At the turning of the year, as the days ever-so-slowly begin to lengthen, nature offers a first step toward Easter. With this as our cue we make a great festival. We call it Christmas, the "festival of Christ."

It's not so much that Christmas is a solstice celebration, as sometimes is said, but that it is a festival *after* the solstice, a rejoicing in the return of the light. Advent, when the light is waning, is the season of preparation for this festival. We begin Advent four Sundays before December 25. The season ends at sundown on Christmas Eve.

In its scriptures and psalms, poetry and melodies, Advent shares much in common with the rest of the harvest season. But now the images are more intense, more somber, and even at times more desperate: "And still we are not saved."

During Advent the church listens carefully to the prophets, but it's not to help us pretend that Jesus isn't here yet. Isaiah, Jeremiah, John the Baptist and Jesus together announce God's reign, which, so they say, is like a wedding, like a path through the wasteland, like the consolation of the grieving, like the birth of a child.

The prophets speak to a people at risk of being crippled by their fears, of being overwhelmed by the work at hand, of lapsing into despair. To hear their words well, during Advent the church holds off on many signs of celebration.

Good listening requires silence, patience and a disciplined refusal to be distracted. That probably accounts for much of Advent's somber character; it's purposes are to help us face our fears, to unite with the suffering and troubled, to hear the prophet's words that "comfort the afflicted and afflict the comfortable."

Advent has two parts, the days before December 17 and the final week, from December 17 to Christmas Eve. Why this division? Early in Advent the days continue to grow shorter, as they have been doing since June, but

the rate of decrease lessens and then, wondrously, stands still. (That's what "solstice" means.) Throughout the final week of Advent, the days are shortest. This week was once called the Halcyon Days, a time of peace and perfection: Supposedly all creatures stood still in sympathy with the sun, almost holding their breath to see whether the sun would turn in its course and the days would grow longer again.

The church, too, holds its breath in anticipation. Liturgical poets have written romantically about these final days of the season—if Advent is like the night, now are the last moments before dawn; if Advent is like a courtship, now is the betrothal; if Advent is like a pregnancy, now the child is kicking in the womb.

This is the week of the O Antiphons, the seven prayers that each begin with the acclamation "O." (The seven verses of the hymn "O come, O come, Emmanuel" are the O Antiphons rewritten to rhyme.) In each antiphon, through powerful biblical images—like "Lady Wisdom," "Flower of Jesse's root," "Sun of justice" and "Cornerstone"—we call on God to come quickly. The prayers are urgent, almost demanding.

During these final days, the church begins to tell perhaps its favorite gospel stories about the coming of the reign of God. The characters are familiar and beloved—Elizabeth and Zechariah, Mary and Joseph—and there are angels as well, who more than anyone come bursting into Advent's darkness and silence to announce: "Fear not." In the gospels, these are crazy words to their hearers, who want to know, "How can this be?"

We can speak of Advent as the church's winter and Christmas as a "second spring"—second only to Easter. Take notice of the readings for Mass on December 21, which is usually the shortest day of the year, the centerpoint of the solstice. From the Song of Songs we hear, "For see, the winter is past!" From Luke we hear, "Blessed is she who trusted that the Lord's word to her would be fulfilled."

As the time of waiting is drawing to a close, the beloved bounds across the hills, Mary hastens through the hill country to embrace Elizabeth, and John leaps in his mother's womb.

As amazing as it sounds, when Christmas arrives, the winter is past. These are Gabriel's own words: "For nothing is impossible with God."

Overview

During Advent we stare the approaching winter in the face. We grow accustomed to the dark. We take notice of winter's subtle beauty. We prepare to defend each other against the season's difficulties.

How does December look in your own neck of the woods? Is it a time of tourists and ripe oranges? A time of mud and gray skies? A season of bitter cold? For many of us in North America, Advent outside our windows usually looks a lot like November, only the frost has muted autumn's glory and perhaps snow has whitened the landscape.

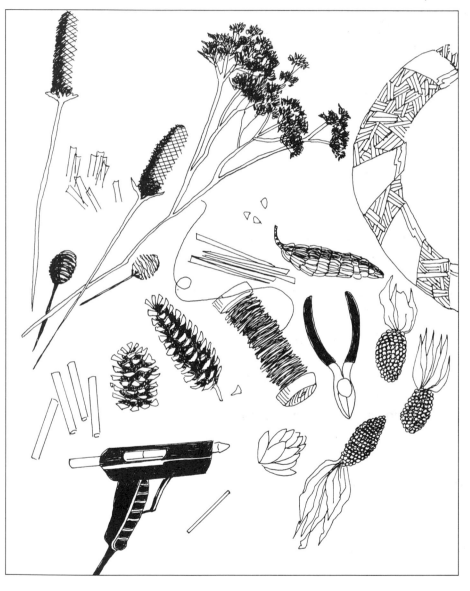

The worship environment for Advent can be plain and simple. Here's where you might begin your efforts:

1. Clean and simplify the whole place.

2. Perhaps retain some of the autumn decor but mute the colors.

3. Although not essential to the liturgy, hang a large Advent wreath and keep it lit for every gathering. (See page 222.)

4. Decorate Mary's shrine. (See page 215.)

5. As a witness to the neighborhood, decorate outdoors in a way that speaks of Advent and not of Christmas. (See page 218.)

An abundance of evergreens is for Christmas, not for Advent. The exception is the Advent wreath, a foretaste of Christmas's lights and greens. It's not that evergreens are inappropriate during Advent; a small amount are. Nor is it that they should not evoke winter, because they do. It's just

that we Christians have a longstanding tradition of using evergreens at Christmas, in the words of an old carol, "to drive the cold winter away."

On the First Sunday of Advent in Year B, the sixty-fourth chapter of Isaiah offers a remarkable seasonal image: "We have all withered like leaves, and our guilt carries us away like the wind." In any year, the Advent worship environment might include dried leaves, dried grasses and an alteration of the harvest time decorations to deaden bright colors, remove flowers and perhaps add pine cones and seed pods.

If you go beyond these first steps, it's wise, efficient and liturgically sound to use some materials during Advent that remain mostly in place for Christmastime. At Christmas, evergreens and flowers can be added to what is already in place.

The span of time from the First Sunday of Advent to the day before Ash Wednesday is not very long, 15 weeks at most. Use common elements of decoration throughout these winter weeks, things that draw the season into our common prayer and bring light and cheer to what can be a depressing time of year.

For example, we hear about John the Baptist often throughout these days —in Advent, during Christmas and then again during the first weeks of Ordinary Time. That suggests displaying a beautiful image of the Baptist as our companion in prayer.

Another example is of a parish that fills the vestibule ceiling with paper snowflakes crafted by parish households. (Instructions for doing this are sent home soon after Halloween.) The snowflakes are hung on the First Sunday of Advent and then are taken down and tossed into a bonfire at a Mardi Gras party. (This sort of "busy" decoration, of home-crafted ornaments, will be more attractive and suitable in a vestibule or hall than in the main body of the church.)

Another parish has fabric hangings made of multiple strips of cloth. Some of the strips are silver and include images of ice crystals. These stay up throughout the winter, but other cloth strips (intermingled among the silver ones) change depending on the season: deep purple and blue for Advent, gold and forest green for Christmastime, and forest green and deep blue for Ordinary Time.

There is both continuity and discontinuity between the seasons. Many of the scriptures, psalms and hymns of one period seem to prepare for the next; as the weeks pass, there is a gradual shifting of imagery.

But there is also discontinuity between seasons. Some images do not carry over. These abrupt changes can bring an unsettling discomfort (not always

a bad thing) but also delightful surprise. One of your tasks is to strike a balance between connections and breaks.

The start of Advent is a time for change in the liturgical environment. Elements that are visually unexpected or even jarring may have a place if only as a "voice in the wilderness" to keep us from growing complacent or too comfortable.

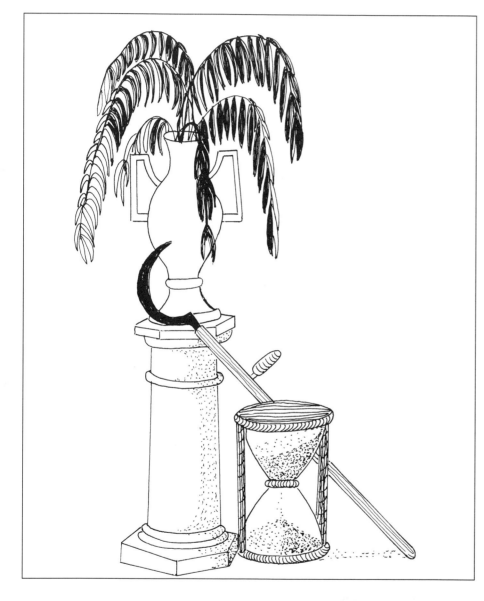

On the First Sunday of Advent we hear a discomforting gospel about the end of the world. In many old churches it was traditional to sprawl a depiction of the Last Judgment over the inside back wall. It offered a warning as people walked out of church. (If your church has a wall or window with this image, it deserves highlighting at this season. Can it be well-lit? Can something be written about it and published in the bulletin to draw people's attention to it? Can it be referred to in the homily or with a brief announcement?)

Trumpeting angels, death's heads, open graves, Christ in glory, the assembly of the saints, the Lamb of God—these are worthy images to use in adorning the worship environment during November and Advent.

John the Baptist was not known for courtesy or tact. Imagine him today preaching in a shopping mall. Advent itself, like John, can be impolite and loud in railing against injustice and in warning against corruption—but how can something of that spirit translate into the worship environment?

There are several traditions that do this, but all of them would be strange to Americans: Many customary Advent images look like Halloween decorations—grinning skulls, devils and other *memento mori,* reminders of death. Throughout the season, costumed demons would bang on windows, disrupt services and harass churchgoers with dire warnings against an

unrepentant life. (Dickens's three Christmas Eve ghosts and St. Nicholas's filthy companion are in this tradition.)

Of course, the spirit of these folkways might best be reflected in vigorous and honest preaching. But those who prepare the environment could see to it that the Advent atmosphere is stripped of anything that is cute, sweet or too soothing. We can be sure to emphasize the figures of the Baptist and of the Last Judgment. We also can become involved in helping the parish

appreciate the depth and serious-ness of the church's prayer during Advent, a prayer that is often missed if Christmas is celebrated before its time.

Advent also bears a decidedly mystical dimension. The long nights can stimulate our wonder, our yearn-ings, our imagination, so that we see beyond our small corner of the uni-verse. Advent can have us longing to talk to angels. As Isaiah reminds us in the scriptures, we are preparing for something more than personal salvation; we are preparing to take part in the renewal of the cosmos.

That may be a reason why Advent seems to require the backdrop of night and the subtlety and mystery of darkness, and why Advent's atmosphere often is imagined to shimmer with distant lights. Celestial imagery of sparkling stars and comets, of diaphanous clouds and snow, can be very appropriate to the season, but they are hard to exe-cute well. And unless this sort of decoration is handsome, noble, well crafted, in scale and appropriately located, it can look ridiculous.

Keep in mind that although Advent is divided in two (before and after December 17), the division of imagery is not totally rigid: Especially in the liturgy of the hours, Gabriel and Mary are mentioned even during the first weeks of the season. The Last Judgment and the preaching of John are mentioned in the liturgy throughout Advent and Christmastime.

Some parishes use a seven-branched candlestick to mark the seven days of the O Antiphons. At the Magnificat of Evening Prayer or at the gospel acclamation of daily Mass (when each day's proper O Antiphon is sung) on December 17, one candle is lit. On the 18th two are lit, and so on until December 23, when all seven are lit.

Perhaps a parish artist could fashion images of the O Antiphons, with each image displayed on the correct day; or the images could go up cumulatively during these days, first one, then two, until all seven are up. They could then stay in place through the Christmas season.

From December 17 to 24 the figures of Mary, Joseph and the donkey could be moved from place to place throughout the church on their journey to Bethlehem. (This changing location might be a good place for the seven-branched candlestick mentioned above or at least for a smattering of vigil lights.)

If Christmas decorations will be elaborate, during this final week of Advent you might begin the process of decorating instead of waiting until after the Fourth Sunday. The notion here isn't to jump the gun on Christmas but to make decorating one of Advent's final prayers-in-action. That's really a very old and practical tradition for this solstice week, and it also might be a way to lessen some of the pressure.

Here's a scheme for how such pre-Christmas decorating might proceed in a parish:

Especially if the Fourth Sunday of Advent falls on December 23 or 24, during the week before the Fourth Sunday put up the evergreens, but do not add decorations to them (the bows or ornaments, if any) until after the final Sunday Mass. Also wait until after this Mass to put up the Christmas flowers.

If you are using electric lights to decorate (which takes time to do well), put them up before the Fourth Sunday but do not light them until Christmas Eve. Be sure to schedule time for cleaning up after your work in time for Sunday worship.

No matter when the Fourth Sunday falls, it might be a good custom each year to have the nativity scene up by this Sunday, but with only the manger and the ox and no other statues. (For more about the nativity scene, see page 251.)

During the final week of Advent and on Christmas Eve and Day, parishioners can be invited to take a bit of straw home to put in their own nativity scenes and to place under the tablecloth (a custom from eastern Europe). It signifies that we are making our own tables into a manger where Christ will feed all who are hungry.

THE ASSEMBLY'S PLACE

High over the main aisle can be a wonderful spot, maybe the best spot, for a suspended Advent wreath. It can be our crown, our wedding ring, an emblem of our communion in Christ. (See page 222.)

Other possibilities, depending on the nature of your assembly and the architectural style of your church:

Hang a cascade of prisms, small mirrors, glass teardrops, snowflakes, or stars, each attached to monofilament (fishing line). (With anything that shimmers, the simpler the objects, the better.) This cascade calls to mind the words of Isaiah, "Drop down dew, you heavens, from above." Perhaps the objects tumble down and through the hole in the middle of the Advent wreath.

Hang an arrangement of bands of fabric in purples, fuchsias, roses, blues, silvers, whites, greens, browns or grays. The bands can hang vertically on a handsome pole, or they can be arranged on the wall horizontally to evoke a winter landscape.

For many people, purple is the color of Advent and for this reason alone it belongs somewhere in the worship environment. Something simple and effective is to sew or glue a constellation of stars onto purple cloth. Stars can be silk-screened onto the cloth or, with luck, you might acquire a star-covered fabric.

Advent's purple calls to mind the night sky, a winter dawn or even the gloominess of an overcast December day; it is also identified as the color of royalty, of ardor, of passion. Stars are signs of the cosmos, destined to fall into ruin and, God willing, be made new and eternal on the last day.

The Book of Daniel tells us that those who loved justice will rise from the dead to shine like stars. This image was borrowed by Venerable Bede, who wrote: "Christ is the morning star, who, when night is past, will shine on the saints the light of life and raise them into eternity."

More complicated images on fabric can intermingle stars with human faces of all ages and races. Perhaps, if this can be done well, bodies rising from the dead or even a full scene of the Last Judgment can be depicted; but unless this is done well, it surely will appear comical.

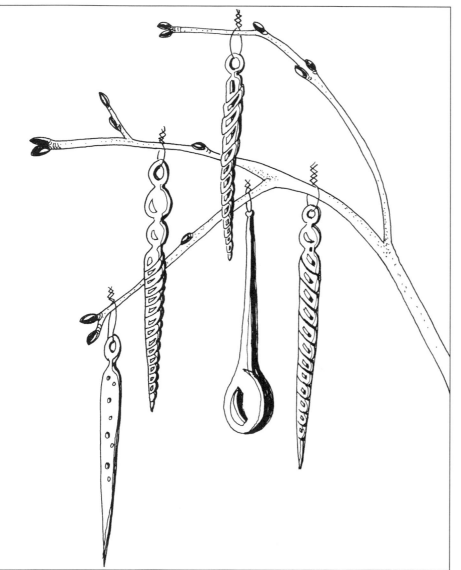

In many depictions of the Transfiguration, the Resurrection, the Ascension and the Last Judgment, Jesus is shown seated in an oval-like shape called a *mandorla,* which means "almond." The shape is created by slightly overlapping two circles. It represents the meeting of heaven and earth.

A simple cross drawn within an almond shape has become an image of the incarnation and of the glory of Christ. Almonds themselves are Advent symbols; in Israel the trees bloom in midwinter and are known as the "watchful ones" because they seem to be so eager for spring.

Another Advent image is the four archangels—Gabriel blowing the trumpet, Michael with the scales of justice, Raphael with healing gall, and Uriel darkening the sun and moon—all assisting in the resurrection of the dead. (Some would say that their feast, September 29, is one of Advent's first heralds in the liturgy.)

Angels are favorite images for banners, but they shouldn't appear saccharine and sentimental or all of the same race or gender. "Angel" means "messenger." In traditional iconography, John the Baptist is shown with wings because he is Christ's messenger and is identified as the "messenger of the covenant" in the prophecy of Malachi. (For more about John's imagery, see pages 161 and 169.)

In many regions, birches and their kin—aspens and poplars— can be cut for indoor decoration without much harm to the environment. There are few trees that look more wintry. A clump of three or so looks magnificent against a light background and will look even better if the clump is set underneath a light.

Short trees can be anchored in a pot of plaster, although the pot will be heavy to move. You can arrange tall trees if you have a spot where they can be attached to the ceiling; once a tree gets stood upright and most of its weight is supported by its trunk, it doesn't take too strong a wire to guy it at the top. (Flat black paint can be sprayed on wires to make them less noticeable.)

Three or more trees fastened to each other midway up can make a stable grouping, provided the trees are also fastened to the ceiling at their tops and the pot or other container is weighed down with sand or bricks.

Brown oak leaves, moss or small pots of ivy can make a beautiful filler for the pot. Artificial snowflakes (the kind used by hobbyists for miniature villages) also make an attractive filler over cotton batting. Perhaps anything artificial is out of place, but artificial snow (flakes of white mica) can boast a centuries-old heritage as a Christmas decoration.

Another attractive branch is red- or yellow-twig dogwood. Where it is native, it's almost a weed. Short branches can be arranged in dry sand. A spiral of grape vines or bittersweet could be handsome rising up a wall; the spiral shape is an emblem of time itself. Florists may have an array of interesting branches and small trees, but they're usually expensive and sometimes are rare species that really should not be cut down in the wild.

Plan to keep the vines, branches or trees in place for Christmastime, too. Then you will add the flowers and evergreens. A Christmas tree can look especially beautiful in front of bare trees. Branches and trees are seasonal reminders of the shoot rising from the root of Jesse that will spring forth and flower. They are signs of potential and of promise.

Branches will be beautiful without ornaments. Whether or not to ornament them is a judgment call: In some settings and with certain species (especially those with especially colorful bark or contorted limbs), ornaments would distract too much from the natural beauty of the wood.

Whether to use ornamentation also depends on what you are trying to emphasize. Bare trees are one sort of symbol. Decorated trees are another. As symbols they share much in common, but they have significant differences. There is a long tradition of ornamenting trees for various seasons and festivals, perhaps because the effect can be magical; an ornamented tree is a sign of fruitfulness and delight.

If the ornaments are handsome and in scale, bare branches can look especially wintry during Advent with simple glass icicles, stars or prisms hanging from them. From a distance, even plain silver glass balls will appear like sparks of light. At Christmas you can add gold, red or other "warm" colors among the clear and silver ornaments. (But be sure they are fastened securely, or else they are sure to fly off when branches are bumped.)

Decorating bare branches can result in either something garish and frivolous or something noble and beautiful. The difference depends on scale, proportion, simplicity and lack of contrivance. The branches should be beautiful. Broken ones or stubs should be removed. The branches should be arranged to appear as if they were growing there naturally. Ornamentation should be evenly distributed, and ornaments should be simple and beautiful. Every one must hang freely and hang straight.

ALTAR, AMBO AND CHAIR

Some parishes "vest" the altar (and sometimes the ambo) with colored fabric in keeping with each season of the year. Is this done well and in proportion? Does the fabric's color and texture match or complement the ministers' vestments?

Advent (and Lent) may be good times to leave the altar mostly exposed, especially if it is beautifully made. A simple altar cloth, well made but much less full than the one to be used at Christmas, can speak of anticipation and incompletion.

For Advent the area in the vicinity of the ambo and altar can be left free of decoration or perhaps with just a single but amply large wintertime (not Christmas) arrangement—of witchhazel or osmanthus branches, of magnolia or rhododendron foliage, of blue-berried junipers, evergreen barberry or dried foxtail grass. You can prepare the arrangement yourself—take a walk in the wild, and where permitted, gather signs of the season.

There's no liturgical requirement, as there is during Lent, to avoid using all flowers during Advent. However, the *Ceremonial of Bishops* (236) says that during Advent the "floral decoration of the altar should be marked by a moderation that reflects the character of the season but does not anticipate the full joy of Christmas itself."

In many places the December garden is without bloom, and almost none of the usual florist-shop flowers look right during Advent. Make an effort at this time to give away leftover funeral arrangements and especially to avoid using poinsettias or other red flowers—these are too associated with Christmas. One flower that looks right during Advent is the paperwhite narcissus. But its small scale means that a pot of these would probably look best in a shrine or in some other place where it can be appreciated (and smelled) up close.

Vessels and Vesture

Some parishes have a plain set of communion vessels for Advent and Lent. During these seasons, books with festive covers are cloaked in plain fabric. It's not that Advent is the same as Lent, but both seasons share a sobriety and a simplicity; both seasons are observed in anticipation of a festival.

It can be appropriate to use the same variety of wine, type of bread and fragrance of incense throughout the days of Advent and Christmastime. (It's not hard to find incense that smells of balsam and other conifers.)

The time of year offers an opportunity for making improvements on liturgical practice and on materials. People may be more willing to accept and appreciate worthwhile changes.

Some parishes have special Advent vesture used exclusively during this season. It's one thing to acquire such a set, but it's another to ensure that it's used every year by all the ministers who serve the parish, including visiting priests and deacons.

The simplest way to make sure that a particular purple set is used is to put away any other purple vesture. During Advent the sacristy closet would hold only the Advent set, the funeral set and a simple white set and a red set for the few feast days when these are worn.

On the solemnity of the Immaculate Conception and on the feast of Our Lady of Guadalupe, you might use a white set different from the vesture to be worn during the Christmas season. Notice that from December 17 to 24, Advent's purple is worn even if a saint's memorial is observed.

It's amazing how much ink has been spilled on the subject of the color of Advent vesture. Here's the argument in a nutshell: Advent isn't Lent. How can the vestments make that clear?

The answer in the Lutheran tradition is to use deep blue during Advent and purple during Lent. Deep blue can be a beautiful color for vesture. It has a liturgical history in certain countries and seems right as an emblem of the night, of winter, of vigilance and of hope, even as an evocation of the Blessed Virgin Mary. But for Roman Catholics in the United States, blue is not approved for use at worship.

One problem with not using any purple for Advent is the loss of an important touchstone. This color might be one of the most straightforward catechetical tools we have in reminding ourselves that it's not Christmas yet, that Advent is a period of preparation and not of celebration. Blue does not yet have that association.

There may even be an advantage in using the same vesture for Advent and for Lent, which is not to suggest that the seasons are the same but that they share certain characteristics—both are times of preparation. If you use two different purple sets for the two seasons, most parishioners won't even notice. (Although people don't need to notice an element in the liturgy in order for it to be worthwhile.)

It has been suggested that Advent's vesture could be a particular shade of purple and Lent's vesture another shade. However, generalizations about what it is that shades of color signify are subjective and easy to contradict. Visit a museum that displays medieval vesture; the vestments come in all sorts of colors. Just as today, many of the fabrics are made of a mixture of colors. The dyestuffs available to vestment makers didn't necessarily yield a distinct or even predictable color but a range of shades.

The ancient tradition of liturgical vesture did not specify a particular shade but rather a mood; vesture was either somber, festive or plain. Vesture for somber times was mostly dark and simple—the exact shade might be reddish, blackish, brownish, purplish or bluish, but it was always a deep color.

Vestment makers often mix colors, and these mixtures contribute to the look and feel of the finished vestment. What then would be the colors of Advent? Would white, blue and silver evoke ice? brown, rust and gray evoke the bare earth? black, purple and blue evoke the night? or purple, red and blue evoke royal blood? (Ambiguity can be a welcome delight.)

What rarely looks good is appliqué symbols on vestments. Leave this sort of thing to athletic jackets. Especially ridiculous is adding representations of the things that would ordinarily be found elsewhere in the church, such as the Advent wreath or candles. And it is certainly inappropriate in Advent to use purple vestments that have on them symbols of the passion—a crown of thorns and nails, for example. There is, however, some tradition for applying images of the saints to vesture, for example, the prophets. And while this is hard to do well, it can be magnificent.

In anything, let the beauty and handiwork of the fabrics shine out, and be sure to use the same vesture throughout the season, no matter who wears it.

There is the tradition that remains with us of wearing rose-colored vesture on the Third Sunday of Advent (Gaudete Sunday), although the practice is optional. If you have beautiful rose vestments, of course you would use them. This color is not pink but a dusky rose.

Gaudete means "rejoice." It is the first word of Paul's admonition to the Philippians and is the entrance antiphon for Mass this day: "Rejoice in the Lord always; again I say, rejoice! The Lord is near."

FONT

In some places, green plants are kept year-round near the font and in other places in the church. However, tropical plants are not reflections of the season unless you live in the tropics. They are especially out-of-place next to materials that evoke late autumn and winter.

The gospels for the Second and Third Sundays of Advent and several Advent weekday gospels focus on John the Baptist; during the last days of Advent we hear from Luke's gospel about John's birth. Then during Christmastime on weekdays and on the feast of the Baptism of the Lord, we hear more about John. During the first days of Ordinary Time we hear once again about the Baptist. An icon or other image of John can be kept in the baptistry throughout Advent *and* Christmastime and perhaps on through winter Ordinary Time. Especially in churches where the font is near the entrance, this may be the right place for the Advent wreath.

If the parish placed a book of the names of the dead in the baptistry throughout November, it is not necessary to remove it when Advent begins. You might keep it in place through Advent and Christmastime. The dead are very much in our thoughts during this time of the year; the O Antiphons are perhaps most fittingly sung in a cemetery.

Perhaps in November the paschal candle was ornamented with a wheat wreath or with other harvest emblems; these too can remain through Advent, especially if a few adjustments are made, if necessary, to tone down the colors.

SHRINES

Mary's shrine deserves special attention during Advent. Keep candles burning there each Sunday and feast. Hang a wreath of dried herbs or rosebuds near the image or place a pot of paperwhite narcissus or a white amaryllis in front of it. Roses, in particular, are Marian symbols. As in the story of Our Lady of Guadalupe, roses in December connote, in the words of G. K. Chesterton, the "things that cannot be and that are." Of course, these words reflect Mary's conversation with Gabriel.

In searching for additional imagery with which to grace the shrine, you might be inspired by invocations of the Litany of the Blessed Virgin

Mary—"Mystical Rose," "Tower of ivory," "Ark of the covenant," "Gate of heaven," "Morning Star."

In iconography, Mary is usually shown wrapped in two significant colors—a dark, bloody red and a deep, midnight blue. The blue signifies mortality, the red, immortality. Mary is clothed in blue but overwrapped in a red mantle. Either the red or the blue dominates, depending on the event being depicted. In the Christmas icon, the red mantle is most visible—Mary is the mother of Life. In the Ascension icon, in which Mary lifts her hands in longing for Christ to come in glory, the blue robe is most visible. Mary is like a wise bridesmaid who keeps her lamp lit through the night in expectation of the bridegroom.

The parable of the wise and foolish bridesmaids (Matthew 25:1–13) is an Advent classic. Perhaps Mary's image can be graced by a single or even five real oil lamps, or by another representation of this parable.

An interesting bit of seasonal folklore identifies five women martyrs as "wise bridesmaids": Cecilia (November 22), Lucy (December 13), Agnes (January 21) and Agatha (February 5). The fifth? Some say Catherine of Egypt (November 25), Barbara (December 4), Anastasia or Eugenia (both remembered on December 25), and some say the Virgin Mary, queen of all martyrs.

Pregnancy is a powerful Advent image that mixes trepidation and tranquil joy. The usual depiction of the Immaculate Conception has much in common with Our Lady of Guadalupe—both show Mary pregnant, wearing the traditional sash of expectant women. With candles or a wreath of berries you might give honor to one of these images throughout the season, especially on Mary's feast days.

Mary is an image of the church. The preface of the eucharistic prayer for the Immaculate Conception speaks to God of this imagery:

> Full of grace, Mary was to be a
>   worthy mother of your Son,
> your sign of favor to the Church
>   at its beginning,
> and the promise of its perfection
>   as the bride of Christ,
>   radiant in beauty.

In some places during Advent it is customary to veil the statue of Mary with a shroud so that only her face is visible, or to drape the veil in a way that makes the statue look expectant (a lovely tradition). Depending on circumstances, there may be ways to do this nobly and handsomely.

Three-dimensional images can be powerful signs of the incarnation of God in flesh and blood, but they also can be idols. It's wise to be wary when using them. Despite this risk, for as long as the church has used religious images for prayer and devotion, the church has clothed its images in seasonal attire, crowned them, wreathed them in herbs and flowers, processed with them and extended to them affection and devotion.

Some parishes have windows, paintings or other art appropriate to the season—of the prophets, of the Annunciation, of John the Baptist, of the Litany of Loreto— that can be highlighted with flowers, pennants, candles and other illumination. And perhaps there is art associated with Christmas that can be veiled or darkened now. This sort of thing can be hard to do attractively, but it's worth trying because it shows high regard for the parish's treasury of sacred images.

In some parishes, people will be leaving poinsettias and other Christmas offerings in the shrines throughout Advent. It's not fair to remove these, which is one reason shrines belong out of sight of the main liturgical space. However, if shrines are in full view of the assembly, especially for the Sundays of Advent, Christmas flowers will need to be removed from them.

SEASONAL CORNERS

Ministers of art may want to teach parishioners about the significance of the Advent wreath, the Christmas tree and other traditions, especially those of the ethnic groups represented in the parish. Surely there will be Advent calendars and other take-home materials for domestic prayer.

It's a real service to parishioners to inform them of where they can buy good religious art, cards and gifts—quality ones are hard to come by. Perhaps the parish wants to make available certain gifts, such as copies of *Catholic Household Blessings and Prayers*. As Christmas draws near, some parishes distribute or sell candles, lanterns, straw, wafers, wreaths, tree decorations, baked goods and other materials for the home.

All these materials and activities deserve a handsome display, not merely a card table set in a corner, because they, too, are part of keeping Advent. Alongside this activity there might be a display of the folk arts of the season, a collection of Christmas books, a particularly fine Advent calendar (LTP publishes a dandy) or images of St. Nicholas and St. Lucy.

The gathering place, vestibule or entryway might be roomy enough for some of these things. Here, too, even on parish bulletin boards, an effort can be made to hold off on Christmas until it arrives.

VESTIBULES, DOORWAYS, OUTDOORS

During December we often encounter outdoor displays that say it's Christmas; perhaps many of us would appreciate a public reminder that it's Advent. The right outdoor decorations can welcome the neighborhood to enter into the spirit of the season.

Perhaps grapevine wreaths ornamented in purple and silver are hung on doors. Perhaps doorways are bunted with strips of fabric in shades of purple and other wintry colors. The use of the traditional purple in outdoor ornamentation is a particular reminder for some people that Christmas isn't here yet, that something wonderful is coming.

Some parishes set up a sign to advertise the times of Advent and Christmas liturgies; if you do this, add the times of worship for January 1 and

Epiphany, which helps invite everyone to keep the season and not just its first day.

If the parish sets up an outdoor nativity scene, perhaps it is put up on December 17 (but not earlier) with only the manger and the cow. The other figures are added on Christmas Eve. Well-crafted images of Mary, Isaiah and John the Baptist can be highlighted outdoors, although the best place for likenesses of our holy ancestors (including a nativity scene) is one suitable for reverence, not on a street corner.

An outdoor Advent wreath can be wonderful. There can even be a nightly kindling of its lights, perhaps in the form of torches. During Advent, we probably need to avoid using other evergreen wreaths or garlanding outside because these speak too strongly of Christmas.

Lights on shrubbery also look too much like Christmas, although it's hard to imagine something more wintry than blue lights—these are not merry at all. Perhaps these can be woven into grapevines put around the main doorway. At Christmas the blue lights can be changed to white and evergreen garland can be added to the bare vine.

OTHER LOCATIONS

What good is accomplished during Advent by holding off on Christmas music, vesture and decorations at worship if the parish center, school and rectory, as well as our homes, are decked out in red, white and green? The split between the liturgical calendar and the calendar we live by is an unhealthy sign, to be sure.

During Advent, the reason a Christmas tree should not be shining, carols should not be sung or parties should not be held, is not because someone issues an edict against these things. The reason must be that we are filled to the brim with Advent. We are occupied with the season's own scriptures, songs, customs and prayer.

Of course, Advent is also a time of anticipation and of the hard work of preparation for the season to come. This anticipation is so wonderful and the preparations are such hard work, how could anyone jump the gun on Christmas?

Those who prepare the worship environment might be better able than most people to appreciate the connections that can be made between the liturgy and the ways we celebrate the year. These ministers can lead the way in imagining what Advent could look like in the school, in the parish hall and in homes. They can help us keep Advent as Advent and then keep Christmastime throughout its many days.

A lot of this is helped to happen if the parish social calendar conforms to the seasons. Christmas parties, concerts and children's pageants are scheduled for Christmastime, not Advent. This sort of scheduling happens months and even a year before the actual events.

If it's your responsibility to suggest to teachers ways to decorate their classrooms, it's much more effective to offer positive suggestions than negative ones. For instance, you might explain that Advent is the church's winter and that snowflakes and icicles are better signs of the season than holly or bells (and are just as easy to find in paper goods stores).

Instead of using red and green, bulletin boards and borders can be prepared in purple, blue and silver. The figures of Lady Wisdom and Mary, of Isaiah and John the Baptist, of Nicholas and Lucy have become important to Advent. Classrooms and meeting rooms can have their own Advent wreaths or even a single candle (also an old custom) lit for prayer every day of the season.

After December 17, preparations for Christmas can begin in earnest, and a part of our preparation is decorating and housecleaning—in the classroom and in the parish center as well as in our homes. If you urge others to hold off on Christmas during Advent, you will also need to build enthusiasm for keeping Christmas when the season arrives.

SPECIAL OCCASIONS

Advent is short but jammed with special days, almost too many. Even if you had the time to do it, there's no reason to alter the worship environment from week to week or for Advent's feast days.

For instance, although John the Baptist is mentioned at Mass on the Second and Third Sundays of Advent, John is one of our "companions" at worship throughout the season and on into Christmastime. The Blessed Virgin Mary is celebrated during Advent on December 8 (the Immaculate Conception) and on December 12 (Our Lady of Guadalupe), and she is mentioned in the gospels at Mass on the Fourth Sunday of Advent. But Mary, like John, is also our companion throughout these days.

Of course, if the parish owns a fine image of Our Lady of Guadalupe (December 12), of Andrew (November 30), of Lucy (December 13) or of other saints of the season, these would be honored on their feast days with candles and flowers.

In many cultures, the final nine days of Advent are devoted to the expectation of Mary and to Mary and Joseph's journey to Bethlehem. The days echo nine months of pregnancy as well as the nine days after the Ascension of Jesus, when the disciples awaited the descent of the Holy Spirit. (Not surprisingly, in some places—like England—the O Antiphons began on December 16, not 17, to reflect these nine days of intense anticipation.)

In some parishes, especially among Filipinos, Mexicans and Central Americans, these days are very important. Mary and Joseph's search for lodging calls to mind all who are refugees, all who are pilgrims, all who are homeless. The parish observance can be tailored to include every ethnic group and to keep the Advent spirit. These nine days aren't for their own sake: They are meant to build enthusiasm for the celebration of Christmas, Epiphany and the merry days in between.

Out of respect and love for people in need, many parishes collect gifts and charity throughout Advent. Ministers who prepare the environment may be responsible for preparing a place for the gathering of these gifts. Large hampers in the vestibule might be needed, or a side shrine or the parish hall might be used as a place to collect gifts.

It's not a good idea to set up a Christmas tree for people to put their gifts around, because Christmas trees are for Christmas, not Advent. It's also a bad idea to surround the altar with gifts, because it's never proper to create an obstacle between assembly and altar.

The giving of charity during Advent can be the beginning of parish almsgiving all year long, especially through the winter. Use the vestibule or bulletin boards to tell the parish about the recipients of its alms. That, too, is a part of the atmosphere for worship.

The Advent Wreath

In the circling of the year
Light and life to us appear
When the Son of God draws near
de virgine Maria.
— from a fifteenth-century carol

During winter, dirt roads become mostly impassable. Either they grow muddy or they become frozen and rutted. In times past, wagon wheels—precious, hard-to-construct possessions—were brought inside and hung high and dry to protect them from the elements. This annual winter ritual may be the origin of the Advent wreath.

Among central Europeans (who invented the custom), an Advent wreath is a circle of evergreens suspended horizontally from the ceiling by ropes. That way it appears to be a hole through which we can peek into heaven.

At the beginning of the season we gaze up into this circle and shout the words of Isaiah, "Oh, that you would rend the heavens open and come down!" Wondrously, the Christmas season will reach its conclusion on the day we hear that the heavens are torn apart and the Spirit descends like a dove. On that day a voice from heaven will call, "My beloved!"

Like the Christmas tree and nativity scene, there is no liturgical requirement to have an Advent wreath. It is not, unlike the paschal candle, a ritual necessity, and its use in the liturgy is not well defined. Maybe that will change. The Advent wreath does have a wonderful history of use in communal settings; even its shape suggests communion.

Perhaps even before we concern ourselves with the Advent wreath in church, our efforts would be well spent fostering this custom in parishioners' homes; the parish Advent wreath can offer a model.

Making an Advent wreath in scale for a church can be difficult, mainly because of its weight and the difficulty of getting candles to stand straight. Perhaps, instead of in the church, a home-sized wreath belongs in the parish center or in the vestibule.

Putting the wreath in the church suggests that it be used within the liturgy, but the *Book of Blessings* (1513) says:

> When the Advent wreath is used in church, on the Second and successive Sundays of Advent the candles are lighted either before Mass begins or immediately before the opening prayer; no additional rites or prayers are used.

The wreath is blessed on the First Sunday of Advent. Curiously, according to the *Book of Blessings*, if the blessing takes place during Mass, it happens as part of the prayers of the faithful. The first candle is lit afterward.

Lighting a large-scale wreath can be awkward, even dangerous. Many parishes find that the best practice here is to have the candles lit before people arrive for worship.

In the liturgy there are very few times when candles are lit ritually, although there's probably no good reason for this lack of tradition. Perhaps the parish can evolve a practice for graciously lighting the church candles at appropriate times during the liturgy (perhaps during the entrance rites or during the preparation of the gifts). After the First Sunday, the Advent candles could then be lit, as the *Book of Blessings* says, before the opening prayer of the Mass. This book gives no words to use, and so the wreath is lit in silence—which means that this action deserves our full attention. But it also seems right to use the simple verse and response, "Jesus Christ is the light of the world: A light no darkness can overpower."

A beautiful practice is to place a bowl of burning incense beneath the suspended wreath. Fragrant smoke is an emblem of prayer rising to heaven. There are few lovelier sights at worship than clouds of incense rising into an Advent wreath.

An Advent wreath has four candles. (There have been versions, however, with as many candles as there are days of Advent!) Customarily one candle is lit from the Saturday evening before the First Sunday until the Saturday evening before the Second Sunday. The next week, two candles are lit. Then three are lit, and then all four are lit from the Saturday evening before the Fourth Sunday until Christmas Eve and beyond. A German rhyme summarizes the pattern:

First one, then two, then three, then four:
And then the Lord knocks on our door.

The tradition is fairly loose about when the wreath gets taken down. In many parishes (and homes) it stays up through the Christmas season, although its greenery and candles may need freshening. Some manufacturers have Advent wreaths with a fifth candle set in the center of the wreath; the fifth candle is for Christmastime. However, this fifth candle tends to obscure the shape of the circle.

An interesting home custom is to hang a star (made out of straw, foil or paper) from the wreath each day of Advent. (This calls to mind the falling stars that are signs of the end of the world.) At Christmas a large, usually illuminated star might be hung in the center. The Moravian people have an exquisite and fragile paper star that would be lovely for this purpose.

Probably the nicest way you might transfigure an Advent wreath for Christmastime (besides by refreshing its greenery) is to add berried branches, such as deciduous holly, haw-thorn, Brazilian pepper or barberry, and other small fruits. A chain of cranberries draping from the evergreens can be richly beautiful. In a cool setting they will look good for about two weeks.

Most central Europeans use red candles for the Advent wreath. (It is, after all, a foretaste of Christmas.) Americans were introduced to the wreath by liturgically-minded folks who taught the use of one rose and three purple candles, which matches the Roman Catholic liturgical colors of Advent. At the time using purple and rose candles was a newfangled idea, but now many people think these colors are essential.

Unless the parish uses rose vesture on the Third Sunday of Advent, it does not make much sense to use purple and rose candles. Ordinary white ones are fine and beautiful, no matter what color your vestments.

Candles should be in scale with the size of the wreath. A well designed, safely burning candle is the only type to use near evergreens.

It's hard to imagine a better Advent wreath than a wagon wheel. In that spirit, a handsome circle of wood makes a good wreath. The easiest and perhaps most attractive way to fasten evergreens to a wooden circle is to use garland, not branch tips. Evergreen garland can be tied to the circle at several points to form loops (which enables people to see the wheel), or it can be attached tightly to the circle (which hides the wheel and may not be the best thing to do if it's handsome).

If the available garland is skimpy, braid several strands together. You might mix greens—balsam, cedar and pine. Avoid hemlock and spruce for indoors; these species will drop every needle when dry. Broadleaf evergreens such as holly look fantastic when fresh and awful when not. Boxwood is an exception; it stays good for months.

Think twice before adding anything other than evergreens to a wreath. Avoid anything that interrupts the circular shape or that distracts from the beauty of the greenery.

Strips of fabric, ropes or chains work better than ribbons for suspending a wreath; ribbons usually tear easily, and they are expensive. To suspend the wreath, use something bold, not merely functional—thick ropes or large chains look better than thin materials, even if thin ropes or chains will do the job. If these attach at a single point, the wreath may tend to spin. If they attach to a single rope that descends for some length from the ceiling, a large wreath will certainly turn slowly, which can be wonderful.

For a large wreath with appropriately large candles, candle holders can be bolted or screwed into a wooden wheel or soldered onto a metal one. (This is a job for a professional; the candles have to be able to stand perfectly upright or the wreath will look awful.) The right combination and dimensions of plumbing fixtures can be turned into candle holders; paint them a dark color and mask them with the evergreens if needed.

Obviously, it's a lot harder to get a long candle to stand straight than a short, thick one, such as a pillar candle. But a fat candle usually is not predisposed to being repeatedly lit and extinguished, because the volume of wax tends to drown the wick. Maybe you will need to put a smaller candle into some sort of larger lamp (such as a glass bowl with a prismatic surface) so that together they will create something in scale with the wreath.

Glass-enclosed votive candles also are not designed to be lit and extinguished repeatedly. If they are lit and left burning they can be satisfactory for the Advent wreath, but don't use votives with colored glass. That just makes it difficult to see the flame.

For a smaller wreath you can use an already-made evergreen wreath. A "double-faced" wreath won't curl as much as a single-sided one. Central Europeans have a device that makes it easy to attach ordinary candles to an evergreen wreath; it looks like a typical candle holder with a nail sticking out the bottom. You can make one by driving a long nail through a small wooden candle holder; the trick is to keep from splitting the wood.

Another customary way to hang ordinary table candles on evergreens is to use a counterweight method. One of the loveliest is from Sweden: Two small apples are tied to the base of each candle and the apples hang over the branches to balance the candle, keeping it upright.

It might be necessary to wire holders into place on the wreath. As the wreath dries, holders usually tilt and will need to be adjusted.

Flames and dried evergreens are dangerous together. There's no practical way to flameproof evergreens. And in a heated building there's no effective way to keep evergreens fresh. (Artificial evergreens can be just as flammable as the real thing, and liturgy is no place for fake evergreens.)

It's heartening to know that for all the real greenery used at this time of year, there are very few accidents. One safety measure is to use flame-proof glass vessels that surround candles, such as hurricane lamps. These can be beautiful as long as the glass is kept clean.

Another precaution (and this one is often ignored) is to use great care when lighting or extinguishing an Advent wreath. It is unbelievable that in many parishes young children are given the task of lighting the wreath. Especially unsafe are lighting devices with long wicks; it's easy for pieces of burning wick to fall off into the greens.

Maybe because it can be difficult to attach candles to a wreath, and maybe because evergreens need to be kept at a safe distance from burning candles, people have come up with other ways to make use of the symbols of the wreath and of light during Advent. One is to hang a wreath on a wall behind four candlesticks (which loses the symbol of a suspended wreath as a hole in heaven).

Another way, which seems ingenious, is to hang the Advent wreath horizontally but rather than put the candles on top of the wreath, hang four lamps well below the wreath or at some distance from it. Perhaps long swags of fabric arc from the wreath to the hanging lamps; if the wreath is

centered over the people, the fabric would appear like a canopy. (For a discussion of this image, see page 257.)

Suspended oil lamps can be beautiful and may communicate a sense of keeping vigil. Clear glass globes can be put in macramé hangers and small candles can be put into the globes. (For any festival, this is a lovely thing to put outdoors hanging from a tree.)

It's a shame that we've grown content to think of the Advent wreath as a tradition set in stone, when only a few generations ago there was great variation and ingenuity in customs for counting the weeks of Advent and the days of Christmastime.

For instance, in addition to the four-candle wreath used for Advent, central Europeans devised 12-candle wreaths to use for the Twelve Days of Christmas and other wonderful 12- or 13-light contraptions to celebrate the days of Christmas with increasing light.

Sometimes the suspended candelabra took the form of spheres of interlocking hoops—a globe constructed of three rings is a beautiful variation on an Advent wreath. Sometimes these globes would be attached to poles to make processional staffs, also a splendid idea, so that the Advent candelabrum would be carried into the community celebrations. Sometimes there were lanterns made out of tin, gourds or cut paper to hold the candles. Before creating your community's Advent wreath, explore the world's folk traditions that employ festive illumination, and explore the significance of the circle and the counting of days or weeks.

The Europeans who devised the Advent wreath also originated the Christmas tree. In some homes the wreath is hung over the place where the tree is to be set up on Christmas Eve; during Advent the wreath is like a promise of

the coming season, and during the Christmas season the wreath forms a shining crown hanging over the tree. In this way the four lights of Advent "blossom" into the countless lights of Christmas.

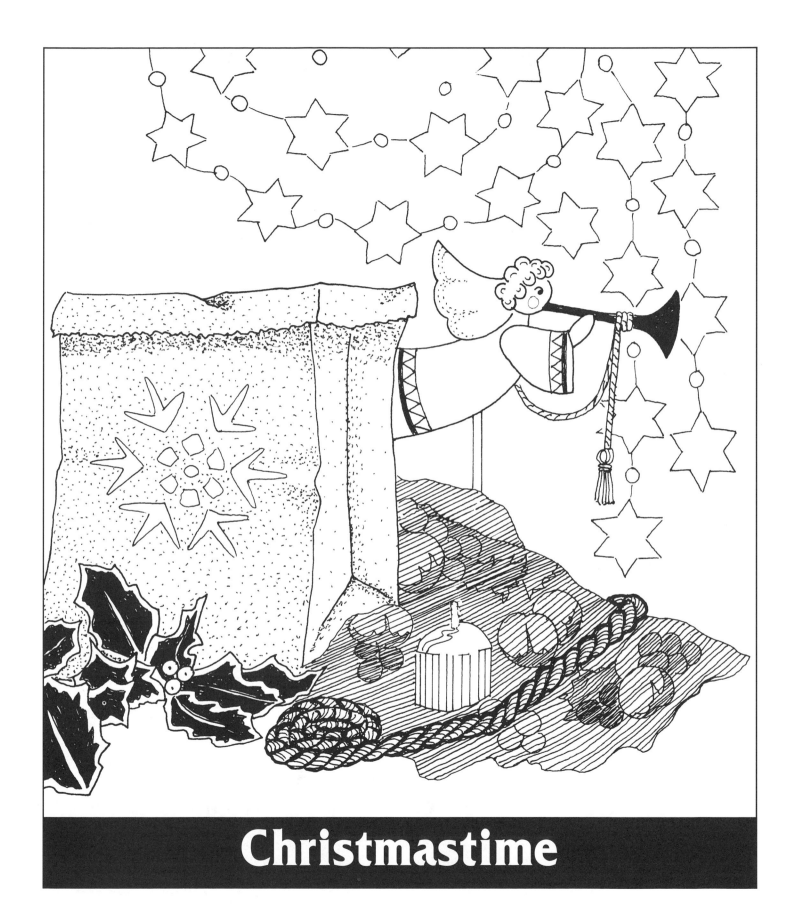

Christmastime

A Sense of the Season

The Christmas festival has had many names. These names can help us get a better grasp of what it is we are celebrating.

Some people called the festival "Lights," which seems to sum up these days pretty well. Others called it "Epiphany," meaning "showing forth." Epiphany comes from a Greek word used again and again in the scriptures to describe the appearance of Christ in glory at the end of the world.

Advent begins with gospel stories of the end of time. But Christmas also has its end-of-the-world scriptures. For example, there are the readings for Christmas Mass at midnight and at dawn from Paul's Letter to Titus, which repeats the word "appearing"—*epiphaneian*—as if to drill it into our heads: ". . . as we await our blessed hope, the appearing of the glory of our God and Savior Christ Jesus." The end is joined to the beginning, birth to rebirth. In naming this festival Epiphany, our ancestors were celebrating the end of the world!

Many people call the festival "Birth" (*Natale, Nadolig, Noel,* Nativity), but they do not mean "birthday." This is no anniversary of a past event but a birth that happens right now. It would never have occurred to past generations to put candles on a cake and to sing happy birthday to Jesus.

Instead, perhaps they make images of swaddling clothes for the newborn child (which is what *stollen* is—baby clothes in dough). They may have created images of the birth showing gospel characters in contemporary dress (which is how old-time nativity scenes most always were fashioned).

Or, to the best of their abilities, they make their homes new Bethlehems; Bethlehem is a Hebrew word that means "house of bread." In messy delight, in some places wheat straw is scattered on floors, sheaves of grain are hung high and every blessed creature in the household—from family members to barn animals—shares in a single loaf, with a healthy portion scattered on the graves of the dead.

Christmas means "Christ's feast," and that title gives us a good notion of what we are celebrating this season—the fullness of Christ. The festival requires many days and includes several gospel stories, especially about Jesus' birth and baptism. These passages have heaven's own words about who Jesus is—a Savior, Christ the Lord, the beloved child of God.

Scandinavians use a peculiar word for Christmas—*Jul.* It once meant "the turning of the year." This word and its English equivalent, Yule, come from a rich family of words that includes the English "all," "whole," "holy," "health," "wealth," "well" and even "wheel." In other languages, this family includes words for festive breads, circle dances and carols, royalty and crowns, and words for beauty and goodness, too.

These words have something to do with perfection and fulfillment—with Epiphany, the appearance of Christ in glory. In Christ all hungers will be sated, all fears comforted, all sicknesses healed, all troubles ended.

The Romans called the beginning of each month *kalenda.* Of course, January's *kalenda* was the best-celebrated. The word lives on in the English "calendar" and in other words, too: Lithuanians call Christmas *Kaledos.* Poles call Christmas carols *kolendy.* Even the Spanish word for Christmas gifts, *aguinaldo,* so the linguists tell us, is a variant of this word. For Christians, the turning of the year has become a season to anticipate the end of time and, even more, the fullness of time.

Many of the customs and images of the festival make sense not so much as celebrations of the nativity but rather as signs of fulfillment in Christ. We stuff breads with harvest bounty and bake them in the form of crowns and wheels. We drive the dark winter away with lights and greenery and blazing flowers. We go door to door singing, we send greetings of peace, we seem to spend our last nickel in our desire to love and to be loved.

A passage (4:23) from St. Paul's First Letter to the Thessalonians reads like a Yuletide greeting:

> May the God of peace sanctify you entirely;
> and may your spirit and soul and body
> be kept complete and blameless
> at the coming of our Lord Jesus Christ.

We still approach the Christmas festival with these hopes—that the days will be a time of peace, abundance, wholesomeness and consolation. We come to Christmas hoping beyond hope that this year our home will be hospitable, our relatives will kiss and not quarrel, people will deal justly with one another, the earth's environment will be restored, nations will lay down their arms and the wrongs of the world will be made well.

Christmastime begins on December 24 at sundown. In folk tradition, when the first star can be seen on Christmas Eve, Advent melts away and Christmas descends, according to the words of a carol, "like a radiant bride from heaven."

In medieval times, it was a village custom to toll funeral bells throughout the day on December 24; it was the death of Death. At midnight, pealing bells would announce the birth of Life.

Christmas is a paschal festival customarily kept with signs of Christ's passing over. In many places people take special delight in celebrating this time with traditions associated with Easter. Branches and flower bulbs are forced into bloom, grain is sown indoors to sprout, sweet breads and other rich foods are prepared, and bonfires and candles are lit to burn through the night.

In much of Europe, pots of red tulips and pink cyclamen are popular at Christmas. Perhaps you never thought of poinsettias as paschal images, but these blazing, tropical plants offer an almost defiant contrast to the winter cold.

The Christmas tree began as a custom for dispelling the darkness of the "Twelve Holy Nights" from Christmas to Epiphany. A shining tree of life seems a celebration of those gleeful words of the Easter *Exsultet,* "O happy fault, O necessary sin of Adam, that gained for us so great a Redeemer!"

The most popular Christmas custom is gift-giving. A few generations ago among many Roman Catholics, Epiphany was the gift-giving day. The custom was connected with the gospel of the magi. (Imagine how a return to this custom would change the "shape" of the season in our homes.)

Gift-giving has an ancient heritage. Pagan Romans exchanged gifts on New Year's Day. They also spent, ate and drank too much, and embarrassed themselves in celebration of the holiday. It sounds familiar.

Some of the early Christian bishops (Augustine, for one) thought that all of this excess was a good reason to greet the new year with a few days of fasting and penitential processions. But other bishops (Gregory of Nyssa, for one) didn't see the harm in celebrating the new year. Perhaps gift-giving could speak of the *sacrum commercium,* the "holy exchange," in which "the divine becomes human that humans might become divine." (Augustine himself had said this.) Perhaps the new year would bring us closer to the final epiphany, the day of the resurrection of all who have died.

In the year 567, the Council of Tours said that fasting is inappropriate between Christmas and Epiphany. January 1 could be as merry as the days that flank it.

Sometimes people say that Christians adapted pagan holidays, but they did more than that. They turned them inside out. The pagan Roman New Year was steeped in nostalgia, a word that once meant "homecoming." The evidence was plain enough to them: Time was a gradual slide into decay. Sensible people should yearn to go back to the good old days, to the "age of gold." That was where comfort would be found. (This too sounds familiar.)

But Christians in those days (who were far from sensible) looked to the future, to God's reign, to the days of the Messiah. True, there was inequity now, and suffering and illness and death, but, as the prophet Malachi wrote, the "sun of justice will arise with healing in its wings."

In Christ, the years are not circles that take us back to where we started. Time is a spiral, like Jacob's ladder, leading us to a vision of angels, rising ever upward into bright glory, rising to an endless festival of lights.

Overview

Christmastime begins after dark on Christmas Eve and lasts until the feast of the Baptism of the Lord, and it echoes in the liturgy until Candlemas, February 2, the feast of the Presentation of the Lord.

The season includes a string of days ranked as solemnities: the Birth of the Lord (December 25), Mary, the Mother of God (January 1) and the Epiphany of the Lord (January 6 or the nearest Sunday). There also are a number of feasts: Stephen (December 26), John (December 27), Holy Innocents (December 28), Holy Family (the Sunday between December 25 and January 1, or else December 30 if there is no Sunday between these days) and the Baptism of the Lord (the date varies). All of these have their own scriptures and perhaps some special customs (see page 243), but all of these are Christmas days. They share that in common, and the worship environment must make that clear.

Don't take decorations down until after the Baptism of the Lord—and that includes the nativity scene. However, you probably will need to spend time keeping decorations at their best. Large crowds on Christmas Day or bad weather might require extra housecleaning.

The decorations get put up before Christmas Eve, but the worship environment on the Fourth Sunday of Advent should keep the Advent mood. Schedule the times of decorating well enough in advance so that volunteers can plan their time for these busy days. See page 208 for some recommendations about what to do when Christmas Eve falls on the Fourth Sunday of Advent or soon after.

As an act of hospitality, perhaps you can arrange to leave the church open for visitors during the afternoons and evenings of the Sundays and solemnities of the season. Invite people to come visit the church with family and friends to enjoy the decorations and to visit the crèche, a home away from home.

Arrange to have security staff. Leave a tape of Christmas music playing. Leave entrances and vestibules lit, but subdue the lighting in other places and leave candles and Christmas lights burning if this can be done safely.

Set priorities for the Christmas worship environment and try to get certain things accomplished. Here's where you might begin:

1. Keep the area around the altar fairly simple. A beautiful and festive altar cloth may be all that is needed here.

2. Cluster flowers handsomely in a few locations in the church instead of putting all of them near the altar. (See page 239.)

3. Decorate the assembly's place (with pennants, swags of fabric, evergreen garlands or baskets of flowers, perhaps hung overhead rather than on walls).

4. Put special effort into the nativity scene. (See page 251.)

5. Decorate outdoors. (See page 242.)

At Christmas we can be hindered by past practice. Maybe the parish seems always to have banked poinsettias along a back wall, several ornamented trees have been used in a particular location, or some other form of decoration has been part of Christmas in the parish for many years. That alone is good reason to think twice before changing patterns.

In the past, many parishes seem to have put more effort into decorating the entire space—with garlands on the walls, the nativity scene on a side altar and even the choir loft receiving wreaths and garlands. But in more recent years (maybe because evergreens and flowers have become more and more expensive), it has become common to see decorations massed around the altar (where even the nativity scene gets placed).

It might be a return to an older tradition to focus instead on the other areas of the church rather than on the area around the ambo and altar.

Be prepared for criticism if changes are made in the regular ways of decorating for Christmas. A parish environment and art committee ordered pink and white poinsettias in place of their usual red. They wound up getting a lot of complaints (and plenty of compliments, too), even though all they changed from past years was the usual color.

What they had done, without intending it, was to invite comments on their taste. The usual red would have been accepted as typically Christmas, but pink was different enough to spark discussion. The committee decided for the next year to stay with what they had done. Why? The change back to red would have restarted the discussion of taste.

It's true that many Christmas decorations are too commonplace, even hackneyed—poinsettias, wreaths, trees, tiny white lights, and so on. They're in every mall in America. What can happen is that these otherwise beautiful things are seen in such profusion that they have a numbing effect. In church they may call to mind the store displays. And because the parish's budget and abilities are not likely to match the mall's, your efforts can come across as poor imitations of commercial decorations.

This is not to suggest eliminating these materials entirely. It would be downright peevish to skip using poinsettias or other familiar decorations. But there are other equally rich ways to decorate for Christmas, using different materials that also can become part of parish tradition.

One way to help keep Christmas visuals from being hackneyed is to expand the ordinary palette of colors. (That was the thinking behind using pink poinsettias instead of red ones.) Instead of the usual red, white, gold and green, perhaps other color schemes could be employed. Rich autumnal colors—plum, rust, gold and forest green—might look good in buildings with wooden interiors. Hot oranges, fuchsias and yellows can be perfect in buildings with tile and stone floors and walls.

Chrysanthemums

Azaleas

Kalanchoes

Amaryllises

What will not work, in any season, are materials that are too small or too busy or that block sightlines or hinder movement. What works in every season is respect for the past, respect for parish practice, and plenty of enthusiasm, creativity and good will.

In addition to poinsettias, Christmas flowers can include amaryllises, kalanchoes, azaleas, chrysanthemums (white varieties with frilled petals are reminiscent of snowflakes) and (forced) flowering spring bulbs such as tulips and narcissus. Cyclamens are wonderful winter flowers with marbled foliage; they come in an array of red, white and pink shades. Most of these flowers do best under cool conditions and are perfect in buildings where the thermostat is set to drop the temperature at night.

Northern Europeans use straw and wheat sheaves in abundance at Christmas. Straw has both a fine aroma and a lovely golden color. Customarily it's woven into garlands, stars and sunbursts. It can be used as "groundcover" around trees and potted flowers—wonderful for hiding pots or tree stands and for visually uniting several separate pots of flowers.

Wheat sheaves can be trimmed with pine boughs and berries and then hung high. They can look magnificent on their own or in the center of an evergreen wreath.

Americans are falling more and more in love with non-European expressions of the season—those from Africa, the Middle East and the Americas. Colored papers and foils can be turned into flowery festoons, lanterns and sheathes for processional poles. Because Christmas includes strong emphasis on the restoration of paradise and on the "grand finale" of the harvest season, fruits, nuts, seedpods and dried vegetables can be used generously.

The American Christmas celebration includes borrowings from many different cultures; often this results in delight and surprise, but at other times this mix gets bewildering, especially when it results in duplication of imagery—a star hanging over the crèche, a star on the top of a Christmas tree, a star-shaped piñata hanging in the vestibule.

It's best not to multiply symbols in the worship environment. One splendid Christmas tree (and not several) communicates that the tree is a powerful symbol and not merely a mood-setter. One fine, large wreath can speak of time and eternity. Of course, if the Advent wreath remains up through Christmastime, additional wreaths may be redundant. They might be pretty, even glorious, but they are duplications of a symbol.

Several trees together are an image of Eden if one tree receives the principal focus as the tree of life. Perhaps that tree is decorated with apples. See page 260 for more about this custom.

Also as a general rule, the nativity scene performs its function best in a shrine away from the liturgical action. A crèche does not belong under the altar or flanking the ambo. See page 251 for a discussion of the nativity scene and its place in the parish's celebration of Christmas.

If for years now the scene has been placed under the altar, a practice that began in many parishes about 20 years ago, it has in fact become part of parish custom. Altering the practice must be done carefully, respectfully and with humility, and only after discussion and catechesis. (The people who first started to put nativity scenes under altars also broke with tradition; we're inheriting a problem they began.)

Another consideration: Easter, not Christmas, is the church's principal festival. Will that be apparent to the eye? It can be, not because there are more lilies purchased than poinsettias but because the worship environment receives at least as much attention (and budgetary allowances) at Eastertime as it does at Christmas.

THE ASSEMBLY'S PLACE

Here is the premier place for evergreen garlands, fabric hangings, lights and other emblems of festivity. Materials must be large, elementary and beautiful. The effect needs to be warm, welcoming, bold and stately, but not busy and fussy or pompous and exaggerated. For a discussion of the use of evergreens and lights, see page 246.

Many typical Christmas decorations may not work well in this area: poinsettias are too fragile to use where they can be brushed against, evergreen wreaths and branches become brittle within a week of being hung and so need to be hung out of reach, and evergreen trees often are too wide for the assembly's area.

Because deciduous trees are wider at the top than at the bottom, they might be used among the people. Arrangements of evergreens, flowers and berried branches can be beautiful if hung in baskets on the walls. (Poinsettias are not attractive when viewed from below).

A canopy or tent is an important Christmas image for this part of the building. One can be constructed from evergreen garland or fabric strips. If the Advent wreath was hung in the center of the assembly, it can now form the center point of this canopy. See the discussion of this image, beginning on page 256.

ALTAR, AMBO AND CHAIR

Is the altar cloth beautiful? At Christmas, is the altar vesture especially full and flowing? Does the fabric appear handsome at a distance, and does its color complement the vestments?

The processional cross can be ornamented with a fine, double-faced evergreen wreath. Candlesticks can also be bunched with evergreens and flowers as long as this looks good from a distance and not just up close.

In most churches, the area around the altar is the most visible place to locate a large number of flowers, and so that's where they get put. The location may be visually effective, but unless there is ample room and the flowers are located several feet from the altar, putting flowers here may not be appropriate to the liturgy. Perhaps you can figure out an alternative location, one where the flowers can be appreciated but that does not hinder ritual movement or block sightlines.

Poinsettias, like lilies at Easter, usually come from the florist as separate plants. A parish orders a certain number and then arranges the plants into groupings. A lot of separate pots can look busy, even if the massed plants are beautiful.

Consider using large baskets or pots in which to put several plants each. Line the large containers with plastic, and add some shredded paper so that the plants sit at the right height. Plants at the periphery of the container may need to be tipped slightly outward.

A few containers with several plants each can be grouped together. For example, perhaps in one grouping there could be a large basket with five red poinsettias, a smaller one with three white poinsettias and a smaller one still with three pink cyclamen. Maybe in the middle, for height, is a pot of white branches (perhaps with small glass ornaments on them).

Vessels and Vesture

Christmastime, especially at its full flowering at Epiphany, calls forth our "brightest and best." And yet that can never come across as pompous or triumphalistic.

Christmastime can be a season for bringing into worship our most precious and exotic materials, if only to call to mind the gold, frankincense

and myrrh of the Magi. In your parish, perhaps the season seems best with shimmering, richly jeweled gold vessels. Perhaps the vestments are magnificently embroidered, expensive silk.

Christmas can also be a season to worship with clay or wicker vessels and with homespun fabrics, if only to call to mind the shepherds of Bethlehem to whom the birth of the Good Shepherd was announced. There is joy in making sure that the vessels and vesture of this season appear as the work of human hands, that their materials and the methods of their making are apparent to the eye and to the touch.

Whether made of gold or earthenware, worship materials cost money. Wasting money and resources is certainly offensive, but also offensive is the notion that miserliness reflects the gospel. The good news doesn't demand that we pretend to be poor but that we break down the barriers between rich and poor. If ethnic customs are any gauge, the poor know the value of flamboyance during festivals.

Communal celebration means the pooling of resources to enable those who live in everyday simplicity to share in festival abundance. Our fasting begets feasting. Perhaps we shouldn't judge the material things used at worship only by the amount of money spent but by the efforts invested by poor and rich alike, all made able to contribute their gifts and talents to one another.

White is the liturgical color of Christmastime. Gold vesture also can be used on festival days. It's fine if the parish has a set of vesture that is worn during both the Easter and the Christmas seasons. It's also fine if the parish has a special set just for Christmas. What would distinguish this set is not Christmas ornamentation but simply the fact that it was chosen and that it is to be used only at this season of the year because its colors and fabrics complement the other materials used at Christmas.

Of course, the Christmas set would also be fine to wear on the Presentation (February 2), St. Joseph's Day (March 19), the Annunciation (March 25), the Visitation of Mary and Elizabeth (May 31) and the Birth of St. John the Baptist (June 24).

FONT

In some churches Epiphany is a baptismal day: The baptism of Christ is one of the mysteries we celebrate at this festival. Baptismal water is blessed on this day in Byzantine churches. In past generations the Roman church blessed "Jordan water," which was used especially in the blessing of homes. There's no reason this custom can't be kept up.

A depiction of the baptism of Christ is fitting in the baptistry throughout the year but especially during Christmastime. For Epiphany and the feast of the Baptism (a continuation of Epiphany), perhaps the font could be surrounded with candles, flowers and even sea shells, and a well-crafted image of a dove can be suspended over the font—unless, of course, it's already part of baptistry art, in which case the Spirit-dove could be illuminated with lights or encircled by a wreath.

SHRINES

The Christmas crèche is a seasonal shrine; see the discussion beginning on page 251. In some churches, Mary's shrine is where the nativity scene goes—an appropriate site.

Mary's shrine deserves attention throughout this season. It can be a good place for icons or other art appropriate to each feast of Christmastime.

Blood-like red is a color associated with Mary at this time of year: Mary is a new Eve, whose name means "the mother of life."

In the Roman Catholic Church, January 1 is the solemnity of Mary the Mother of God. Perhaps a bowl of burning incense can be placed in her shrine at the beginning of worship this day. Pink rubrum lilies, sheaves of wheat, oats or corn, clusters of acorns and almonds, lady apples and pomegranates, bunches of herbs, and other signs of fecundity can be used, *della Robbia*-style, to adorn the image of the Blessed Mother.

SEASONAL CORNERS

Parish decorators could see to it that any such areas are kept clean and uncluttered. Here is the right spot for decorations that are richly detailed, for materials for people to interact with—by thumbing through a book of Christmas art, by smelling a bundle of winter-blooming eleagnus, by reading over a description of the charity that has received the donations to the toy drive.

The Bethlehem scene is also a kind of "seasonal corner." It is a place to visit before and after worship. That might be the right place to make Christmas wafers (optłatki) and calendars available or to offer Epiphany chalk, incense and Jordan water for the blessing of the home.

VESTIBULES, DOORWAYS, OUTDOORS

Make an effort to wait until the last few days of Advent before decorating outdoors for Christmas. At least wait until Christmas Eve before turning on the holiday lights. We have a liturgical witness to perform here.

Outdoor decorations for the Christmas season are difficult and even dangerous to put up when the weather gets bad. Below-freezing temperatures make evergreens and electrical wires brittle. It helps to untangle and stretch out these things in a room-temperature environment before carrying them out into the cold.

You might want to highlight the many feasts of the season by changing some elements of the outdoor decoration. For example, if there's an outdoor nativity scene, move the Magi around the parish property before bringing them to Bethlehem at Epiphany. Hang an illuminated star somewhere prominent at that time. Add a depiction of a dove to the scene at the Baptism of the Lord.

Is there an outdoor Marian shrine? This too requires seasonal attention. Perhaps it can be graced with torches, especially on the night of January 1.

Epiphany is the high point of the Christmas season. Some people think the day is the liturgical grand finale and an even grander beginning to the entire year. Three mysteries are celebrated—the adoration of the Magi, the baptism of Jesus in the Jordan and the wedding feast at Cana. It is a time for turning what was private, quiet and homey about Christmas into something public, boisterous and communal.

If only to make the world aware of the grandeur of this day, plan something extraordinary outdoors—a children's parade with lanterns and clouds of incense; or foil crowns, sea shells and water jars on poles with fluttering ribbons; or three snow-Magi surrounded be a sea of luminaries.

OTHER LOCATIONS

In small or big ways, the parish center, school, rectory and all other parish facilities would be kept decorated for Christmas until at least the Baptism of the Lord. That is a witness to the neighborhood of the holy season we are celebrating.

Students and teachers reassembling after Christmas break can benefit from returning to a building still shining with Christmas—although it may be necessary to remind everyone that it still is Christmastime.

The Epiphany blessing of the home (see page 263) might also be done in the school, in the parish center and certainly in the convent or rectory. Because Christmastime is a season for plays, parties and pageants, parish facilities may get a workout and might require some housecleaning and a refreshing of decorations.

SPECIAL OCCASIONS

The Christmas season is short. You won't have enough time to make major changes in the worship environment from day to day, and you shouldn't do that anyway.

Of course, if you have an image of one of the saints of the season (for example, Stephen, December 26, and Elizabeth Ann Seton, January 4), surround it with candles on his or her feast day. On the feast of the Holy Family, you already have a nativity scene. On the solemnity of Mary, Mother of God, you should have already given Mary's shrine extra attention for the season, but at least be sure candles are kept lit in the shrine for that day.

Epiphany, however, calls for something special. Church documents only rarely have anything to say about seasonal decoration, but for Epiphany the *Ceremonial of Bishops,* 240, specifies, "there will be a suitable and increased display of lights."

Figure out a good way to "increase" the lights; no doubt there are already plenty in evidence for the season. Perhaps for this day most every nook and cranny in church receives a votive light (which can be ordered from any church supply store). For safety's sake (glass votives crack on occasion), you might put each votive in a glass tumbler.

The usual way of increasing light in the liturgy is to give everyone a burning candle before the proclamation of the gospel. In some places Epiphany candles are, naturally enough, set to burn in star-shaped lanterns. These lanterns are made by many cultures, but Poles and Ukrainians have especially magnificent versions constructed out of wood and paper, which allows the candles to glow from within. At Christmas the Filipinos have wildly exuberant light sculptures called *faros,* which can be splendid indoors or out at Epiphany.

The feast of the Baptism of the Lord is a celebration of the most mystical of the three Epiphany mysteries. You'll notice that in the gospel accounts of the baptism, the Holy Spirit is identified as a dove. (The account of Pentecost, from Acts, speaks of fire and wind, not a dove, as signs of the Spirit.) That makes the dove a premier symbol for the Baptism of the Lord.

Sometimes we divorce this feast from Christmastime, at least in the way we think, if we regard Christmastime as "a season of the infant Jesus," which it is not.

The gospel accounts of the baptism speak strongly of the appearance of Christ in glory, of the incarnation of God in human flesh, of the union between heaven and earth. This is the same good news found in the accounts of the nativity. Christian poets speak of the similarities in these stories and of the unity of Christ's birth and baptism: If at Christmas we delight in seeing Jesus in his mother's lap, then today we rejoice in seeing Jesus embraced by his Father.

In the worship environment, emblems of the baptism of Christ (the dove, the waters of the Jordan, a sea shell, John the Baptist, the opening into heaven) have a place throughout the days of our Christmas celebration, just as Epiphany's star has a place throughout this time. There is another strong image we shouldn't forget: Lord Jesus (in another form of the name, "Joshua") leads us through the Jordan of baptism into a land flowing with milk and honey.

Evergreens and Lights

Green grows the holly, so does the ivy:
The God of life can never die.
"Hope," says the holly.

—sixteenth-century carol

PINE

FIR

SPRUCE

HEMLOCK

Nowadays we use evergreens for decoration only at Christmas, but in past generations, yew, boxwood, laurel, holly and ivy were used as "palms" on Palm Sunday; they were woven into victory wreaths and garlands for Easter; and they were planted in cemeteries as promises of resurrection. Their use at Christmas echoed Easter as signs of a life that is stronger than death.

If bare branches and trees were used during Advent, leave them in place for Christmastime but add evergreens, flowers and candles. The same is true if grapevines and arrangements of dried grasses were used during Advent. Simply add to these some pine boughs and berried branches.

Certain evergreens will not stay fresh indoors. If kept dry, holly quickly turns grayish and ugly, and if kept in water, it drops every leaf and berry. The only place holly looks good for a couple of weeks is in an unheated but not too frigid place.

Spruces and hemlock are species that drop every needle when they dry out. In much of the nation, the spruces are the easiest to grow of the evergreens and so are the most commonly available conifer in parishioners' yards. You can keep a freshly cut spruce tree in good condition in church if it is kept standing in water, but there's no way to keep cut branches fresh. Even in water they will drop every needle within a few weeks.

In contrast, pines and firs are relatively long-lasting, and even when they dry out, most species stay green. White pine and frasier fir are the longest-lasting and are available most everywhere.

If you've ever made your own wreath or garland from sprigs of greenery, you know how much work it is and also how many evergreen tips you need—a mountain of them. Be thankful that already-made wreaths and garlands are available. Happily, it has become easier and easier to find quality products.

In past years it was more likely that wild areas were being stripped of evergreens for Christmas—a terrible practice. "Princess pine," which is really a species of club moss, is still gathered from the wild, but most Christmas evergreens are grown on farms that are replenished.

Florists and tree lots probably are the most expensive sources for Christmas evergreens. Keep your eyes open: Garden centers and hardware stores may have fine materials for sale at good prices, as long as you shop early.

One problem is that we can't always depend on the supply from cheaper sources, and so we order evergreens months ahead of time from expensive sources. In general, it's often easy to find Christmas trees and wreaths in good condition discounted just before Christmas, but fresh garland is chancier. Supplies run out. (Evergreens will stay fresh for many weeks if kept in plastic in a chilly place out of direct sunlight.)

You can combine evergreens and fabrics in wonderful arrangements. A few days before Christmas, small evergreen wreaths can sometimes be purchased for next to nothing. They can be linked together using strips of fabric to form chains, an interesting image; a cluster of three or five small wreaths can be hung from the ceiling with varying lengths of fabric; or a wreath can be placed near the ceiling and a long swag of cloth or garland festooned from it.

Think big. A common mistake is to use materials that are much too small for the space. Another mistake is to add ornamentation to evergreens that detracts from the simple beauty of the greenery. See if something "reads" well at a distance, and also check if ornamentation, even a bow, really adds anything to the decoration.

That's not to say that everything should be as plain as possible or that bows and sparkling ornaments are always inappropriate. It's just that it is hard to use these things elegantly; it's usually most effective to keep things elemental and natural.

Real evergreens are much easier to use than fake ones. To look decent, fake garlands or trees require every branch tip to be fluffed out, a tremendously time-consuming task. Also, they lack that great aroma and are almost as messy as real ones; both require a thorough cleaning after they are put up and after they are taken down. Anyway, worship is no place for anything artificial.

It's especially hard to use Christmas lights in church. There are ways to use them well but even more ways to use them poorly. The worship environment is almost always better served by candles. A constellation of flickering votive candles—perhaps lining a beam or clustered in a corner—is a lot more magical and unexpected than electric lights.

If you use Christmas lights, use enough. The eye tends to "connect the dots" in a string of lights, so if you want the lights to appear randomly arranged, you will need to spiral them loosely around a garland or wreath and not stretch them tightly through it.

Electrical outlets, especially outdoor ones, should have ground-fault indicator outlets that cut off power instantly if there's a short. (These aren't expensive.) Electrical timers for outdoor outlets cost about $20.00. It's not a good idea to leave lit Christmas lights unattended indoors. Outdoors, use waterproof tape on plugs and on exposed outlets (or stick them into plastic sandwich bags and then seal the bags with tape). It's also good to tape over electrical connections within reach of worshipers.

With miniature sets, be sure no more than six 35- or 50-light sets (or three 100-light sets) are plugged together; otherwise you might overload the fuses built into the plugs. With ordinary C9 Christmas lights (the old-fashioned, large lights), don't plug more than 50 lights together. Again, you may blow the fuse in the plug.

It's usually more attractive to use all one size of lights rather than mixing tiny ones and large ones. The effect of tiny white lights is magical to some, cold to others. Different brands of miniature lights come in all sorts of degrees of brightness. Sometimes that's indicated on the box, sometimes not. Mixing regular lights with "super brights" will give an uneven effect, which you can avoid if all the light sets are of the same brand. Outdoors, the old-fashioned-style large, colored bulbs can be merry and yet tasteful, especially in combination with evergreen garland.

When putting strings of lights on a tree, it's best to begin near the trunk, come out along one branch to the tip, go back to the trunk along the same branch, come out to the tip along another branch, go back to the trunk, and so on. Try to get lights to the very tips of the branches, and begin at the top.

With tiny lights, work with lit strings (and in dry conditions!). That way, if the string flickers or goes out, you can more easily find the problem. (It's not a bad idea to wear rubber gloves when doing this work.) With larger lights, to avoid cracking the glass or breaking the filaments, screw in the bulbs after you have finished arranging the strings. Plug them in only after you have finished screwing in all the bulbs.

The Nativity Scene

> They come into the stable,
> the furred and feathered,
> As they once boarded the ark,
> a place of safety,
> Only tonight they have entered
> into paradise.
> —from a Silesian carol

St. Francis of Assisi arranged to have Christmas Mass celebrated in a stable, among barnyard animals. Most people, then as now, did not think that animals were proper companions at worship.

Francis's motive was compelling. At the time, Muslims and Christians were killing each other in battles over the ownership of the Holy Land. This slaughter disgusted Francis. In worshiping in a stable, he was saying that any place can be Bethlehem. Every place is sacred. All the earth is holy ground.

There are Christmas customs for turning living quarters and churches into stables. Some people on Christmas Eve spread their floors with straw. Animals are given high honors, and chief among these is abstinence from eating meat. In some places, animals are welcomed into churches this night—imagine that. A favorite bit of folklore is that animals kneel and sing praises at midnight on Christmas Eve, and that they do so again at midnight on Epiphany, as the Twelve Days depart, so that "heaven and nature sing."

There is in the Christmas festival a great longing for the world to be set right, for creation to be made new again, for the earth itself, in Isaiah's words, to give birth to justice.

In a traditional nativity scene, the birth of Christ is shown to occur not years ago but now. It seems that no matter who fashions it—the Pennsylvania Deutsch, Hondurans, Neapolitans, Catalonians, Poles, Filipinos—a nativity scene is a depiction of its creator's own community.

In some scenes, just about everyone in town is represented in miniature. This has a chastening effect: The scenes offer gentle (and sometimes harsh) criticism or parody of the goings-on among people, especially the leaders.

Sometimes other scriptural characters are included in the scene (in contemporary dress): Eve and Adam (and the snake, too), Noah and his ark full of animals, the twelve sons of Jacob and the twelve prophets walking arm-in-arm with the twelve apostles. But human beings aren't the only ones there; any creature might be shown making a pilgrimage to meet God face to face.

What is clear is that creation is being restored to the goodness it had in the beginning. The cosmos is being set free from separation (the meaning of the word "sin") so that angels, humans, animals and even inanimate things are in communion. Here is an image for our times!

A star-topped Christmas tree may be used as a perch for representations of all sorts of critters. The tree arches over the nativity scene, which makes it clear what the scene is meant to reveal—a homecoming in paradise.

A traditional nativity scene is not and never has been an attempt to depict a gospel event. Nativity scenes combine Matthew's star and astrologers with Luke's angels, shepherds and manger. To the gospels are added a host of other scriptural allusions, most commonly Isaiah 1:3, "The ox knows its owner, and the donkey its master's manger." (The gospels themselves tell us nothing about an ox and an ass.)

Matthew tells us that a "star stopped over the place where the child was." In many old nativity scenes the star is shown not in the sky but sparkling inches from the head of Christ. That's not so preposterous if you imagine stars to be points of light, as ancient peoples did. That's what the gospel writer imagined—a star that came down from the heavens to give witness to Christ.

In several traditions, strong reminders of the baptism of the Lord get blended into the nativity scene. Perhaps Mary is washing diapers in the river Jordan, or a dove is descending on the newborn child, or John the Baptist—as a child or as an adult—is pointing toward Christ and to a lamb nuzzling the child.

Put effort into the parish nativity scene. It can be far more than just a gathering of statuary, but it needs space to spread out.

A nativity scene doesn't belong around the altar. It isn't part of public worship. In fact, the 1989 *Book of Blessings,* the ritual book that contains the order of blessing for the crèche, says that *if* the scene is set up in church, it *must not* be placed in the sanctuary (#1544). If your building has a spot that can be visited by parishioners before and after worship, that's perfect.

What will not work is a mediocre Bethlehem scene in an out-of-the-way location. You've got to make it worth visiting. Something else that doesn't work is putting the scene in an area that gets too much traffic or is not appropriately reverent. If this is the first few years that you are putting the scene in a new location, then be sure to advertise it well.

You might be lucky enough to have beautiful nativity figures along with a handsome stable. Get around to any needed repair while there's still time to do it. At the very least, be sure the figures are clean.

Well-made crèche figures can require a considerable investment. Their facial features should not be exaggerated or juvenile; figures of angels and shepherds that appear to be of different ages, genders and races are traditional. Especially lovely are figures of the elderly.

If you do not have fine figures, make it a year-round priority to acquire them. Interestingly, some of the greatest old cathedrals have homespun nativity scenes—the figures may have been fashioned by parishioners from papier maché or even from cardboard. However, often the faces are exquisitely painted and the other elements surrounding the figures are lavishly detailed.

Perhaps all you need, besides the figures, is an abundance of straw and flowers. (Don't be parsimonious with them.) You may be able to purchase straw bales at horse farms and at racetracks. Before you buy, be sure the straw is in good condition. Bales should be totally dry. A bale left out in the rain is ruined—it will mildew and may even begin to ferment—a fire hazard. Be warned: Mice love to make nests in straw.

Instead of placing poinsettias near the crèche, consider using some of the more unusual, more delicate potted flowers. Small kalanchoes seem perfectly suited to being nestled in straw. Spring flowers—the kinds usually associated with Easter—are glorious in a nativity scene. Order them from the florist or raise your own. At this time of year, if cut and placed indoors in fresh water, forsythia or quince branches can be forced into bloom in about a month. Paperwhite narcissus bulbs will bloom in about three weeks.

A stable can be constructed from wood or from logs with the bark still on. Walls of reed matting or grasscloth can be attached to a frame of branches. A carpenter might construct a more elaborate stable, perhaps using a wooden folk design as a model. Examples of classic folk buildings are Bantu huts, Native American lodges and Norwegian meeting houses.

To the walls of the stable you can festoon pine garland, strung cranberries, clusters of crabapples and dried flowers.

Perhaps more ambitiously, a replica of your town could be put together, with the stable set in the middle of the town. Or, you might surround the stable with a backdrop with images from your community. (Traditional scenes keep getting more elaborate each year as new materials are added.)

One parish created a lovely collage of hundreds of photos of parishioners to use as the backdrop for the nativity scene; the photos were arranged against a velvet blue curtain studded with silver stars.

A woodland scene can have great appeal as an emblem of paradise and of the healing of our damaged environment. You might tier the scene so that higher levels are in the back and lower ones are in the front. Then "landscape" the scene with bare branches, clusters of berried branches, and small and large evergreen trees of different species.

These will have to be arranged with the same eye as in landscaping a naturalistic garden, asymmetrically. Begin with large materials and then

gradually add the smaller elements. Begin in the back and work toward the front. Don't add tiny white lights or anything else artificial.

Some details to include are moss, dried fern fronds or small live ferns arranged in a group, bracken fungi, mushrooms, a bird's nest and a tracery of bittersweet vines "growing" up a tree. (Pennsylvania Deutsch nativity

scenes, in common with their German predecessors, often use thick carpets of living moss lifted from the woods and placed on waterproof sheeting; the moss must be misted each day.)

You can add all sorts of representations of animals and birds if these also are lifelike and not sentimental or weird. Unless the scale of the various figures is grotesquely disproportionate, the eye is forgiving of discrepancies in scale among the figures.

When you're nearly finished, add to the crèche any potted flowers, and add a few individual flowers in water-pics near the feet of some of the figures.

In thanksgiving for the harvest, also fitting would be piles of gourds and pinecones, *ristras* of peppers or herbs, a straw wreath studded with straw flowers, a great cluster of pampas grass or phragmites, thistleheads, a cornucopia filled with fruits and vegetables, wheat sheaves and even a bundle of corn stalks with the ears partly stripped back to reveal the golden corn.

(Beginning on page 256 is a discussion of the Bethlehem scene as a "harvest home," a biblical image of the incarnation.)

In some parts of Central and South America and Europe, the nativity scene is left up from Christmas until Candlemas. The nativity scene helps establish a connection between Christmas and Candlemas. (And this is not so outlandish, considering that the nativity scene is placed in its own out-of-the-way shrine.) In the reformed calendar the connection between these days is still there, of course, even in the old custom of keeping the same Marian antiphon, *Alma Redemptoris Mater,* at Night Prayer throughout the time from Advent until Candlemas Eve.

If the nativity scene is understood as part of the Christmastime worship environment, then of course it is disassembled after the feast of the Baptism of the Lord, when the Christmas season ends. However, if the scene is instead a shrine to visit, as it should be, in a place somewhat apart from public liturgy, then it can remain until Candlemas.

A lovely Candlemas tradition is to surround the image of the infant Christ with spring flowers. They set the heart yearning for the days to come— Lent, the Triduum and Eastertime.

The Tent

In the birth of Christ, our tents, so easily knocked over by death, are raised up again by the One who first built them in the beginning. For how does our Creator arrive? Not in a great boat or flaming chariot but in a frail tent of human flesh, born of Mary.

Let us welcome Christ with green branches while we sing, "Blessed is the one who comes in the name of the Lord!"

—Gregory of Nyssa †395

Christmas has a privileged place in the course of the agricultural year: The harvest is completed. If the harvest has been good, larders are now as full as they will get.

Christmas is a harvest festival, an act of thanksgiving for what is past and of hope for what is to come. Think about this when you slice into a fruit-cake or a minced pie. These are Christmas foods that seem to gather in one dish the bounty of the harvest. Bethlehem scenes also were gathering places for signs of the abundance of the earth. All of that, in representation, was placed before the image of the newborn Christ.

Luke tells us that Mary placed her newborn son "in a manger, because there was no place for them in the inn." Luke says no more than "manger," a trough where animals feed, but Christian imaginations have embroidered the scene to depict the manger in a setting in which mangers are likely to be found—in a stable or cave.

Eastern Christians most often portray the manger in a cave, a reminder of the tomb and a sign that Christ has come to bring the dead to life. Among Western Christians, the manger most often is imagined to be in a rickety stable. The stable calls to mind a "harvest home," the tents of natural materials built by harvesters so that they could live in their fields at harvest time.

These tents have rich, biblical significance, too rich to do them justice in a few words. A harvest tent is a symbol of creation. The tent is frail as a sign of mortality. In Hebrew it is called a *sukkah* in the singular and *sukkot* in the plural. Sukkot is the name of the Jewish autumn festival of the ingathering of the harvest.

For the festival of Sukkot, many families build a harvest tent in their backyard. It's decorated with fruits and flowers, and the roof is left partially open so that the sun, moon and stars can be seen. And everyone, including the dead, are invited to enter.

Psalm 118 is sung, with its many cries of "Hosanna," and green branches are waved to herald the end of days, when the living and the dead will stand before their Judge.

In the days of the Exodus, God dwelled in a tent to keep company with the people on their way to the Promised Land. But even after Solomon built God a stone Temple, the holy of holies inside the Temple was a frail tent. In Jewish folklore, at the end of time the Messiah will slaughter the sea beast Leviathan, death itself. The Messiah will sit us down to a "feast of roast beast" and turn its scaly skin into a tent of peace to encircle the world.

In the prologue to John's gospel, in the passage we translate, "the Word became flesh and lived among us," the word "lived" is a translation of the Greek *eskinosen,* which literally means "pitched tent." John's gospel borrows a symbol from the festival of Sukkot to describe the incarnation: God pitches a tent of mortal flesh to live among us.

That is what we can be fashioning when we construct a Christmas stable. We are building a *sukkah,* a frail tent, a harvest home, where all the world is welcome to the banquet of the Messiah.

Another way to employ the image of the tent in the worship environment is to build a canopy over the assembly. Several strands of evergreen garland can be attached to a single point in the ceiling; then each strand is drawn to a separate corner of the room.

Strips of fabric, which will much more readily be recognized as a tent, can be used in place of garland. (It's not good to use mixed colors of fabric for these strips, because the effect can be that of a circus tent!)

If the Advent wreath was hung over the assembly, it can form the center point of the canopy. This arrangement is magnificent. Depending on the height of the ceiling, it may be necessary to remove the candles of the wreath and to raise it very high.

An amazing, strange custom from Finland is to pleat wheat sheaves into a large canopy. The canopy is either hung from the ceiling or stood on poles. From it are hung a multitude of stars fashioned out of straw or silver paper. The construction is called "heaven."

This kind of arbor or trellis of all natural materials may have a fitting spot over the altar or, better, over the ambo, where it would form a tent pitched over the proclamation of the word.

A Christmas canopy is one of those primordial symbols that may be unfamiliar but that has a venerable history. Sometimes it's best to let such symbols speak for themselves rather than to try to explain them too much. As with anything (such as the Advent wreath or Christmas tree), it must be large enough to fit the scale of the room and it cannot hinder movement. The materials used in its construction must be simple and beautiful.

Perhaps this symbol of the tent is included in the construction of the Bethlehem scene. Perhaps it is reflected in the arrangement of the decoration over the assembly's seating. Perhaps it becomes a canopy over the ambo. You may very well find this image worth returning year after year.

The Christmas Tree

The mountains and the hills before you
    shall burst into song,
and all the trees of the field
    shall clap their hands.
– Isaiah 55:12

Christians in times past created all sorts of contrivances for holding candles for use in festive celebrations, not just for Christmas but for other occasions as well. There were spinning wooden towers, suspended chandeliers, and fantastic forms that either hung from a ceiling or were fastened to a table. (The Advent wreath is one of these customs.)

In some places, Christians also developed the custom of the paradise tree: A small tree or large branch was hung with fruits and foods; the edibles would be off limits for a while until it was time to taste the "forbidden fruit." The ceremony was a way to celebrate Christ, who has brought us back to Eden's garden.

Paradise trees were used at weddings, at births, at Mardi Gras or at Midsummer. Sometimes they were carried from door to door. The maypole is a variant of this custom—the ribbons often were festooned with food. To this day, the fantastic "palm trees" carried on Palm Sunday in many central European and Central American towns are hung with pretzels, eggs or other treats to be eaten at Easter.

Christmas was a favorite day for a paradise tree, especially because December 24 was the feast of Saints Adam and Eve. In Sweden the tree must remain untouched until January 13, the old octave day of Epiphany; then its fruits, cookies and candies are stripped and eaten in a ritual called "plundertime."

Years ago it was more common to use tree-shaped frames that held evergreens than to have whole trees—probably because ordinary folks had no easy access to trees and probably because getting a tree to stand up indoors can be difficult without the right equipment. (Is this the year to get a better tree stand?)

The custom of creating a great burst of light to welcome Christ got blended into the custom of the paradise tree. Some Italian households have a candle pyramid called a *ceppo*—from *presepio,* "manger"—to hold the nativity scene. Germans continue to use candles to illuminate their trees; not only are candles tremendously beautiful, warm and bright, the lighting of the tree is then a ceremony, not the flick of a switch, and the tree, out of necessity, must be watched carefully while it is lit.

Because of the meaning of the Christmas tree, it doesn't make sense to set up two or more. It's true that Christmas trees in quantity can be beautiful, but beauty is not the sole purpose of a Christmas tree.

If it has already become your custom to use several evergreen trees in the worship space, perhaps only one is the "Christmas tree" and the others are left undecorated as its companions in paradise.

In your "Eden," instead of using trees of all the same size and variety, different species of conifers and leafless deciduous trees of different heights might look wonderful together. An asymmetrical arrangement works well in some buildings, but some churches seem to demand symmetry—if something's on the right, the same thing belongs on the left. But that still isn't a compelling reason to decorate two (or four, or six) Christmas trees.

How can the parish tree be used in a ritual way? In a home the tree is used ritually by being set up and decorated, by gifts being opened around it and by it's being lit each evening. And in some homes the tree is a place for prayer, song and even dancing each evening of the season.

The parish tree also deserves to be blessed (see the *Book of Blessings*), to be lit each evening, to become a part of the way we worship. Perhaps it is the centerpiece during the lamp-lighting at Evening Prayer. Perhaps on Christmas Eve it is lit during the course of the Christmas vigil. If you lit the Advent wreath as part of the entrance rites at Mass, why not light the tree at that time during the Christmas season? Jesus Christ is the light of the world: A light no darkness can overpower!

A Christmas tree isn't essential in the worship environment. In fact, it may even be inappropriate in some buildings if the only place it will fit will block sightlines.

Even though a tree isn't necessary to liturgy, there are few things as wonderful or as fragrant as a beautiful conifer. It brings with it a royal and holy presence that seems to embody the whole of creation.

There can be big differences among tree species as to how well they last indoors and how easy they are to work with. In general, spruces (which have short, sharp needles) are hard to handle and the needles drop when the tree dries. Firs (with short but soft needles) and pines (with long needles) are easier to handle and hold their needles well. Any tree, if it was cut too soon before it was sold, cannot be recuperated.

No matter what species you use, within minutes before standing the tree in water be sure to cut a few inches off the bottom of the trunk. (A cut quickly clogs with resin if exposed to air.) If there has to be a short delay between its being cut and its being stood in water, wrap the cut in foil to keep it from drying.

Unless the cut is perpendicular to the trunk, the tree may tend to topple in its stand. Play devil's advocate after the tree is stood in its stand and shake the tree a bit; if it's easy to push over, a crooked cut may be the problem— or the stand may be too small or too flimsy.

A frozen tree can take several hours to thaw completely. And as it thaws it tends to loosen in its stand, so you may need to tighten any screws after the tree defrosts.

Ornamenting a Christmas tree has the potential for trivializing or obscuring its natural beauty. Even something as simple as white electric lights can disfigure the tree with electric wires. It's easy to understand why some people think candles are the only way to illuminate a tree. It's also easy to understand why some people decide to leave the tree bare rather than risk spoiling it.

Bright red apples (with stems) are wonderful and simple adornments for a paradise tree. Although Genesis does not tell us the species of the tree of knowledge, the apple got the blame because, in Latin, *malus* is "apple" and *malum* is "evil." You may want to use apples, and that's all, to make clear the significance of the tree, but other traditional ornaments are oranges (which long have been symbols of the sun) and straw stars, a handsome folk custom. Straw itself makes a traditional and beautiful carpet underneath a tree (to catch the sap and the wax drippings).

The tree of paradise is a resting place for creation. Everything has a home among its branches. Perhaps that is why old-fashioned ornaments included just about every animal and vegetable and fruit, as well as every "work of human hands."

Some parishes ornament their tree very creatively—with photos of parishioners and with ornaments hand-crafted by most every household, by parish schoolchildren, by seniors or by anyone and everyone. If a parish Christmas tree is to be wonderfully complicated, it may need to be placed somewhere it can be appreciated close at hand, such as in a shrine, in the vestibule or even in the parish center.

The Mystical Marriage

Today the Bridegroom claims his bride, the Church,
    since Christ has washed her sins away
        in Jordan's waters.
Today the Magi hasten with their gifts to the royal wedding.
Today the wedding guests rejoice,
    for Christ has changed water into wine.

– from Morning Prayer for Epiphany

The gospels identify Jesus as the bridegroom and the church as the bride. John the Baptist is the best man, the witness to the wedding between heaven and earth. Jesus often compares God's reign to a wedding, but the parables are not all sweetness and delight: Without the right garment, we run the risk of getting tossed out of the festivities.

In Jewish folklore God's Wisdom is called a bride, as are the Sabbath day and the scriptures, so strong is the people's affection for them. Creation is like a wedding garment that surrounds the bride and groom.

Christian poets have seen in the baptism of Jesus a strong nuptial image. The Spirit-dove is wedded to the Father. In Jordan's waters—an image of creation's womb—their beloved child is born.

Poets also have spoken of the many days of the Christmas festival as a marriage. Advent is the courtship and Christmas is the exchange of vows. Epiphany is the wedding feast and Candlemas is the wedding night. An antiphon for the procession with candles was composed with this imagery in mind: "Zion, adorn the bridal bower!"

Where is this mystical marriage seen in seasonal decorations and rituals? It's just about everywhere, except it's never explicit and always enigmatic. The image is woven through the season like a theme song.

Christmastime's white vesture is like a bridal gown. We may be familiar with the Jewish wedding custom of the *hupah,* the canopy held over the couple as an emblem of their new household. Christians also have used this primordial symbol, and at this season it is often reflected in depictions of the nativity stable, which is like an old-fashioned canopy.

Holly, ivy, rosemary and mistletoe are plants associated with love and remembrance; they're customary in bridal bouquets and in Yuletide decorations. Grains, fruits, festive cakes, ornamented trees and other signs of fecundity have a long tradition of use at weddings as well as at Christmas.

Circular symbols are ancient tokens common to marriages and to Christmas. Crowns are an important part of the wedding ritual among Eastern Christians. Every Christian marriage can be a reflection of the bond of love and fidelity between Christ and the church. Of course, crowns and rings are royal images; they speak of dignity, responsibility, fidelity and eternity. But they also establish a fundamental equality among those who are crowned.

An evergreen wreath is a leafy crown, in Greek, *stephanos* (which happens to be the name of the first saint of Christmastime, the martyr Stephen). To past generations, wreaths called to mind athletes, heroes and graduates, as well as newlyweds and even corpses. Wreaths were used especially at weddings, at funerals, at the turning of the year and at other of life's "passovers" —the times we celebrate time itself.

It can be difficult today to muster enthusiasm for wedding imagery. Calling Christ the groom and the church his bride might suggest that men are dominant over women, as the Letter to the Ephesians asserts. But that isn't necessarily all that wedding imagery implies, nor is it the dominant theme in the scriptures.

To be married to God can mean something that takes our breath away— that somehow we are partners, that the relationship requires continued faithfulness and love, that our embrace gives birth to Christ.

Another paschal image common to weddings and to Christmas is the threshold. In Latin, doorway is *janua.* "January" means "month of entrances and exits." The Romans personified the new year as Janus, a fellow with two faces, one to look forward and one to look back.

Psalm 24 ("Lift up, O gates, your lintels") is one of the royal psalms the church sings often at this time of year. Parish doorways deserve extra attention at Christmastime. Most of the traditional ways of adorning our "lintels" can be wonderful, but especially in winter something more is necessary: Doorways must be kept safe, swept and perhaps salted, and certainly well lighted. All of that is the task of janitors working hand-in-hand with parish decorators.

It's a grand custom to bless doorways at Epiphany, perhaps because of the hospitality of the Holy Family toward the Magi (and vice versa), perhaps because doorways are symbols of the new year, and perhaps because an open doorway is a sign of the coming of Christ.

In many parishes at Epiphany, chalk, water and incense are blessed and distributed for people to take home for blessing their front doors. The chalk is used to write over the door:

19   +C   +M   +B   96

The C, M and B stand for the legendary names of the Magi—Caspar, Melchior and Balthasar. The numerals are those of the new year.

In some parishes, at the end of the Epiphany Mass the magi arrive with as much pomp and circumstance as possible. They write their own initials to bless the front doors of the church, and then after the liturgy they help distribute the chalk, water and incense. (It's not too expensive to order through a supermarket a large quantity of sealable containers for this "Jordan water.")

A grand Epiphany custom is the announcement of the date of Easter for the new year. (This custom is mentioned in the *Ceremonial of Bishops,* and the text is part of LTP's annual *Sourcebook for Sundays and Seasons.*) Epiphany is also the perfect occasion for the blessing and distribution of parish calendars.

Environment and art ministers will likely be the folks responsible for assembling any physical requirements for handing out chalk, water and calendars, for robing and crowning the magi (with wise women among the wise men) and for making sure the day appears to be the brightest and best of the days of Christmas, shining with gold and fragrant with frankincense and myrrh.

Winter Ordinary Time

A Sense of the Season

The winter weeks of Ordinary Time last from the day after the feast of the Baptism of the Lord (when Christmastime ends) until the Tuesday before Ash Wednesday (when Lent begins). The time between the Christmas season and Lent can vary from one to two months long, depending on when Ash Wednesday falls.

Keep in mind that Ordinary Time isn't a church season; it's a term used to describe the days in between the seasons. We use this term to help us organize our liturgical books so that we know which scriptures to read and which prayers to pray. Lent, Eastertime and the other liturgical seasons are rich in mystical significance; during the seasons the church is summoned to do certain things, to orient itself in certain ways. But Ordinary Time is not a season, and there's no point in searching for significance where none is intended.

The Christian imagination wouldn't be able to sink its teeth into Ordinary Time, but there's plenty to digest in the imagery of the Lord's Day, in the feast days and in the individual days with their scriptures, psalms and prayers. Winter itself gives us food for the imagination, and so does Carnival, a period concurrent with winter Ordinary Time.

On winter Sundays we begin to read from the year's gospel. These passages from the beginning of Matthew, Mark or Luke give winter Ordinary Time a definite "atmosphere" much the same way that November receives its atmosphere mostly from the end-of-the-world scripture passages of those weeks, when we conclude our reading of the year's gospel.

Christmas and Epiphany, at the turning of the year, are rich in gospel "beginnings": Matthew's story of the visit of the Magi, Mark's account of the baptism of Jesus, Luke's stories of Jesus' annunciation and birth, John's prologue ("In the beginning was the Word . . .") and the story of the wedding at Cana.

In winter Ordinary Time we continue these beginnings, and we quickly come upon harsh and challenging words: John and Jesus appear on the scene with demands that come close to the heart of the gospels: "Reform your lives. The reign of God is at hand."

There are scripture passages on these winter Sundays that seem to spring from Epiphany: "The people who walked in darkness have seen a great light." "The world as we know it is passing away." "Before I formed you in the womb, I knew you." "Jesus appeared in Galilee, proclaiming God's good news." "Is not this Joseph's son?" "The light shall rise for you in the darkness." "You are the light of the world."

At the same time, there are important and powerful Lenten images during these winter weeks: "Forty days more and Nineveh will be destroyed." "Seek justice; seek humility." "Share your bread with the hungry; shelter the oppressed and the homeless." "Is not our life on earth a drudgery?" "Here I am. Send me." "Your sins are forgiven."

These are words for people in need of sustenance and hospitality, for those suffering from winter blues, for catechumens and for those working to strengthen their relationship with the church.

Looking back to Epiphany and looking forward to Lent: This doublefold imagery is a strong component of the brightest feast of this part of year, February 2, the Presentation of the Lord. This day is also called Candlemas. Turn to page 275 for more about this feast of lights.

In the old days, there was a liturgical pattern to winter that would have been helpful to the imaginations of parish decorators. From Christmas to Candlemas, the images of Epiphany dominated. From Candlemas to Mardi Gras, the Lenten images came into focus.

These two periods were never tightly defined (mainly because Easter's date and the days that rely on Easter change from year to year), and that loose definition can be helpful to us in our own day. Perhaps the worship environment can show some kind of transition and refocusing throughout winter Ordinary Time, with Candlemas as a kind of "hinge."

Overview

Many people find wintertime a productive and busy season. Parish life is usually in full swing, and in addition to regular programs and meetings, there can be almost an overdose of social activities and fundraisers (but better now than during Lent, when they would interrupt the season).

This is probably the hardest time of year for parish decorators. We're often exhausted from Christmas, and much of the energy we can muster will need to be directed to preparations for Lent and the Triduum. Although the word "ordinary" in Ordinary Time means "counted," not "plain," we probably welcome a few weeks of plainness during winter.

On the one hand, it's wise to establish a mostly simple treatment of the worship environment during these "counted" weeks of the year. On the other hand, this busy span of winter weeks seems to call for something more than what's fitting during the lazy days of summer.

But where are we supposed to find the time to prepare the decorations that go up when the Christmas decorations come down? December is preoccupied and so is November. It seems that decorations for January need to be organized months ahead of time if they're going to happen at all. No wonder that even in parishes that wisely put energy into advance planning of the seasons, Ordinary Time can get lost.

Customarily the church keeps the days between Christmas and Lent with a merry heart. It's Carnival time. However, simply removing Christmas decorations will leave the worship space plain. This stripping can make it appear that we're jumping the gun on Lent. Plainness isn't the problem; the problem is contrast. In August, for instance, the church might be dressed appropriately with a splendid bouquet of sunflowers. But in the weeks after Christmas, a single arrangement, no matter how grand, can appear gloomy compared to the Yuletide exuberance.

For winter, perhaps the church could receive seasonal ornamentation akin to the amount it received in November. For instance, perhaps in November in certain sites there were autumnal colored hangings and a gathering of dried grasses, chrysanthemums and harvest produce. So now in January there would be wintry-looking hangings (perhaps in shades of whites, blues and silvers) and a return of November's dried grasses along with branches of blooming filbert and a few pots of white cyclamen.

We might be able to reuse some of the materials used during autumn and in Advent. One reflection of the season may be found in the shade of green used in the vesture of Ordinary Time. Perhaps winter's color is a dark, forest green or a deep olive combined with brown, gold, russet, gray or silver.

In the Deep South, because this is the time of the budding of trees and the first flush of growth, winter's vesture might be a pastel green highlighted with other pastels.

It's a challenge to keep wintertime expressions honest to what is going on in our own neighborhood, whether in South Dakota or South Carolina. As always, keep these expressions conformed to the needs of the liturgy and to the scale of their location.

The usual materials that speak to us of winter—pine, birch and brightly berried holly—can seem more like emblems of lazy housekeeping than expressions of the season, as if we neglected to take down the Christmas finery. But don't let this keep you from using wintry materials in the worship environment.

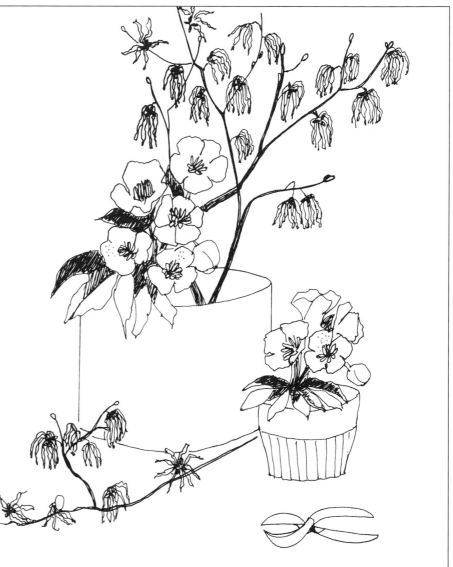

It helps if we avoid hackneyed materials, such as spray-painted white branches, and also if we avoid the color red, even for red berries, which are beautiful but can speak too loudly of Christmas. It also helps now in Ordinary Time, and back in Christmastime, too, if we make use of a wide range of seasonal materials—which means keeping an open eye to the natural world around us.

At this time of year, many of the usual florist flowers, such as gladioluses, are out of place. Instead, why not use an arrangement of winter-blooming plants, such as witchhazel and hellebores mixed with branches of broadleaf and coniferous evergreens? (Maybe you never noticed that winter can be so lively.) As in late autumn, brown grasses and dried flowers have seasonal appropriateness. For January we might leave out the oranges and yellows and focus instead on the earthtones and russets.

If you've never taken a good, long look at the winter appearance of plants, you're missing out on much subtle beauty. Cherry, birch and aspen, as well

as some maples, euonymus, gums and many others, can have splendid bark, perhaps brightly colored, exfoliating or corky. Some branches have fat buds that can communicate anticipation and potential.

What do we do with leftover poinsettias? Judging from most parishes, the plants remain in church to deteriorate until Lent. Is it inappropriate to leave poinsettias in church after Christmastime? Yes and no. Many varieties stay in good shape for months (especially if they're kept near a window), and it seems wasteful to get rid of such expensive plants. But why take down other Christmas decorations only to leave up the poinsettias, often the most vibrant signs of the season?

Maybe for Ordinary Time the poinsettias could be arranged less dominantly in the worship space. Or maybe the white ones would stay but the red ones would be removed. Maybe they could remain until Candlemas and then be thrown out. (That's perhaps the best plan.) And perhaps next year the parish could buy a few less and use the money for other decorations to use during these weeks of Ordinary Time.

For generations, human beings have taken delight in getting a jump on spring by bringing into their homes flowering plants to coax into early bloom. During winter, florists are especially well-stocked with cool season flowering plants—cyclamens, primulas, azaleas and cinerarias in a fantastic array of colors. "Forced" spring bulbs, such as crocuses and tulips, are in abundant supply.

Why anticipate spring? For the delight of it! Winter cheer is an act of hospitality; it can even be necessary therapy for those prone to seasonal depression. Flowers are like lights at the end of a tunnel. Of course, many of these flowers are strongly associated with Easter, and their modest presence at worship can convey an eagerness for the arrival of the church's paschal time.

Spring flowers brought into early bloom also convey another kind of eagerness; they are signs of the hastening of the reign of God. Amazingly, they are something like the wedding at Cana. Jesus tells his mother that his hour has not yet come, and yet she persists in hastening that hour, the arrival of the fullness of time.

THE ASSEMBLY'S PLACE

Because the assembly's place is so large, appropriate decorations here can consume a good portion of the budget. Naturally, Ordinary Time is last on the list in budgetary priorities. Even in parishes that have become accustomed to decorating this part of the church for the seasons, often during Ordinary Time the area is left bare, which may be what's needed for a few weeks.

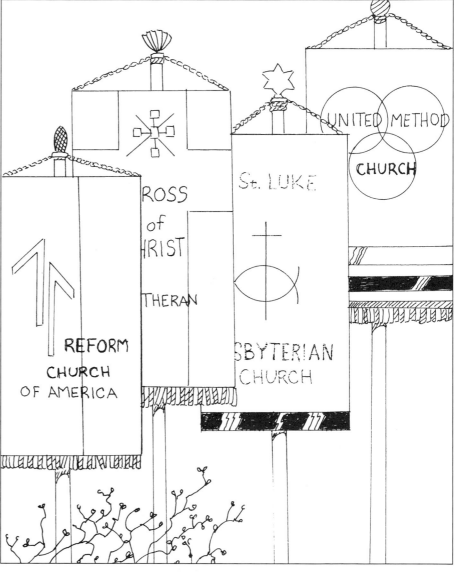

However, attention to visuals in this space would be especially warranted during winter because they can be the most effective way to keep the worship space from appearing drab after all the Christmastime finery has been removed.

The natural environment during winter may be austere, and in many places even life-threatening, but winter is far from being an austere time in an active parish: Its programs are in full swing and there is a flurry of social activities before Lent—parish school plays, theater trips, fundraisers, dances, and especially a grand Mardi Gras party to get us ready to settle down into Lent.

There is also a flurry of liturgical events—for the Octave of Christian Unity, Catholic Schools Week, Candlemas and St. Blase's Day—as well as the prayerful pondering and preparations that lead up to Lent and some of the catechumens' election for Easter baptism.

Something of this—this sense of heightened activity—can be reflected in the church. Winter brings before us the contrast of nature's dormancy and human enterprise.

Besides decorating the assembly's place, scrutinize the effectiveness of the church's lighting. That just may be the job of environment and art ministers, who even if they are not ultimately responsible, can at least work together with the pastoral staff and building custodians. (There's nothing but good to be gained from parish artists, decorators, janitors and others responsible for the physical plant having open lines of communication.)

The long nights make it a good time of year for this review. Before days get too long, you might ask Saturday evening Mass-goers what they think of parish lighting inside and out.

And while we're on the subject, in what shape are the church's candles and candleholders?

ALTAR, AMBO AND CHAIR

Some parishes dress the altar with a full "gown" of fabric during the seasons of Eastertime and Christmastime (which hides the table), but during Ordinary Time use far simpler clothes. So at least for a major portion of the year, the holy table can be clothed in a manner that reveals and doesn't hide its materials and construction.

Some parishes use altar cloths in seasonal colors. This is not especially traditional, though it does keep the color in sight throughout the week. If the seasonal green is evident in other places besides the ministers' vesture, make sure the shades match or are compatible. A jumble of shades can be jarring and sloppy.

Of course, deacons and priests sometimes bring their own vesture from home to wear at worship. To be attractive, this vesture needs to be coordinated with the other materials in the worship environment. It probably would be helpful to have a good sit-down discussion once or twice a year to make sure that all of the ministers are tuned in to aesthetic concerns.

FONT

John the Baptist is mentioned often in the liturgy early in winter; if the parish honors an image of the Baptist during Advent and Christmastime, why not leave it in place until Lent? The baptism of the Lord is celebrated on the final day of the Christmas season, but this event is referred to in several of the gospels of early Ordinary Time. Perhaps an image of the baptism can be specially honored throughout the winter.

Indoor plants sometimes get miserable-looking during winter. Give them a critical look. Sometimes they need more than care; they need replacement.

Now is a fine time of year for a review of the physical beauty of parish procedures surrounding infant baptism. Consider the worthiness and usefulness of the font, its regular upkeep, the chrism stock, the paschal candle (which by now is about as burned down as it gets) and the baptismal candle that the parish gives to the newly baptized.

The gradual burning down of the paschal candle can be a sign of the progression of the year, of how our year flows from Easter and returns to Easter. That's why it's best if one candle is large enough to last the year. If you misjudged, you'll need a new one midyear. The paschal candle requires regular care to keep it attractive. If the candle burns down to any painted ornamentation, there's a serious hazard because paint can burn explosively.

SHRINES

In some places, the Bethlehem scene is left up until Candlemas, February 2. Think of it as a temporary shrine. Even if you take the scene down at the end of Christmastime, be sure to decorate Mary's shrine for Cndlemas. Snowdrops and flowering heath have long been associated with this feast (See page 275).

Many parishes have gotten into the good habit of displaying appropriate feast day images. These never go in front of the altar, and in most churches probably work best in a shrine, on a pedestal in the vestibule or even smack in the middle of the main aisle. Four sturdy floor-standing candlesticks set around the pedestal can define a kind of sacred space for the image.

Another day ranked as a feast is the Conversion of St. Paul, January 25. Can you add an image of Paul or highlight one already in church, say, one in a stained glass window? A customary way to highlight an image is to circle it with a garland of flowers and herbs—it's hard to improve on this tradition.

SEASONAL CORNERS

Lent is coming! See the information beginning on page 36 about devoting some corner of the church to sharing information, making materials available for prayer in the home and for opening eyes to the imagery of the liturgical seasons.

A month before Ash Wednesday is not too early to direct parish attention toward the keeping of Lent.

VESTIBULES, DOORWAYS AND OUTDOORS

Custodians often have their hands full clearing walks of ice and snow and getting salt and sand out of entryways. (One more reason not to carpet a church!) These responsibilities may be shared by janitors and parish decorators if only to bring to worship an extra measure of hospitality, safety and beauty. Think of this work as an extension of the entrance rites. It's especially important work at funerals and weddings, when our parish home is open to visitors.

Candlemas

At Christmas we gain an eyeblink more of light.
At Epiphany we gain the time it takes to wash.
At Candlemas we gain the time it takes
    to make breakfast.
Rise and shine!
– a Central European proverb

February 2 is the feast of the Presentation of the Lord in the Temple. An old English title for the day is Candlemas, a name that continues to be used in our own day, probably because it evokes the connection with Christmas, 40 days prior. On Candlemas the church blesses candles and then marches in procession to acclaim Christ the Light of the world.

At Christmas the light came into the world. At Epiphany it rose to shine in glory like a star on high. At Candlemas the light is placed in our arms. Like old Simeon, we embrace heaven's eternal youth.

The Presentation comes midway between the winter solstice and the spring equinox. No wonder today we take a final look back at Christmas and a first look forward to Lent. Candles and oil lamps seem apt symbols for the day because they are lights that consume themselves in order to shine.

The images of light shining in darkness and self-sacrifice are strong common denominators throughout winter. This imagery suggests that we need not be too quick to say farewell to the lights of Christmas. Bear in mind that Ordinary Time is not really a church season; it is a time between seasons.

It simply is not that critical in the worship environment to highlight the distinctions between the Christmas season and Ordinary Time. Instead, perhaps worship during these winter weeks can be a bit like Candlemas, reflecting the great mystery we celebrated at Epiphany and moving us toward the great mystery we will be celebrating at Easter.

Processions are emblems of exodus, of our journey through life, of our march toward the kingdom. In the liturgy, processions have special association with the conclusions to 40-day periods: for example, on this day, on Palm Sunday, the days leading to the Ascension, and at least in the Middle East, the fortieth day after someone dies. These occasions mark a kind of crossing of a threshold, a homecoming.

Liturgical processions share much in common: Two favorite "traveling songs" are Psalm 24 ("Lift up your heads, O gates") and Psalm 118 (with

its lines "Open to me the gates of justice," and "Blessed is the one who comes in the name of the Lord"). It is appropriate to adorn parish "gates," especially the main doors, with bunting, victory wreaths, even a triumphal arch. (Maybe these are simply some of the outdoor Christmas decorations left up until today.)

Prepare the physical accouterments of the procession—censer(s), candles, processional cross (made merry this day with an evergreen wreath and red ribbons?), banners and other pole-mounted signs of festivity. Think of these as "walking sticks" that can show those in the middle or rear of the procession where everyone is heading.

Many parishes would like to give away handsome candles on this feast, but the cost is great—no doubt about that. Byzantine parishes, in a stall somewhere in the back of church, often have available rather hefty candles and the windguards necessary to walk with them in procession. People contribute what they can, but contribution is not required. The system works.

Lousy weather or ice-slicked sidewalks work against outdoor festivities at this season. However, there's something splendid about a wintertime procession as an act of defiance against the elements, as a hastening of spring. Foretastes of spring surely have a place in our communal prayer throughout this time of year. Even in the north, an open eye can usually locate some stirring of nature—the flash of a bird's wing, the first snowdrop, even icicles formed from the melting and refreezing of snow on a roof.

Perhaps those are the best reasons of all for marching outdoors. They are the signs that the sun is gaining power. For us they can be sacred signs that the love of God is stronger than death.

Our hastening the spring can speak of an eagerness for Easter, a longing for resurrection. That is the ultimate destination of liturgical processions. Most years, even in the north, the elements cooperate and a procession is possible. The journey ordinarily leads to the eucharist. Perhaps a logical adaptation in cold weather is to have the procession follow Mass and lead to warm refreshment.

At an evening liturgy the church can be kept in candlelight alone, at least through the liturgy of the word. The sacramentary offers the option of a "solemn entrance" in place of a procession, an option that can be lovely with a little adaptation: After everyone has gathered in church (itself a kind of procession), the ministers go to the main entrance to bless the candles. (Everyone turns to face the blessing.) Then the ministers (perhaps including the choir, lectors, eucharistic ministers and servers) might carry lit candles into the dark church and circumambulate the assembly. Perhaps along the route other candles (votives perched on window sills?) could be lit to encircle the church with light.

Upon first entering, people might receive unlit candles, and they also could bring candles from home. The assembly's candles would be lit once the procession of ministers is complete; this pattern allows the light to draw attention to the encircling of the ministers and then to illuminate the proclamation of the word.

If the nativity scene is left up until February 2, on Candlemas morning it would be surrounded with spring flowers before being dismantled in the evening. It would not be farfetched in some parishes to use Bethelehem's straw and evergreens for an outdoor bonfire this night and even to use the bonfire's ashes for Ash Wednesday. Perhaps Candlemas can be the right occasion each year for this necessary act in preparation for Lent. See the next page for more about the preparation of ashes.

Ashes

*Memento, homo, quia pulvis es
    et in pulverem reverteris.*
Remember, human, that you are dust
    and to dust you will return.
—Genesis 3:19

Burning something is an age-old way to declare "out with the old, in with the new." In early spring in many cultures, an effigy of old man winter is set on fire. Winter burns up so that spring can be born. In some places field stubble is set on fire to clear the land for plowing. The ashes fertilize next year's crop. The church also has its fiery rites of spring: We burn up the branches from the previous Palm Sunday to make Ash Wednesday's ashes.

Ashes are a memento mori, *a reminder of death,* but the ashen brand we receive is in the shape of the cross of Christ. For us it is the tree of life, the ark's anchor, the bronze serpent that saves us from dying in the desert.

The brand goes on our foreheads. We are marked like Cain. To see the disfiguring mark on ourselves we need a mirror, a reflecting pool, and baptism is that pool. Lent leads us to the water's edge that we might see ourselves as we are. And when Lent is done and the pasch has come, the water and the dust together will form the clay of a new creation.

Those who prepare ashes are struck by the acrid smell of burning palms, and some think that this aroma is too nostalgic to keep to themselves. It is a nostalgic aroma, a kind of unpleasant incense, and it may deserve a place in the parish's experience of the changing seasons.

There is no tradition for burning palms within the liturgy, but the preparation of ashes still can be a parish event. In the weeks before Lent, parishioners can be asked to bring last year's palm fronds from home. A large basket in the vestibule would be marked for collecting palms. Perhaps after each Mass on the Sunday before Ash Wednesday a quantity of branches could be burned outside, or perhaps this could happen at a Carnival party held that night or on Mardi Gras night. (Or maybe Candlemas is the annual day for this fire.)

At this party a snowman piñata can be smashed to send the woes of winter packing. A bonfire, into which are tossed the palms as well as the bashed remains of the piñata, can end the evening, and this would be a time to sing a final round of Alleluias.

A large heap of palms burns down into a relatively small amount of ashes. A metal garbage can or washtub is the right shape to contain the fire, even if it is inelegant. Under no circumstances should a quantity of palms be burned indoors. To make them easier to use on Ash Wednesday, the ashes can be sifted through a screen, a loosely woven basket or a wire colander.

The logical container for ashes is a large urn, which might be kept on display in church throughout Lent, perhaps on a handsome pedestal in the baptistry.

Good containers for distributing ashes are clay bowls—this material calls to mind the creation of Adam and Eve. Please don't use vessels that are clearly meant for other purposes, such as custard cups. Invest in something special. Of particular beauty for this purpose are hand-thrown Japanese tea bowls, each a unique, fragile creation.

Occasional Celebrations of Sacraments

A Sense of the Sacraments

Like other forms of liturgy, occasional celebrations such as baptisms, weddings, anointings of the sick and funerals require ministers to serve the assembly—a presider, readers, a cantor and other musicians, a sacristan, and perhaps servers and ministers of hospitality. The ministry of environment and art also is needed for wholesome celebrations; don't let anyone tell you that your ministry is nice but not necessary.

What would be the role of the art ministers? As always, our task is twofold because it involves a thorough knowledge of the rituals—what we're going to do—as well as a sense for the materials of the rituals—what we're going to use.

Fitting what we're going to do with what we're going to use requires cooperation among the parish staff, musicians, art ministers, sacristans and the other people who are preparing the celebration of the sacrament. In this cooperative effort, an art minister would share her or his expertise with the group. For example, some of the those getting ready for a baptism may need a refresher about the use and design of the baptismal garment. That could be the art minister's task (although if it isn't, it should be *someone's*). After explaining the garment's purpose in the ritual, perhaps the minister lends or gives the family of the soon-to-be-baptized a beautiful garment; perhaps the minister suggests to the family how to refurbish an heirloom or how to design a new one. Or, maybe the minister puts the family in touch with a parishioner who will do this work.

The church has a traditional approach to how the actual candidates for the sacraments are involved in the preparations. According to tradition, candidates aren't supposed to be bothered with rehearsals, with explanations of the rites or with the concerns of getting together the materials for the rites. Instead, the parish itself (which includes the candidate's godparents, sponsors, attendants and family members) is responsible for knowing the rites and for providing materials. During the liturgy the parish guides the candidate through the ritual and gives any requisite materials to the candidate as gifts.

According to this tradition, only after the celebration of the sacrament are the newly baptized, newly confirmed or newly wed offered explanations of what they have experienced. This post-sacramental teaching is called "mystagogy" (which means "the learning of mystery").

The notion behind this tradition is that the sacraments are gifts given to us by the parish and done for us by the parish community, which, as the body of Christ, shares its gifts of the Spirit.

Most sacraments share in common certain images and gestures: the sign of the cross, the laying on of hands, the robe, the crown, the branch, the carrying of a lamp, the anointing with christening ointment. These are the physical accoutrements of the saints. They are the property of all who have been baptized.

These fundamental signs take various forms. Some are essential to the rites, some are optional, and some (thanks to the twists of history) have fallen into disuse or are now merely suggested. For instance, the "robe of the saints" may take the form of the baptismal garment, the bridal gown or the funeral pall. The "crown" might be a wreath placed on a coffin or it might be suggested by the fragrance of chrism surrounding the heads of the newly christened. The circular form of the crown might be suggested by wedding rings or, in some Latino weddings, by the *lasso*.

A few churches have tried to restore the ancient signs to readily apparent and fundamental forms. For instance, the newly baptized, the newly confirmed, the first communicants, maybe the wedding couple and even the dead are dressed for the liturgy in albs—basic baptismal robes—instead of any substitute clothing. There are store-front churches in which all the worshipers don white robes for any assembly.

Maybe we won't begin doing that, but certainly every parish should stop using those skimpy "baptismal garments" (that look like baby bibs) sold in religious goods stores. We have no right reason not to get back to using full robes. Of course most families clothe their babies in christening gowns that are in fact glorious for this purpose, although to conform to the ritual, the gowns should be put on the babies after, not before, the baptism. This means that we need to suggest appropriate ways to clothe babies before their baptisms (they might be brought to church naked and bundled in blankets) and to provide useful, safe places in which babies can be dressed after being baptized.

Getting back to the church's sacramental basics is a worthy goal for art ministers, but hard work, too. And it will probably take several generations. No decoration or other visual elements should take precedence over sacramental basics—the water, chrism, oil, bread and cup, robes, rings, candles. More basic even than these are the candidates themselves in the company of the gathered people. In our use of visuals we can echo these emphases.

For instance, for a communal celebration of the sacrament of the sick, figure out an appropriate spot to put the oil. Certain sacramental signs (such as holy oil) can be placed on the altar, but we might avoid using the holy table for anything but the eucharistic sacrifice. A good alternative is to put the oil on a large pedestal, perhaps with candles or oil lamps set around it to make the vessel glisten, and perhaps also with olive branches as a noble reminder of the source of the sacred substance.

Rather than placing the pedestal for the oil in the area around the presidential chair, you might consider, if there's room, placing it in the main aisle or somewhere the people can see it up close as they arrive. Nearby you might put an image of Jesus healing the sick or perhaps an icon of the Good Samaritan, whose wounds were dressed with oil. Up front such imagery would be nearly invisible, but in an approachable location this arrangement can invite those assembling to idle a moment and ponder the mystery of the sacrament.

Sacraments Require Hospitality

Sacramental celebrations may lead many to spend money lavishly and generously. "Festive excess" can be a natural and healthy response to great moments in life.

The trick is to find ways to share these moments without showing off or being wasteful. Who will benefit from the money being spent? How can flowers and the other visual signs be used to express love and concern for those who have gathered? How can these signs be an expression of gospel values—of joy, simplicity and charity? And, most importantly, how do these signs point toward the reign of God? How are they emblems of eternity?

When a family begins its preparations for a baptism, confirmation, first communion, ordination or wedding, or when a family makes the hurried preparations for a funeral, it really should think first about the people who will gather there—friends and family, yes, but especially the many people who may be strangers to one another.

In this gathering the whole church comes together in spirit: the living and the dead, the saints and the angels, and all the company of heaven. That is the mystical and lavish gathering we call liturgy. For a time on earth all of us have a doorway into heaven, where differences are put aside, where no one is left a stranger, where, despite all the evidence to the contrary, we know that love is stronger than death.

Hospitality is an ancient and important sacramental tradition. It is one of the customary tasks of godparents, friends of the dead, the wedding party and the soon-to-be-ordained to attend to the needs of guests, many of whom may be arriving from a distance and some of whom may be unacquainted with the ceremonies of the church in which they now gather.

Hospitality, above all, is the proper "atmosphere" of the worship environment. It is in essence the climate to be created by any decoration.

Through hospitality—perhaps by offering arrivals a refreshing drink, a hearty hug, a flower poked into buttonholes, a beautiful and useful participation booklet—as well as through decoration that may begin in the parking lot and be focused on the assembly, we communicate that the people who have gathered are necessary for the liturgy, not incidental to it.

But hospitality is more than cozy friendliness, and it definitely isn't chuminess where some folks get more attention than others. A climate of hospitality encourages us to participate more fully in the liturgy, perhaps to sing with more vigor and certainly to know that our presence is essential for what we are about to do together.

Sacraments Are Processions

When done right, there can be a lot of walking around as a part of sacramental liturgies. The walking is a sign of life's journey toward God's reign and of our entrance into paradise. This exodus is physical participation in the paschal mystery.

Most processions would surely include the processional cross (which can be ornamented with a wreath of flowers and hung with bright ribbons), processional candles (which also can be decorated with flowers) and an incense-bearer (church incense comes in an amazing array of scents).

There also might be processional banners and other sacred signs hoisted high on poles. A portable image of the parish's patron saint or the patrons of the sacramental candidates might have a place in the liturgy. A bunch of dried flowers, a sheaf of wheat, or a balsa-wood or papier-mâché star, dove or lamb can look splendid attached to the tops of poles.

A procession might include a maypole, which is basically a wreath hung horizontally from a pole with fluttering ribbons attached to the wreath. It is a token of God's scepter and crown and an ancient symbol for marriage. A canopy (described on page 256) might be carried over the newly baptized, the bride and groom, or the coffin. A canopy is a sign of God's watchful presence, an emblem of the incarnation, of God-with-us; at weddings a canopy also represents the establishment of a new household.

Especially at funerals the church's liturgy involves several sites and the movement among these sites. The liturgy for the dead begins at the place of death. Then there is the wake (ordinarily in the home or in its substitute, the funeral home), where we keep watch before moving to the church. After the rituals in the church we move to the cemetery, where we make the earth itself the site of our liturgy.

How would these several sites be decorated for their purpose? A wake, for example, invites small-scale, homey decoration, such as an attractive collection of photos and other memorabilia—materials that are wonderful at a wake but out of place at a eucharist.

The graveyard also can be decorated, and here is where processional cross, candles, incense and banners are especially fitting. Can these items be transported to the cemetery? Can they withstand the elements? Funeral directors already spend much time and energy on "decorating" gravesites with things that emphasize safety and comfort, often at the expense of the authentic images of burial—most importantly, the earth itself, which in too many places gets hidden under astroturf and gladioluses.

A funeral involves complex liturgical rites (and a family reunion) that must come together at a moment's notice. Weddings, ordinations and other sacraments, especially baptism, also can have rituals that take place at several sites. For example, when people wed, what communal prayer is possible at home, at the rehearsal dinner, at the reception? All these sites can be part of the liturgy of marriage. That's why the parish needs fairly established ways and means to help the sacraments be filled with beauty, grace and worship.

Most liturgical processions are not given the attention they're due. Maybe they aren't recognized as processions. For instance, the taking of communion to the sick can be made more beautiful and more decorous if perhaps along with the body and blood of Christ, some seasonal flowers are brought each week to the sick. Perhaps the vessels containing the eucharistic bread and wine are transported in a case surrounded by these flowers. Perhaps the communion vessels are wrapped in richly detailed fabrics in seasonal colors. Perhaps different vessels are used that reflect the time of year— maybe clay during Lent, wicker during summer. Certainly all vessels should be worthy and beautiful at any time of year.

A processional journey common to every public liturgy is the journey from home to the place of worship and then back home again. Many decorators put some effort into ornamenting the church parking lot, doorways and other outdoor locations, using banners, bunches of flowers and decorated wreaths; or perhaps a long swag of lightweight fabric can be used to arch over the main doorway. These are ways of announcing the liturgy to the neighborhood and can be a gracious sign of welcome to all who will gather —and, as a bonus, it can help out-of-towners identify the church.

CREATING LINKS BETWEEN CHURCH AND HOME

People can be greeted or bid goodbye with a flower or fluttering flag. After confirmation, one parish handed out rather exquisite paper fans painted with phoenixes and purchased in quantity from an Oriental import store.

A newlywed couple gave out packages of nasturtium seeds at their springtime wedding. Tulip bulbs make lovely favors at an autumn event. Tree seedlings can be bought in bulk from the Department of Environmental Resources and distributed. A couple could use potted herbs, geraniums and other bedding plants to decorate their springtime wedding and then give them to parishioners to plant outside for the summer.

A rural couple planted a row of zinnias in spring; then at their September wedding they harvested the zinnias and handed them to arriving guests.

A south Florida couple did something similar with pink cosmos for the christening of their child. The people themselves were "decorated" with emblems of paradise.

Ordinarily, anything the church hands out can be more than a "favor." It can be the focus of our thankful blessing lifted up to God. Flowers, seeds or other handouts can be blessed, and the usual time for doing that would be right after the homily or right after communion. Or, in the case of weddings and funerals, perhaps the blessing and distribution is part of the gathering (the night before at a rehearsal dinner or wake) or the meal (reception) afterward.

We need to encourage a renewed sense of the connections between church and home. The reformed liturgical books put fresh emphasis on many of the links. In particular, look through *Catholic Household Blessings and Prayers*. It's filled with the domestic rites that can lead to and follow from the sacraments—blessings for an engagement or anniversary, for moving or other new beginnings, for conception, birth, adoption, and for times of sorrow and sickness. These blessings, too, are liturgies, and they need the right environment for celebration.

How can the home be made more decorous, "fitting," for prayer? What are appropriate ways for Christians to decorate a hall for a wedding reception? What are some ways to decorate a home for a christening or first communion party? How can we make more beautiful the sacrament of the sick celebrated in a person's bedroom? What could hang on the front door after there's been a death in the family or when someone in the family is being baptized or confirmed or ordained? The answers to these questions can be an aspect of the church's ministry of art.

Toward a Parish Policy on Decorating for the Sacraments

Someone in the parish should coordinate visuals. This person might even have a title and certainly should have some authority. The role is "pastoral" in that it receives commission from the pastor for the sake of the parish.

The coordinator would be responsible, for example, for advising the families of engaged couples on how to use flowers and other decorations at weddings; for advising expectant parents about the baptismal robe and candle and other physical elements at the christening; for coming up with an appropriate manner to dress *confirmandi* and first communicants; and for helping the bereaved in any decoration for the wake, the funeral eucharist and the grave.

The coordinator's purpose is not to put brakes on parish creativity and enthusiasm but to help parishioners make best use of their talents and time. Two things go far in helping a coordinator work with households: a parish policy statement on the use of decorations and a photo album to show what worked in the past and what didn't. (Included in the album would be the church in its various seasonal adornments.)

It's best to put parish policy on the use of decorations into writing. That way everyone is expected to play by the same rules—including parish families, program directors, florists and funeral or wedding directors. It may feel restrictive, but it also feels fair.

The emphasis shouldn't be on the negatives, although some of that will be necessary. Make clear where photographers shouldn't stand, where flowers shouldn't be placed, and why photographers and even flowers can be counterproductive if they're in the wrong place. Also suggest effective, practical ways that the visual elements of sacramental celebrations can be made graceful and hospitable and invite participation.

Of course, a policy statement or photo album won't cover every possibility. There is always the need for one-on-one guidance, which makes the job of coordination essential. As an example, if two weddings are scheduled on the same day, the coordinator might suggest that both can share in buying flowers and then put the parties in touch with each other.

What would go into such a policy? Every building is different, but in any church the decorations shouldn't be placed in such a way that they block people's view or interfere with movement. The altar, a lectern or a chair are never to be used as flower stands. In most churches there are more

attractive and more liturgically appropriate locations for flower arrangements than right in front of the altar or on either side of it. Where are these alternatives?

Of course, size and scale are important. For instance, a small arrangement can be overwhelmed by the size of the space. Usually a single large bouquet is more effective (and less costly) than several small ones. You might make a point of recommending when less is more.

Florists sometimes have decorations to rent, such as archways and candelabra. You might discourage the use of these things because they usually are too small to look right in church, and their design can clash with furnishings and create the ambience of a photo studio. Couples have a right to want extra signs of festivity in church on their wedding day; therefore the parish would be wise to provide couples with appropriate decorations that fit the building and that are placed appropriately.

Cleaning up afterward is an important responsibility. Many churches do not have janitorial help, or the help arrives days later. Folks can make their participation in the sacraments a blessing for the parish by cleaning up any rooms they've used and by leaving flowers in the church to continue to grace worship.

Regarding the matter of whether or not to leave flowers in the church: Perhaps the flowers are carried from site to site in the course of the "procession" of the liturgical rites—for instance, from home to rehearsal dinner to church to wedding banquet, or from funeral home to church to grave. Or perhaps flowers remain in church as evidence for what has transpired there.

Notice that the notion here is never that flowers are the "property" of the family or couple, because that makes the church no different than a rented hall. In sacramental preparations, it might be worthwhile to talk over the understanding that the aspects of the sacramental celebration "belong" to the congregation as the common property of the body of Christ.

Coordination among pastoral staff, art ministers and parish households can help great things happen. For example, a couple were getting ready for an Eastertime wedding. They were shown photos of how the church looked last Eastertime. Together with the coordinator, they noticed that the seasonal banners were not the best. The couple gave the parish a bolt of fabric; the color and material were chosen in collaboration with parish decorators. Someone turned the fabric into seasonal hangings for the church, and the hangings graced the couple's wedding.

As another example, one parish had a sorry-looking funeral pall. A parishioner noticed this and asked the pastor if she could make a more beautiful one. The pastor put the woman in touch with an art minister, who worked with the woman to complete the project. In order to match the parish's Easter set of vesture (the set also worn at funerals), the fabric and trim for the new pall were ordered from the manufacturer. From experience, the art minister knew that the pall would be more useful with a cross (formed handsomely from trim) running from edge to edge in both directions from the pall's center. (That makes it easier to unfold on a coffin.)

The art minister also knew that hanging in the back of a church closet was an old but splendid banner depicting the Lamb of God. (In past generations the banner got hung in front of the monstrance during the Masses of the Forty Hours Devotion.) The edges of the banner were falling apart, but the Lamb was hand-done in silk thread, too lovely to lose. The image was too small to be used on a new banner and too large to recycle as a lectionary cover. The Lamb was removed from the old banner and sewn onto the center of the new pall.

To Everything There Is a Season

Decorations for the sacraments are best when they reflect the time of year. The choice of materials from a florist is wider in cold months than in warm, but at any time of year we can take advantage of field and garden flowers and produce. In January a bouquet of evergreen branches may be more becoming (and certainly less expensive) than a bouquet of flowers. In May, garden lilacs and irises surely are more splendid (and fragrant) than a florist's chrysanthemums.

In summer, why not fill a large pot with sunflowers and cattails or Joe-pye weed and Queen Anne's lace? Perhaps a basket of colored peppers or ripe apricots would be as lovely as flowers. In autumn, we can take delight in red and orange oak leaves, in sheaves of corn and in the feathery plumes of pampas grass. It's also the time of year when mums are truly in season.

The decoration for sacramental celebrations needs to fit with the parish's seasonal environment. The parish may have ornamentation in place for a holy day or for a season. For example, in November the church may be decorated for the harvest. In the weeks after Easter Sunday the church may be filled with flowers. It would never be right to take apart the parish's seasonal decor to accommodate a wedding, funeral or other sacramental liturgy. These services should take place amid—and be graced by—the parish's seasonal environment. Any added materials for a special event should enhance and not detract from or compete with seasonal decorations.

Keep in mind that decorations may need to be put up a day or even a few days before a holiday or season. So, for example, on the Saturday afternoon before Pentecost the church may already be decorated with fiery reds and oranges.

If a liturgy takes place during the Easter season—the 50 days from Easter Sunday until Pentecost—the church's paschal candle will be there to shine on our worship as a bright symbol of the presence of the risen Christ. Be sure that the candle is lit and that it will be prominent. Throughout these 50 days, some parishes keep the candle surrounded by potted flowers, or the candle stand itself is decorated with flowers. Check to see if these flowers need refreshing.

The church may have an Advent wreath during the weeks before Christmas, and the right number of candles would be lit for any liturgy. There may be a nativity scene, a Christmas tree and other rather dominant decorations for several weeks after December 25.

According to church law, flowers are not used in church (except at funerals) during the Seasons of Advent and Lent. Because the spirit of Advent and Lent is sober and often austere, engaged couples would be wise to schedule their wedding so that it doesn't fall during these seasons. Many parishes make it a point not to schedule baptisms or confirmations during Lent, and, in contrast, many parishes schedule confirmation and first communion to take place each year during the Easter season.

Traditional Visuals in Celebration of the Sacraments

The church's favorite decorations are living flowers. In the scriptures, flowers represent the things that are here today and gone tomorrow, "which at dawn spring up anew, but by evening wilt and fade" (Psalm 90:6). In this way, flowers can call to mind our hope for the things that are eternal, for a place of endless springtime and everlasting life.

Flowers bring us their own mystery, a sense of the passage of life, of the goodness of creation. Flowers also bring festivity. It's as if they are able to shout God's praises and to lift up our spirits to do the same.

You may need to remind folks that it's not required to have flowers in church. Some couples have a bride's bouquet and a boutonniere for the groom, and that's that. Some mourners choose just a single rose to place on the coffin. The rich symbolism of flowers can be captured in one blossom.

Some people like to do it themselves. Rather than involve a florist, they select and arrange the flowers. This rewarding work may better enable them to make their preparations a blessing for all who will gather. Some people receive help with flowers from a friend; this is a worthy gift. But most people rely on the services of a florist.

It's best to go to a florist with a firm budget. Make notes before going: What are parish policies on the use of flowers in church? Where does the parish recommend flowers be placed? What small things will mean a lot that day—perhaps bringing Mom yellow roses or perhaps placing a bouquet on Grandpa's grave?

Flower colors should be compatible with any seasonal decorations that will be in place when the sacrament is celebrated. Warn brides-to-be so that they at least have a chance to coordinate flowers and attendants' gowns with the church's seasonal decor.

Go to the florist with a budget and a few rough ideas, but don't go with your mind made up. Most florists will be eager to try to accommodate requests without busting a budget. Give them as many alternatives as they will find useful. Like other service industries, some florists offer a better deal than others. But in general, you get what you pay for. Remember also that you're purchasing custom work. Negotiate honestly and be flexible in your expectations.

What about artificial flowers? These remind some people of other things in life that are fake—which is not a good thing to call to mind at worship.

The decoration for baptisms, weddings and funerals can involve more than flower arrangements. Wreaths and crowns are signs of fullness, of unity and of the royal dignity of Christian life. In some churches a wreath of flowers may be appropriate on the lectern, near the baptismal font or on church doorways. In some traditions, crowns of flowers are customary for both bride and groom to wear, to place on a coffin or to put on the heads of the newly confirmed or first communicants.

Many folk-art designs feature knots, chains, spirals or entwining geometric patterns; these are emblems of fidelity and eternity. Fabrics imprinted or woven with these designs can be splendid for banners. In summer or autumn, a spiral of grapevines and bittersweet may look beautiful tumbling in front of the church's lectern.

In times past it was common to decorate for sacramental celebrations with fruits, berried branches and sheaves of grain—these are signs of fulfillment. We still have a token of this practice in the custom of throwing rice at weddings. Garlands of flowers, greenery, nuts and fruits—*della Robbia*-style—are expensive but magnificent.

For their August wedding, a couple decorated the church with bushels of peaches, which were distributed that night at the parish's soup kitchen. Another couple created centerpieces for their wedding banquet out of canned goods and bright cellophane, which were then given to a food bank. At a confirmation liturgy, the vestibule was ornamented with the candidates' donations of gift-wrapped packages of infant and children's supplies, which then were given to a women's shelter.

Small nosegays and clusters or garlands of herbs and flowers placed among the people can be lovely. A custom even older than using flowers in arrangements near the altar is using loose flowers and herbs to tuck into hair and clothing, to ornament the sacred images, the doorways and the walls of the church, and especially to ornament the people who have gathered.

After the liturgy, perhaps a few of the flowers could be brought to those who could not be there. They could be taken later to the cemetery to remember the dead or could be given as gifts to an institution (as long as the place accepts such gifts).

In preparation for the royal weddings of England, sprigs of ivy and rosemary are cut from potted plants kept alive by the couple's parents. The sprigs are woven into the bride's bouquet and the groom's boutonniere. After the wedding, the sprigs are rooted to make new plants that will be tended over the years and eventually used as stock for the couple's children's weddings. In north Africa and the Middle East, fragrant myrtle and laurel are used in much the same way, except that after they are rooted, they are planted outdoors. What a delightful tradition!

A lovely custom in many places is to plant trees in honor of a marriage, when a child is born or when someone dies. One parish marks confirmations and first communions by planting trees. In some places, two trees or vines are planted and allowed to grow together as the years pass, as a sign of love and fidelity—a good image of marriage or reconciliation or of pacts between churches.

Topiaries are potted plants that have been grown to form a beautiful trunk supporting a rounded head of foliage; for weddings, sometimes the trunks of two topiaries are woven together to form a knot.

There are other ways to use plants as tokens of the continuity of life. Many people have a few wedding or funeral flowers dried and preserved to place in a shadow box alongside other memorabilia. Our worship on this occasion could be extended to the community through donations to charity or through the good works of peacemaking and loving service to neighbors. In celebration of a christening, a marriage, an ordination or a funeral, money could be donated in support of a public garden, a hospital or a clinic, or some other institution that fosters life. Donations to the parish can be earmarked for materials such as vesture and vessels.

Aromatic herbs—such as rosemary, thyme and lavender—are said to conjure remembrances of the past. Indeed, this has been shown to be true, for nothing, it seems, brings forth memories as much as aromas. Perhaps that's why the traditional flowers for a bride's bouquet and groom's boutonniere, or for the spray on a casket, include orange blossoms and lilies of the valley, jasmine and gardenias, roses and stephanotis—all intensely fragrant.

Among many families in Africa, the Middle East, India and Eastern Europe, guests are greeted with a sprinkling of rosewater or other flower essences and are sometimes given garlands of flowers to wear. In many places, the path of the wedding party or funeral cortege, or the processional route of the newly baptized or first communicants, is spread with herbs and flower petals that release their aromas when walked upon.

To sweeten the church, we might "anoint" out-of-the-way places in the building with a fragrant flower oil, such as rose or jasmine. Such oils are not difficult to find in bath shops and old-fashioned apothecaries.

For Christians, fragrance can be a reminder of baptism, when we were anointed with perfumed chrism and when we promised to be united with Christ in a love that death cannot part. Chrism is a sign of the Holy Spirit, God's own "breath," which first filled us at our christening.

> Thanks be to God,
> who in Christ always leads us in triumphal procession,
> and through us spreads in every place the fragrance

that comes from knowing him.
For we are the aroma of Christ.

—2 Corinthians 2:14–15

Rehearsing For Heaven

In all we do, we are preparing not a show but a communal ritual. These notions about the use of flowers and other decorations often mean using visuals in active rather than passive ways, so that they aren't just nice to look at but instead become part of the activity of worship. Of course, that probably isn't what we're used to, and it takes coordination and creativity grounded on authentic liturgical practice.

We environment and art ministers who try to do our best throughout the year for seasons and feasts will find that in this work we keep coming back to initiation—to baptism, confirmation and eucharist—and to the celebrations of initiation as liturgies bound up with Easter. And we discover that the more we learn how to keep the many rituals of the Easter Triduum with full gestures, beautiful materials and renovated buildings, the more we learn how to keep all the sacraments—in fact, all liturgy.

The good news is that all of this good and hard work keeps making things better. Each celebration becomes rehearsal for the next.